EXPERIMENTAL SCHOOLS
REVISITED
BULLETINS OF THE BUREAU OF EDUCATIONAL EXPERIMENTS

Edited and with an Introduction by
CHARLOTTE WINSOR
Former Director of Teacher Training
Bank Street College of Education

AGATHON PRESS, INC., NEW YORK

Distributed by
SCHOCKEN BOOKS, NEW YORK

©1973 by Agathon Press, Inc.
150 Fifth Avenue, New York, N. Y. 10011

Library of Congress Catalog Card Number: 72-95965

ISBN: 0-87586-032-X

We are grateful to the Bank Street College
Library for its help in providing the material
from which this book was prepared.

Printed in the United States

CONTENTS

INTRODUCTION

The publication of professional literature after a half century of neglect demands answers to an array of questions. Is the material useful today? Does it present base-line considerations upon which early childhood programs were established originally? Is the contemporary scene a fertile one for reconsideration of those tenets of young children's education propounded by the authors of these papers? And more——

That education has become a major social-political question in the second half of this century is indisputable. It has literally emerged from behind school-house walls to fuel issues as far removed as presidential party politics. Recognition of the prime role of education in the growth and survival of a society has brought in its wake a wide variety of panaceas for instant amelioration of ignorance, alienation, disruptive behavior, and most all the other social ills which plague us.

And more recently early childhood education has followed close upon its parent's heels to take its place as front page news in the hope that the little child holds the answer.

Freud, Piaget, Skinner — to name the most illustrious — have brought to laymen as well as scholars new and deep insights into the critical impact of the early childhood years upon growth. More specifically, the question of the irreversibility of psychological and intellectual deprivation in these early childhood years has produced wide-ranging controversy in the behavioral science disciplines.

The materials in this volume mark the opening of another era in education, an era that saw the beginnings of scientific observation and recording of children's behavior; the development of group experiences for children of toddler age; an approach to school programs built upon maturity levels of children; the design of equipment and materials specific to a proposed educational goal; the pursuit of a philosophy of education congruent with the newer knowledge of the disciplines of psychology and sociology; in short a humanist, environmentalist approach to the study of young children and their learning propensities. Such were the goals of pioneers in the movement which came to be known as progressive education. The term has fallen into disrepute and disuse. The ideals and meanings of the "movement" have been diluted, distorted, and by some opponents scorned and reviled.

In recent years education has sought classroom answers from technology, its hardware and software; administrative answers from the social sciences and even the business world; answers to its social dilemmas from the political and community sectors. But answers are not easily come by and schools are more than ever hard put to serve children adequately.

Most recently the fervor of acceptance of the concept of the "open classroom" bespeaks a deep search for a return to a more human style in that most human of all undertakings—child rearing.

Has a cycle come full circle? Are we ready now to examine primary material, developed as working documents for contemporary workers in the field? Can we find in such material some provocative suggestions for present-day educational thinking?

This volume represents a small segment of a moment in educational history—small but significant. One definition of history (Random House) seems apt—"acts, ideas, or events that will or can shape the course of the f··ture." However, history only becomes a viable tool for ongoing decision-making as it records itself. This historical material is presented in the hope that it is viably useful for today's consideration of educational issues and programs. The Bureau of Educational Experiments, which was responsible for the original publications, held as one of its major purposes the recording and disseminating of primary resource materials which were being developed by the workers engaged in the process of implementing experimental approaches to early childhood education.

In the preface to a pamphlet published in 1917 the Bureau describes its purposes and program.

> The Bureau of Educational Experiments is made up of a group of persons who are engaged in first-hand efforts for improving the education of children, and who have all shared in the general movement that has brought about a more scientific study of them. They feel that the development of some more comprehensive plans for utilizing the results

of the recent interest in "free education" is the next step, and that it depends essentially upon securing a closer cooperation among experimenters.

Among the noticeable features of the present educational situation are: a broader view of education, which makes well-considered experimenting a much sought-for opportunity; the emergence of a considerable number of educators who are really experimentally minded; the accumulation of a large amount of highly specialized experience; the appearance of a considerable literature dealing with experimental procedures; and the gradual sorting out of doubtful experiments from those that have more permanent usefulness. To this situation the Bureau hopes to contribute by affording an opportunity to increase the value of all experiments through cooperative effort, and by preserving and making permanent those experiments that may suitably become parts of an organized system of experimental education.

The Bureau aims to accomplish these ends by giving support to present experiments; by initiating new experiments; by collecting and making available for public use information about the whole field of experiments in education; and by hastening the introduction of newly acquired methods through actual teaching experiments.

A brief summary of the early work of the Bureau is contained in this statement.

The Bureau of Educational Experiments was organized some six years ago by a group of men and women of varied professional backgrounds who wished to further a cooperative study of normal children in a normal environment. Our aim is two-fold: first, to conduct researches which will lead to further and fuller data concerning children's growth, and second, to bring schools and specialists dealing with various aspects of children into intimate and working contact with one another.

These aims are made practical through having a school for our laboratory and through having both research and practical programs for our research staff. But, obviously, a particular kind of school and a particular kind of specialist is also necessary. A school conducted in the spirit of experimentation, one that gives its children a curriculum of experiences as well as of information, will be a good place for children to grow in and so will also be a good laboratory in which to study the growth of children; a specialist who is interested in normal development rather than in cure will see the opportunities in such a school laboratory. In the six years of its experiments, the Bureau has worked in a number of schools, public and private. At present, its work is confined to our own Nursery School with eight to ten children from sixteen months to three years of age, and to Miss Caroline Pratt's City and Country School, an experimental school with 125 children, ranging from three years through eleven. As both schools are in one building and as the nursery children pass on to the three-year-old group in the City and Country School, these two schools for purposes of research constitute one laboratory.

At present our research staff consists of a physician and a psychologist, with assistants for certain phases of their work, a statistician, and a social investigator who gathers home records. From time to time we have had other members—a health worker, nutrition workers, a recorder as well as fellows in special subjects. Reports of the work of several of these have been published in our bulletins, or in technical magazines or in book form, as has been also a report of the first three years of our Nursery School experiment.

The scientific data of physician and psychologist accumulate slowly, and, of course, increase in value the greater the number of years they cover and the larger the number of children they include in each age group. Our physician's records include a thorough yearly examination of each child in both schools; yearly stool and urine examinations; x-rays of the chest and electro cardiograms; proportional measurements; schematograph records of posture for older children, and for the babies, photographs taken against a cross-section screen. Other and more frequent examinations are given children found to have special difficulties. All these records are taken primarily as part of the research program. All are sometimes used currently, however, to contribute data for shaping practical programs which schools and physicians work out together.

The psychologist's records include a yearly examination of each child in both schools. At this examination, the children in the City and Country School are given the Stanford revision and a group of performance tests. For the babies, special tests are being worked out, and observations along particular lines are being made. A number of studies of selected children are being made or have been made on such subjects as fear, fatigue and blood sugar, and muscle coordination. The psychologist's material is being worked up both in the form of individual records of mental growth—in many cases covering five consecutive years—and in the form of studies of age groups. Some of these data, loke those of the physician, are utilized in current programs. Both physician and psychologist use one another's material as well as the histories made for each child by the social worker.

The records of these three members of the Bureau's research staff, combined with the full records of the children's activities and experiences kept by the teachers in both schools, should make a rich accumulation for the study of normal growth in children—source material for scientists and schools alike.

The name and structural organization of the Bureau have long since disappeared but the persistence and growth of many of the undertakings described in this volume offer continuity and hopefully validity to the conceptualization of the programs developed by this interdisciplinary group of pioneers in education. It is interesting to note that none of these "founders" came from the teacher training schools of that time.

The major work of the Bureau was eventually expanded to become the Bank Street College of Education. Within its programs the Children's School carries forward the work of the Nursery School described by Harriet Johnson. In Mary Marot's study, *School Records, An Experiment,* we see in embryo the work of the Research Division of the College. The small beginnings of two prestigious independent schools—Walden School and City and Country School—are described by their founders Margaret Naumburg in *The Children's School* and Caroline Pratt in *The Play School.* The Ethical Culture School, founded some decades earlier, is represented by a report by Mabel R. Goodlander in *Education Through Experience.*

That there were so many functioning experimental schools at this time in educational history astounds us. More than a score are mentioned in a list which is not a complete accounting. It would seem, then, that there is a responsibility to examine what was the dream, how it was expressed and implemented, where it has gone.

The documents in this volume represent the major publications of the Bureau from 1917 to 1924. One unifying theme in this material is the commitment to an experimental approach to education. Whether the purpose of a pamphlet is to assist teachers in choosing toys and materials in *Playthings* (1923), to develop a critique for recording behavior in *School Records* (1922), or to describe the beginnings of school programs in *The Children's School,* there is a universal appeal to regard the content as evidence of process rather than as definitive result. Such a point of view is stated most directly by Caroline Pratt in her report on *The Play School.* She questions the worth of some established practices and views the program thus: "The real purpose of the school lies in its development as an experiment station where children can be observed." However, she places the *child* in the company of the active experimenters and puts special emphasis on an open environment in which the child may discover his world and its meanings.

Many years later attention on the child as discoverer, on the concept of education as a process of forming a style of relationship thinking rather than on the accumulation of facts, led to important and oft-times radical innovations in school curriculum. There is the profound if sometimes naive, expectation that honest evidence, carefully recorded, would lead to a truly scientific approach to education. A beginning to objective evaluation of process is made.

To this end the school programs are presented in a dual format. We find in almost all the reports of schools a statement of goals and practices by the directors, in short, the rationale underlying the establishment of *that* school. But in addition, an observer presents an objective view of the setting, the program, the children's response in each school. A more detailed report on recording children's behavior individually and in group life is offered by Mary Marot in *School Records: An Experiment* (1922). In this study we see that dedication to an open-ended stance demands that even the recording of behavior must stand as an experimental process seeking its own validity and technique.

The most significant documents deal with accounts of the schools or programs in the process of beginning at that time. And here the similarity ends. We are offered a full gamut of physical settings—urban and rural; ages ranging from infancy to fourth grade; a public school experiment; a family setting. Nine of the twelve bulletins published by the Bureau are included in this collection. The remaining three are omitted as being of minor bibliographic or historic interest only.

Child development principles also included a broad range. There is a clear statement of psychoanalytic theory as providing a methodology for education by Margaret Naumburg *(The Children's School)*. A social orientation to child growth is expressed in the report of the work of Mabel Goodlander at the Ethical Culture School. She sees as the aim of education, "to provide leadership in a democracy, emphasizing the need for the fullest development of the individual in order to render the greatest service to society." In most cases child development principles are implicit, with major stress on freedom, self-actualization, and physical and mental health. One report, *The Home School* (1917), states as its purpose, "to bring up children whose emotional expression is so unchecked and spontaneous that they will not need to be psychoanalyzed"!

Thus, we run the gamut from today's quite traditional child development theory to a Summerhillian formulation, pre-dating A. S. Neill by many years.

Conscious expression is given to social principles, psychological theory, educational goal in each of the programs described. Perhaps because the experiments were in beginning stages and the "prophets" themselves were in direct control we are able to discern a pure application of the rationale or philosophy of each of the schools.

For example, the founders of the Stony Ford School were avant garde rebels, political socialists, religious agnostics. The children share all decisions of school management; ethical principles based on social ideals are taught; school experience is explicitly designed to further the goal of developing healthy minds in healthy bodies. Organic foods, scant clothing, rigorous living are viewed as important factors in developing alert minds.

The responsibility of the school experience toward social consciousness is expressed by the other educators in different ways in these reports. For some, the child develops a sense of his social role through an intellectual understanding of his surroundings. The Play School puts major emphasis on a curriculum which opens a world of work processes to the child; provides specific materials with which he recreates his experience in his play; alerts teachers to the need for clarifying and interpreting the complexities of modern life for the child. At the other end of the continuum is the statement of social principle of The Children's School: "The reality of the social group must evolve from the child's own needs: it must grow from his gradual sacrifice or transference of ego-centric aims in favor of the wider sphere of satisfaction that the school as a social group can offer." We also see The Children's School emphasizing "spontaneous creative activities" that bring buried forces to light. For Margaret Naumburg, "true democracy is . . . a complex organization of highly differentiated individuals all contributing their particular creative powers to the life of the community." And in a third grade experimental class in a public school (The Gregory School), social goals are expressed as "honesty to themselves, to their work, and to each other." Such goals are implemented by teacher example, encouragement of children toward establishing and enforcing rules for their own behavior. Concern for social development is expressed by Harriet Johnson in *A Nursery School Report* although the children are at an infant stage—under three years. The role of group life in socializing these very little children calls for sensitive consideration of fundamental needs. At

times one protects the child from too close contact; provides
toys in quantity to encourage similar play by several children.
But encourages sharing by also having a single piece of play
equipment. To bring the child from his one child-one adult
pattern to acceptance of place in a peer group without the
trauma of deprivation is no small task. However, the belief in
group life includes the concept that early peer experience pre-
dicts positive outcome for social adjustment.

What do we find in the schools that one may designate as educational, academic purpose? When earlier we referred to con-
gruence of ideals and practices it was found to be in the experimental stance. Perhaps, one might state this even more strongly,
namely, rebellion from traditional education. There is concern
that children shall achieve mastery, there is reference to areas of
knowledge such as science, history, literature. But in every case
there is belief and expectation that in an atmosphere of freedom
the child will discover his intellectual interests and capacities
and will become sufficiently self-disciplined to pursue the tasks
that lead to competence. One must bear in mind that for the
most part these programs were designed for the young child—
pre-schoolers they came to be called. Yet we find that The Play
School experimented with directed teaching of reading and
several children did learn. However, reading seemed to hold
little interest for most of the children and was abandoned as a
non-functional skill for young children. (In later years this
school and others delayed all formal teaching of reading to the
seventh year or second grade, engendering controversy and explanation which has grown ever more heated as early childhood
education has come to occupy a more central position in the
total educational theme.) In The Children's School materials for
reading and writing were available, but only incidental instruction
was offered. The child's interest in academic skills is interpreted
as the outcome of parental pressure rather than as a response to
his own needs. We read about the notebooks kept by the older
children, sixes and sevens, and wonder how this was accomplished without some skill in writing. The Teachers College
Playground was developed with the avowed purpose of building
a curriculum which encompassed many "subjects" through the
playground experience. Thus a newspaper feeds reading interests;
building a play house calls for skill in arithmetic; a village de-

velops with play life that takes on the character of a community thereby calling for competence in planning, taking on special-ized tasks (someone must buy or sell, or put out fires), and even-tually the discovery of social organization. In this plan we see the precursor of so many schemes for social studies teaching—to name a few that have been time-honored and much publicized, only to be replaced by a new wave of enthusiasm. An early answer to the need for integrating disparate bits of information became the project method, then the activity program, later the unit method, more recently the integrated curriculum. The most sophisticated fundamental approach is found in *Man: A Course of Study* developed by the Education Development Center in the 1960's in response to the critical questioning of a group of cognitive psychologists under the leadership of Jerome Bruner.

In these experimental schools, we see an almost reverential attitude to the child's self-expression, a learning style which emanates from the child and moves outward to the peer group, the school, the community. It becomes a basic tenet of the faith, therefore, that art expression is to be individualized, un-tutored, and comprehensive. Although interpretation of such principle varies, the goal is essentially free expression for each child. In purest form The Play School sees the art experience as bringing forth "buried forces," even overcoming the blocks to expression created by the child's developing language. Abstract art is a major product in this school, seemingly absorbing and gratifying to the children and expressive of differing personality patterns. At the other end of the spectrum in The Gregory School, we see all the children drawing Halloween pictures in October and sheep when they are studying wool in the spring, with the teacher helping toward a more realistic product. But art programs go far beyond graphic expression of paper, crayons and paints; in music and dance programs Isadora Duncan furnishes inspiration in one school, in another the disciplines of body movement foreshadow the modern dance era. Dramatic production—from conception of plot, to dialogue writing, to scenery painting, to acting—is given high priority in the Stony Ford School. Language as an art medium is touched upon in the report on *Playthings*. A concern for the "child's creative power in language" leads one to recognize the "play spirit in words," and to offer language as a "free material" suitable for play purposes and art expression. Lucy Sprague Mitchell, who played a major role in the work of the Bureau, was at this time engaged in writing *The Here and Now Story Book,* which ushered in a radically new approach to the field of children's literature.

One major component of school experience, namely the teacher's role, remains implicit rather than directly expressed in these reports. Volumes of studies have emerged these many years pointing to the primacy of teacher role and style in the school experience. Yet there is no section in any of these reports devoted specifically to teachers—their personality traits, training, and experience; nor are the supervisors or directors described in such terms. How refreshing (!) and how in the neglect of such prescription of roles do we see the rebellion from the traditional teacher training schools of that time. Ten years were to elapse before the Bureau undertook to build a teacher education program to provide personnel for the proliferating progressive schools. The graduate programs of Bank Street College are the present-day outcomes of that undertaking. What then do we find in these records about teachers—their goals, their relationships with children, their responsibilities for planning and providing school experience?

As has been suggested earlier, the children play the star roles in the constellations of these schools. With perhaps more idealism than wisdom, teachers are perceived as the recessive partners in the learning-teaching transaction. The very title of the book, *I Learn From Children,* by Caroline Pratt, is indicative of the stance of these educators! Theoretical approach to child development or pedagogical method is eschewed, replaced by first-hand observation and recording of children's behavior, provision of direct experiences and materials, and the content to be learned (curriculum) originating in the children's interests.

With such an interpretation of the learning process it is not surprising to find a careful exposition of new meanings of children's play in major publications such as *Playthings* and *The Play School.* Here we see playthings as furnishing the child with the wherewithal for recreating his world as its relationships begin to take on meaning. The most careful consideration is given to the materials for constructive and dramatic play to be introduced into classrooms. The ready-made toys and finished materials with which children were usually provided are given

short shrift in these settings. Playthings are to be the raw materials from which the child, through experimental stages, fashions
ever more complex settings for his play. From this it follows
that playthings are subjected to a most rigorous study as to their
educational value before introduction to classrooms. The planned
paucity of things is seen as adding stimulus to children's imaginative ideas and to original production of play settings and experiences. There was the hope and expectation that children,
through their play, would find the need for the symbols of their
culture and thus be moved to acquire the skills of language and
numbers. Such is the respect and concern for the intellectual
processes of play that in *Children in the Play School* a quote
from John Dewey, "To be playful and serious at the same
time . . . defines the ideal mental condition," is offered in support of the thesis.

Devotion to such a concept of play is truly a recapitulation
of the proposition for the new education envisaged by these
pioneers. It furnishes the rubric within which lives experimental-
ism as the process, the child as the free agent and the adult as
provider and understanding observer. A social philosophy of a
better world brought into being by self-actualizing individuals is
inherent in these concepts of education.

In addition to recording and reporting experiments in school
settings the Bureau also undertook to gather and publish specific
curriculum materials. Two are included in this volume. *Study of
Animal Families in Schools* tells teachers as much about children
and programs as it does about the care of classroom pets: how
teachers may see new dimensions in children's behavior; how
they can "loosen up school practices"; how, by indirection, they
can teach basic hygiene lessons of ventilation, cleanliness, nutrition. Measured against the elaborate, slick curriculum materials
of today we have here a simple direct statement of the values
and problems of such experiences in classrooms. But beneath
this deceptively simple statement, there is in this, as in other
materials, a much larger purpose. There is a subtle interplay of
observation of child personality with concern for kindness to
animals. The anecdotes of responses of real children of yesterday serve to bring us once more to a view of the universality of
childhood experience.

Playthings, referred to earlier, is more than *A Catalogue of*

Play Equipment, another publication of the Bureau. It is an original, basic formulation of the meaning of play in child growth and development. Only as one regards the play of childhood as a deeply serious component of education, does one study the value and purpose of each aspect of the setting, the equipment, and the materials of the work-play life of the classroom. The scope and breadth of the ideas contained in this pamphlet go far beyond the date of its publication. Interpretation of children's play has since then developed a multi-discipline sophistication and a massive literature. But there is an almost prophetic vision of the meanings of the child's play as signals of stages of growth.

In *School Records, An Experiment* we have what is perhaps the fullest account of the principles of the study of education undertaken by the Bureau of Educational Experiments. In keeping with one major goal of the Bureau, subjecting education to scientific study, Mary Marot projects the methods of scientific research upon the school experience. She pursues direct evidence with objectivity. But she hopes to put evidence into the service of evaluation of success or failure to the end that teaching-learning methods can and will be changed. The purposes of this early attempt at recording children's behaviors in classrooms are many—among them to find a suitable technique for the school recording process; to assess individual child growth; to examine along several dimensions the continuous interaction between the child and the school environment; to alert teachers to children's differentiated models of response as evidence of learning; to develop the decision-making process as a function of total school personnel; to develop a technique for interweaving the records of peer group life with the evidence of individual children's· behavior.

Varied attempts at recording were unsuccessful. The conclusion was that only the teacher can truly record the total experience over a significant time span. That this calls for heroic effort on the part of the teacher is passed over lightly by these devoted pioneers. Teacher-recorders have not been proven practical since these beginnings. However, analysis of method, formulation of observation guides, definition of outline captions, suggestion for varied approaches so that differing experiences of classrooms may be recorded are presented and given reality by

the wealth of anecdotes of child response. Recording group behavior is viewed as a necessary aspect of the study of the individual child. There is awareness of the "whole child" and some attention is paid to parents' observations but only in so far as they
enlighten the child's responses to the school situation.

As has been indicated earlier, from this early research effort
of the Bureau there has grown at Bank Street College a well-
staffed division of psychologists and social scientists whose major
work has been in the field of educational research. Their assess-
ment of children's programs has taken many forms. One recent
publication* brings into focus much of the early work of the
Bureau founders. Applying highly sophisticated methodology
this volume studies the effect upon children of growing up in
schools that differ along the dimension from a traditional to a
modern philosophy of education. Have we proof positive that
the kind of education envisioned and expounded so many years
ago offers the "good life" to all children? A simple answer is
hardly to be expected if one asks the probing, multi-faceted
questions that true research demands. Nor is there one.

We return to the message of the simple yet basic work of
these pioneers. In the experimental stance, in an approach to
learning as an open adventure, in the valuing of human respon-
siveness, we may find a road to learning and schooling that belongs to our times of upheaval as the radical propositions of
this volume served theirs. We find no blueprints for the schools
of tomorrow here, but we do well to seek and perhaps find the
fundamentals of children's needs to be served by their schools.

Charlotte Winsor
Bank Street College of Education
September, 1972

* *Psychological Impact of School Experience*

ON THE DOCKS

EXPERIMENTAL SCHOOLS

THE PLAY SCHOOL

Caroline Pratt
Lucile C. Deming

Bureau of Educational Experiments
1917

EXPERIMENTING IN CONSTRUCTION

A TRUNK LINE

THE PLAY SCHOOL

AN EXPERIMENT IN EDUCATION

The attempt in the Play School has been to place the children in an environment through which by experiment with that environment they may become self-educated. As the educational elements in every environment are limited, the school has consciously undertaken to provide for them and recognize them in relation to the different age periods in the growth of children. The children are given free opportunity in the enriched environment to occupy themselves according to their individual needs or desires. Their choice and efforts are encouraged; their fears, if they have any, are broken down; their self-consciousness swamped in their interest in the possibilities which the environment offers. Where the school is successful, the children become in the first few months of school life, full-fledged experimenters with all that that implies.

The school had the courage to adopt the experimental method as its educational basis because it was recognized as the child's own method, by which, for example, he learned to walk and talk. All the children were, as a matter of fact, experimenters before coming to the school at four years of age, and the method had become a habit, either strong or weak, as they had lived in free or limited opportunities. In the school, where the children come in contact with other children and receive suggestions from each other, the impetus to experiment is intensified.

The traditions of established educational institutions are against experimentation. The term "experiments" as generally used, refers to the teacher and not to the children, whereas the freedom of the children is the first essential of school experimentation. There are innumerable experiments *on children* in methods of teaching; methods of teaching reading, writing, shop-work, music, and so on. But until these are applied to groups of children free to accept or reject them, the experimental method of education is not being used and the real experiment is still for the future.

Opponents of the experimental method claim that choice of occupation results in specialization. In the experience of the school with children between the ages of four and eight (at the present time the oldest

class is under nine) this is not true. All the children *choose* and undertake to do everything which the opportunity offers. Moreover, the
longer the children are in school, the more diversified do their interests
become. Those children who entered the school at seven or eight
instead of four, are, as a matter of fact, the specialized children. They
have invariably had less opportunity for choice than have the children
in the school.

The usual criticism that comes from educators is that children
never would become educated under the circumstances described. The
community, accepting the educators' ideal of literacy, believes that the
school has accomplished its purpose when such ends as reading and
writing have been accomplished.

To meet the above criticism is not yet possible. A school that is
experimental is concerned with the process and not with any such fixed
end. I cannot prove that the children will become educated under the
Play School method because the school has not carried them over a
sufficiently long period. The school has been in operation only four
years, and it will take another four at least before results can be considered. Also the school has not so consistently followed its own
method as it hopes to. Each year it learns from the experience of the
past year its failures and apparent gains. But I do claim now that
the experimental attitude is the scientific attitude which is as basic in
education as in other fields of inquiry and activity. It is the practical
procedure for a school because it is the scientific procedure. The school
may be wrong in the selection of material, but its use of the material
is scientific.

Another difficulty is the fact that the school has been compelled
to work on assumptions regarding environment in relation to the age
periods. Some of these assumptions are possibly sound, some without
doubt it will be discovered are wrong. The school is constantly on the
watch to revise them. Their valuations would be simpler if the children who came to the school had not been coerced. Before any considerable body of information can be gathered which is based upon scientific observation of children in relation to their age periods, experiment
stations (to speak in terms of the Agricultural Department) must be
multiplied. The teachers must be more scientific than they are to-day
in their observations, and psychologists must bring their material more
successfully than they have done into usable form.

In discussing the Play School, I wish particularly to avoid the
crystalization of any part of our practice or environment. There is

nothing final about either. In the following presentation of our work it should be remembered that it is all open to criticism and modification by anyone who can propose a better plan. In fact it fails in so far as it escapes criticism, and in so far as the work does not attract people who want to experiment. The real purpose of the school lies in its development as an experiment station where children can be observed.

The following are some of the things that the Play School has acknowledged in its environment. First, that the children already live and have developed, and will continue to live and develop, in surroundings with which the school has had nothing to do. Second, that children have always had a tendency to carry out in play the processes which they have seen going on about them. Third, that the complexity of modern life makes it necessary to interpret it for the children if they are to understand and use and adapt themselves to it. Fourth, that to carry out these processes they must have tools and materials suited to their childish purpose. Fifth, that any social enterprise, such as a school, creates its own problems which have to be met, and that these problems may be met naturally in a school by the children themselves.

It is only fair to recognize that the natural place for children in a world devised for grown people is that of onlookers at their pursuits, and as creators or producers only in the field of play. The unnatural or artificial attitude, as we term it, treats the children as if what they do is important in real situations in the grown-up's scheme of life. I do not minimize in saying this the importance of the tasks which children do in their homes, such as caring for their own arrangements, though I believe it is easy to carry this too far. But no scheme of education should centralize in *tasks* no matter how joyfully these tasks are under-taken. We are often misled by a five-year-old child who loves "to help" and disappointed to the point of despair when this desire disappears as it is apt to do a year later. There is no occasion for this feeling. We should be able to look at the change as an indication that the youngster has more of his own life to express and wants to do it in his own way. He is on the road to become a strong little player which argues well for his becoming a strong worker at a later period.

In a world devised for adults, any environment which is arranged for children is open to the criticism of being artificial. Some time in the future when industry, commerce, art, publicity and all social enterprises are developed in the measure to which they contribute to the growth of the race; when libraries, picture galleries and zoological gardens are arranged for children as well as adults; when parks and playgrounds and streets serve the purpose of the whole community rather than the interests of a few, and when the attitude of the grown-ups is an educational one, we may turn our children loose in an environment which will permit them to grow in a natural way, and thus escape artificiality. But until this comes we shall have to adopt some plan of education which is confessedly artificial and try to reduce the artificiality to a minimum.

This is what is attempted in the Play School. The school is but a small part of the environment of the children who attend it. It should be regarded as a convenient laboratory, work-shop, studio, furnished with all the necessary appliances. The school, however, does not depend upon these appliances for the impulse to use them, but rather upon the impetus which the child gets from his interests in outside things.

The youngest children are taken on trips through the streets. The activities they see around them are interpreted, sometimes by workmen engaged in an operation which the children are watching and sometimes by the teacher. The children in their seventh year are taken into work-shops and factories and have an opportunity to observe the processes and discover their significance. The traffic in the streets is explained to the first year children, their attention called to the different kinds of wagons, trucks, trains of cars and steamships. The traffic unexplained is confusion to the small observer. "What is the use of a horse?" I asked a city boy. "To fall down in the street," he answered. The real and vital significance of street life is lost in the general confusion, but the accident separated from the general confusion attracts attention without calling forth intellectual effort. The movement of things like traffic attracts little children, but constant and unexplained, ceases to arouse curiosity. The interpretation of the traffic, that is, getting at its significance, is to simplify the processes for them. From their curiosity about carriers their interest naturally broadens to a consideration of food, clothing and shelter. This is the method which the Play School adopts to establish an acquaintance between the child and the big world.

The children without exception are expected to take the trips. What each child gets is an individual matter depending largely upon what he already has; it may be only an impulse to do *something*. Only occasionally do the children make use of the impressions they gather from the trip immediately after they have acquired them. With the youngest children the Play School does not follow the practice which is usual in schools, of suggesting to them that they interpret the trips, but leaves it to each child to bring out in his own time and his own way what a trip has meant to him. The seven and eight-year-old children,

NOT QUITE FRIENDS

however, are induced to connect the trips with their school play where they do not make the connection for themselves. That is, their attention is called to the informative facts of a trip and the possibilities for reconstruction.

These trips are of great importance in offering the children opportunity for first hand information and in training them in observation. Nor is this information isolated from the children's purpose. For example, the activities of building a subway, transferring the materials dug out, and transporting other materials for construction suggest an adaptation of blocks, toys and other school room materials which is "play" with an entirely new significance. I am not at all sure that this interpretation of play is not a revolutionary step in education; it is newer in the educational process than structural iron work is in building. In the Play School we have not discovered the limitations to this kind of play—I doubt whether there are any.

The ideal is to pass by for the present accidental facts and center the interest in the related facts. There is no necessity for a superficial correlation of science, art, literature, geography and arithmetic in the school program if the whole problem is approached from the viewpoint of human relations, such as industry and its manifestations, because the correlation has already been made fundamentally. When nature study, for example, is applied to human activities, it throws the study of plants and animals into the background, and makes a study of them contributory to the real purpose of understanding human life. The study of past events so approached, becomes a means of interpretation of the present, where the interest is naturally centered. Although employed in a limited way in the Play School, the fundamental human relations are the underlying connection between school processes; a connection which has been one of the main quests of modern educators. An interest in the relation of things human can be begun and is begun in the Play School with the youngest group. The children of seven and eight ask pertinent questions and answer questions which they put to themselves on a basis of related facts. The school expects this treatment of the informative side of the process to lead the children to books to supplement their knowledge. The information acquired by the children is thus the result of their own observation, and the relations between their fields of information are based on observable human relations.

Such treatment of the informational side of the educational process I believe makes the school a living force. The pursuit of information is never regarded as an object in itself. It is the *process* of *getting* the *information* which is important. Giving children answers to no matter how pertinent questions never will educate them. They must be given the power to educate themselves, and this means as far as information contributes to their education they must know the sources.

With the informational side provided for, it becomes a simple matter, if such information is basic, to provide the child with the means to express both himself and the limited bits of the world with which he is becoming acquainted. Toys and blocks and materials of construction such as work-benches and tools are provided for all ages at present represented in the school, that is for children from 4 to 8 years old. It is true that toys and blocks do not respond to the need of a child who has no related knowledge to fall back upon. If a child does not know that a horse's home is a stable, where he is fed and cared for; if he does not know the use either of a horse or a wagon, it is useless to present him with a horse and wagon to play with. Parents, I think, fail to recognize that this is the answer to their query, "Why do my children always destroy their toys?"

A child can do very little with an isolated toy, but a few related toys typical of his environment furnish a stimulus if he is given space as well as blocks and building materials. The Play School toys are related in kind and size, but they are not numerous. It is important

that the children supplement the adult's unfinished stock by constructing toys for their own special use. The construction of those the school
supplies is sufficiently simple and obvious to suggest the possibility of
making other toys. The four and five-year-old children turn the school
furnishings into play materials. In their dramatic activities they use
their floor rugs, tables and chairs, and the screens which divide their
play spaces, turning them into fire engines or locomotives, or using them
to build hospitals, restaurants and all sorts of houses. In innumerable
ways they serve their dramatic purposes.

I think in calling these materials *free* materials I can best distinguish them from the materials of the kindergarten and Montessori
schools. Their uses are various. They are not designed for some special
educational purpose of an adult, but are incident to child life and child
purpose. They offer the greatest opportunity for the children's experimentation. The school is still searching for other materials as the children's play suggests new and wider needs.

The school provides in the first two years for a certain amount of
isolation of each child. The floor is spaced off with the low screens
mentioned above to protect the children's play schemes from outside
interference. Very young children can contribute little to a group until
through their own experimenting they have gained something real of
their own. In their dramatic efforts and common play they use the
school equipment which served to isolate them in their individual play.
It is the intention of the school to extend this double use of equipment
in the play-grounds of the school.

One of the contributions which I hope the Play School may make
to education is in art expression. There are possibilities of an art life
in every individual, just as there are possibilities of an intellectual life,
and by art life I do not mean art appreciation or criticism but art
expression. The failure to develop art impulse in education is partly due
to the non-recognition of the fact that the free play of children *is* art.
When this is appreciated, art expression will be developed during the
period of school experience. As the children play with drawing materials,
with plasticine, with blocks and toys, with words, with dramatics, the
emotions are freed and in a primitive way art is produced. The emotional processes in the children's play are identical with the processes
we call art in adult life, and which, with an acquired technique, give us
art production. It is what the modern school of artists in their simplified
methods of expression try to realize.

The Play School provides a supply of drawing materials for the free use of the children, limited only when they show a desire to waste them. Their desire to draw is not restricted. They are not criticised in their drawings, but stimulated. They are encouraged to represent bits of experience rather than isolated objects. The common practice of giving children objects to draw does not lead them on or stimulate their imagination. A brand new isolated object means no more to a child than it does to a grown person. He will pass it by just as a grown person does unless he can apply it or unless it is bound up in a comprehensive conception. The school has been criticised for stimulating the concept in drawing on the ground that it tends to representation rather than design, but I am confident that with little children the opposite is the case. If the very small children represent bits of experience in their drawings they begin to arrange the elements and gain composition as well as design.

Language expression is provided for through the telling of stories and relating of personal incidents. As the stories are told they are written down by the teachers and kept as a part of the child's record, together with the drawings, which are filed chronologically. As language is as utilitarian with children as it is with grown people it is necessary consciously to design to use it as an art. When a child tells a story he must hold the interest of the group. The teacher does not force the other children to attend. This stimulates the child who tells the story to choose his words. He becomes interested in words and experiments or plays with them very much as he does with his crayons in drawing.

The question of reading and writing for little children is a baffling one. It may be necessary to determine while the children are very young, while they are three or four years old, for instance, which are destined to have difficulties in the use of symbols, and to direct their attention to the value of symbols in their play schemes.

The acquirement of the technique of reading and writing has been met in one group by requiring a half-hour per day of directed effort. This has been done quite frankly and several children have learned to read and write without more time. But it must be acknowledged as a significant fact that at least half our children in the group are totally uninterested in reading as a means to acquirement and in writing as a means of expression. As laboratory equipment they find little use for either.

The approach to arithmetic has been made very simply in connection with bench-work and the carrying on of a real store with real money as the medium of exchange. The children have an interest in using tools, including a rule, and in using money, and through these they are familiar with the fundamental arithmetical processes.

Of the many things toward which we think our plan of work is tending, we are particularly encouraged in the opportunity afforded for imagination. The children are using this so constantly that it escapes observation. Even with those children whom we are inclined to designate as unimaginative the opportunity to think beyond, to anticipate the next step in play schemes for which they individually are responsible results in the training of imagination. In dealing with children we may congratulate ourselves that no young child can carry out imitative processes to any extent. He may get his impulse through desire to do just what some other child has done but he is protected from carrying it out by lack of training. He diverges and in doing so comes as near creation as it is possible to do. This divergence tends to become a habit and if the child is left to his own devices or encouraged to pursue his efforts as an individual instead of being forced into group activity, I believe he will go through life with a tendency to anticipate, plan, imagine, initiate or whatever one may choose to call this quality.

CAROLINE PRATT.

BUILDING FOR A PURPOSE

CHILDREN IN THE PLAY SCHOOL

The Play School experiment is enchanting enough in itself when one considers that its philosophy suggests that all the vivid interest, the activity and color and joyous freedom it produces might belong to life in general. But its setting is also unique and delightful—in a studio at the end of MacDougal Alley, decorated in an unusual variety of gracious colors laid out and planned in shapes of triangles and diamonds that satisfy the mind and quiet the eye. The effect is both child-like and charming. A balcony where the five-year-old children work overhangs the room adding to the amount of floor space sufficiently so that each child can be comparatively alone. This and the adjoining room of the seven and eight-year-old group can be thrown into one for general activities like dancing. Above there is a library room and a good-sized workshop. The school was started five years ago in a little old-fashioned house. Two groups of children are still attending there, but will be moved to rooms nearer the rest next year.

The furniture bears little resemblance to that in the traditional schoolroom. There are individual tables and little chairs, and attractive cupboards and shelves where all the materials lie within easy reach of the children. In the yard with its gaily painted fence a family of rabbits and of pigeons have their homes. Other animals are brought regularly for study. In the yard also are climbing poles, bars, a see-saw, a sand pile, garden tools, and a group of packing boxes recently moved in, which the children are now transforming into a village.

Most of the equipment is something like the raw material needed for the purposes of living. It lends itself chiefly to creative and imaginative activity. There are blocks, short, square, triangular; curved ones that make fine corners for train tracks, and long ones, some of which stand taller than the children who build big houses with them. Other blocks that fit together with pegs make all sorts of things, including automobiles, derricks, and other machinery that the children have seen. The block houses are alive with dolls of different sizes who in the roles of men, women and children, stand, sit, walk and drive and do all the things children see people doing about them in the real world. The wooden horses, cows and other animals are of related size to the dolls, as are also the dump carts, milk wagons and railroad trains. These toys are made of wood and are easily reproduced by the children in the workshop. Some of the professional dolls and all of the animals are painted in characteristic colors. A policeman doll suggests to the child the need of a street corner and when at length a city is built up around this beginning a farm may next be located where the child can keep a cow from which to get his city's milk supply. This indicates the possibilities which the children themselves find in the material.

All of the classes take weekly trips out into the city to visit factories, bakeries and stores, to follow automobile trucks to their destinations and see what happens there, to see the docks where food supplies, coal, and raw and manufactured products from all over the world are unloaded from the ships. Whatever the child gets from these experiences is likely to appear later in his play. The portfolios of drawings on the shelves as they fill up during the year with the graphic records of scenes which have been running through the children's minds, provide a wealth of material from which to study the interests of the individual child.

The plan carried out in drawing is characteristic of the method of the school. Drawing materials in abundance are at hand as if they were the natural right of the child—colored crayons, water color paints and large sheets of paper. The children work with entire freedom. No criticism is ever made by the teachers. The only suggestions are put in the form of a question that relates to action and will raise some visual answer in the child's mind. If he says, "This is a man," the teacher may ask, "Where is he going?" Her attempt is always to encourage in the play the reproduction of "blocks of experience" rather than of unrelated or isolated objects. An eminent artist who has recently seen the collection of drawings exclaimed with pleasure at the composition and color that has been arrived at by the children themselves.

Another material that appeals to the children greatly is clay. The smallest child will pat and pound and roll, and if you happen by he may tell you, "This is a worm! And this is a cake and a flower!" You may ask him where the worm came from, but if you suggest that he can make the flower look more like one (to you), you will be violating the spirit of the school.

The work-shop is equipped with four substantial benches and all of the best ordinary carpenter's tools. Children of four and five discover how to use the saws and planes and chisels for themselves. They make carts and automobiles, Fifth Avenue busses, boats, and toy furniture. A child's standard of satisfaction with his product is the mark of its success for the teacher. If he is pleased, she does not see the crooked edges and corners. A five-year-old, working by himself, who found that he could make the square window he wanted in a box by starting with the augur and bit and then inserting a key-hole saw, had had exactly the kind of experience of trial and discovery the school hopes to provide continually for him.

The Play School has found that the children's impulse to play is real and continuous enough to sustain day-long, spontaneous, purposeful activity in the school. But it is something also easily destroyed by lack of a fostering environment—children who enter the school later than four years old are sometimes already slightly changed by the influences of conventional repression. In activities like the dancing they may join with complete abandon. But in using tools and materials their spontaneous interest may at first be less absorbing. Professor John Dewey has said that "To be playful and serious at the same time is possible and it defines the ideal mental condition." This essential spirit of freedom for joyous and effective living it is the hope of the Play School to preserve.

LUCILE P. DEMING.

LITTLE "HAROLD BAUER"

LIST OF EXPERIMENTAL SCHOOLS

THE BERKELEY PLAY SCHOOL (Summer)—University of California, Berkeley, Cal.
> MR. and MRS. W. CLARK HETHERINGTON.

BOYLAND—Santa Barbara, Cal.
> MR. PRINCE HOPKINS.

THE ELEMENTARY SCHOOL—Boston.
> MISS FAYE HENLEY.

THE ELLIS SCHOOL—Newton Centre, Mass.
> MISS EVELYN ELLIS.

THE ETHICAL CULTURE SCHOOL (First Grade)—
Central Park West and 63rd Street, New York.
> MRS. HELEN SPEER.

THE FAIRHOPE SCHOOL—Fairhope, Alabama.
> MRS. MARIETTA JOHNSON.

THE GREGORY PUBLIC SCHOOL—West Orange, N. J.
> MISS EDITH BARNUM.

THE HOME SCHOOL—Sparkill, N. Y.
> MISS MATTIE B. BATES.

THE FRANCIS SCOTT KEY SCHOOL—Baltimore, Md.
> MISS PERSIS MILLER.

THE HORACE MANN KINDERGARTEN—Teachers College, Columbia University, N. Y. C.
> PROF. PATTY SMITH HILL,
> MISS CHARLOTTE GARRISON.

THE HORACE MANN SCHOOL (First Grade)—
525 West 120th Street, N. Y. C.
> MISS F. MABEL McVEY.

THE LABORATORY SCHOOL—157 East 72nd Street, N. Y. C.
> MISS SARAH FISKE,
> MISS ESTELLE DE YOUNG.

THE LANIER SCHOOL—Greenwich, Conn.
> MRS. MARIETTA JOHNSON,
> MRS. CHARLES D. LANIER.

MARIENFELD PLANTATION SCHOOL—Samarcand, N. C.
DR. C. HANFORD HENDERSON.

THE MERION COUNTRY DAY SCHOOL—Merion Station, Penn.
MISS GERTRUDE HARTMAN.

THE CHILDREN'S SCHOOL—34 West 68th Street, New York City.
MISS MARGARET NAUMBURG.

THE ORCHARD SCHOOL—Leonia, N. J.
MRS. WILLIAM G. NOYES.

THE OPEN AIR SCHOOL—119 East 40th Street, New York City.
MISS LEILA M. WILHELM.

THE PARK SCHOOL—Buffalo, N. Y.
MARY HAMMETT LEWIS.

THE PARK SCHOOL—Baltimore, Md.
PROF. EUGENE RANDOLPH SMITH.

THE PHOEBE ANNA THORNE OPEN AIR MODEL SCHOOL—
Bryn Mawr, Penn.
DR. M. DE CASTRO.

THE PLAY SCHOOL—206 West 13th Street, N. Y. C.
MISS CAROLINE PRATT.

THE PORTER RURAL SCHOOL—Kirksville, Missouri.
MRS. MARIE TURNER HARVEY.

THE SCHOOL OF CHILDHOOD—University of Pittsburg, Pittsburg.
PROF. WILL GRANT CHAMBERS.
MISS MEREDITH SMITH.

THE SOCIAL MOTIVE SCHOOL—540 West 114th Street, N. Y. C.
MISS BERTHA BENTLY.

STONY FORD SCHOOL—Stony Ford, New York.
MRS. DELIA D. HUTCHINSON.
MR. ROBERT H. HUTCHINSON.

TEACHERS COLLEGE EXPERIMENTAL PLAYGROUND—Teachers College,
Columbia University, N. Y.
MISS MARY RANKIN.

Note.—The Department of Information desires the cooperation of persons acquainted with experimental school work in extending the above list and in collecting information regarding such schools.

REFERENCES

REPORT OF EXPERIMENTAL WORK IN THE SCHOOL OF CHILDHOOD.
  University of Pittsburg Bulletin—General Series, Vol. 12, July 29,
  1916, No. 19.

THE DEMONSTRATION PLAY SCHOOL OF 1913.
  University of California, Bulletin, 1914, Vol. 5, No. 2.

EXPERIMENTAL STUDIES IN KINDERGARTEN EDUCATION.
  Teachers College Publication, 1915.

THE FAIRHOPE LEAGUE PUBLICATIONS.
  Greenwich, Conn.

TEACHERS COLLEGE RECORD.
  November, 1916. Education for Initiative and Originality.

THE SPEYER SCHOOL CURRICULUM
  Teachers College Publication, Columbia University.

A YEAR'S WORK IN INDUSTRIAL ARTS (Third Grade), Speyer School
  Ida M. Bennett.

ALEXANDER, F. M. P.
  Conscious Control. Methuen, 1912.

HENDERSON, C. HANFORD
  Education and the Larger Life. Houghton Mifflin Co., 1902.
  What It Is to be Educated. Houghton Mifflin Co., 1914.

DEWEY, JOHN.
  Democracy and Education. Macmillan, 1916.

  How We Think. D. C. Heath & Co., 1910.

  Interest and Effort in Education. Houghton, Mifflin Co., 1913.

  The School and Society. University of Chicago Press, ed. of 1916.

DEWEY, JOHN and EVELYN.
  Schools of Tomorrow. E. P. Dutton Co., 1915.

HALL, G. STANLEY.
  Aspects of Child Life and Education. Ginn & Co., 1914.
  "The Story of a Sand Pile."

KILPATRICK, WILLIAM HEARD.
  The Montessori System Examined. Houghton, Mifflin Co., 1914.
  Froebel's Kindergarten Principles Critically Examined. Macmillan
  Co., 1916.

LEE, JOSEPH.
  Play in Education. Macmillan Co., 1915.

PALMER, LUELLA.
  Play Life in the First Eight Years. Ginn & Co., 1916.

RUSSELL, BERTRAND.
  Why Men Fight. The Century Co., 1917.
  Chap. 1, "The Principle of Growth."

WOOD, WALTER.
  Children's Play and Its Place in Education. A. S. Duffield & Co.,
  1913.

WELLS, H. G.
  Floor Games. Small, Maynard & Co., 1912.

THE CHILDREN'S VILLAGE

EXPERIMENTAL SCHOOLS

THE CHILDREN'S SCHOOL

Margaret Naumburg
Lucile C. Deming

TEACHERS COLLEGE PLAYGROUND

Lucile C. Deming

THE GREGORY SCHOOL

Lucile C. Deming

Bureau of Educational Experiments
1917

LUNCHEON AT THE CHILDREN'S SCHOOL

A Direct Method of Education

Up to the present, our methods of education have dealt only with the conscious or surface mental life of the child. The new analytic psychology has, however, demonstrated that the unconscious mental life which is the outgrowth of the child's instincts plays a greater rôle than the conscious. We have spent much of our time training children to think and act properly by themselves. But we have done this without being aware of the fundamental basis of thought and action. The new psychology has uncovered the true nature of primitive thought and has shown that it still lives on in the unconscious mental being of the adult as well as of the child. Most of our thinking is in this primitive or "fantasy" form; and only a minor part of our mental life occurs as *directed* thought. Yet all our methods of education up to the present time have taken into account only this later type of mental process.

This discovery of the fundamental sources of thought and action must bring about a readjustment in education. School problems can no longer be dealt with as they appear on the surface, for our deeper knowledge must direct our attention to the deeper realities beneath. The nature and the meaning of an·action must no longer be judged by its mere external manifestations. Formerly, if a child forgot what he was told to do, lied, showed fear or disobeyed, that particular matter was taken up, investigated, or solved in some immediate way as a problem in itself. But with this new approach we know that most of such behavior, common to all children in and out of school, is significant not so much in itself, but rather as a symptom of deeper and more intricate states in the unconscious life. And the usual attempt at a surface solution of a child's behavior when, for instance, he lies or shows fear, is similar to the act of cutting off the top of a weed with the roots still in the ground. We are now able to regard such actions as symptomatic and to trace them back, step by step, to their source. Up to the present time, education has missed the real significance of the child's behavior, by treating surface actions as isolated conditions. Having failed to recognize the true sources of behavior, it has been unable effectively to correct and guide the impulses of human growth. In view of this, the new approach furnishes the *one direct method for education.*

By means of it, we are led immediately into the study of the child's unconscious psychic life, which is the outgrowth of the activity and interplay of his inborn instincts. The trend of these complex forces determines the child's adjustment to the objective world. The very young child is absorbed in himself, in his bodily functions and in those individuals who intimately surround him. The problem of gradually weaning him from those ego-centric interests is deeper and more complex than educators commonly realize. These early attachments of childhood are so strong that they may color and affect the entire adult life. The usual processes of education, in combatting merely the *symptoms* of these attachments, may result in repression, so that the emotional connections continue to operate unknown to the individual himself. True education must tend to bring forward these emotional sources so that they may be freed from their infantile stations and consciously re-directed into social and creative channels.

The nature of these deep childhood associations is determined by the fusion of two elements: his own type and temperament and those of his family group in their effect upon him. The emotional tone of these relationships will in turn influence his personal and social reactions in later life. To those who have the technique of tracing symptomatic actions back to their sources, the exact position of the child in his family group is revealed by his behavior in school. For the child who is carried out of the family milieu into the school milieu brings with him all the unconscious reactions by means of which he adjusted to his mother, father, brothers and sisters. He thereupon tends to re-create in the school group those relationships which were peculiar to his home environment. For instance, the child with the all-encompassing mother is apt to run to the teacher for praise and attention; the child who has been dominated by an older brother is apt to imitate his strut, and gain satisfaction by dominating in turn a weaker or younger child in the school group; the child who has been ruled at home by a younger but stronger brother is likely to reveal this family situation by also reproducing it in school, where he seeks out a younger but stronger child to take his brother's place. To the uninitiated these examples may seem special, but in average groups of children I have found them to be among the typical relations. By becoming aware of them and of their meaning the teacher is placed in a position to cope with them; to prevent the mere repetition of narrowing relationships and to help the child broaden and round out his social life.

The intense and unconscious attachments that bind a child to his own immediate appetites and to his family make it far more difficult than is generally realized for him to sacrifice them to the larger interests of the group. As a necessary step in socialization, however, the school group must replace the family. But this readjustment does not come easily. A child's persistent ego-instincts act as an impediment to the socializing process, and create a conflict in his psychic life. The reality of the social group must evolve from the child's own needs: it must grow from his gradual sacrifice or transference of ego-centric aims in favor of the wider sphere of satisfaction that the school as a social group can offer. It must come from deep within, in order to be fundamental. My own experience with the new psychologic method has convinced me that a great part of the so-called socialization in our modern schools is an external form superimposed by the teacher, and that underneath the appearance of a social group, the fundamental interests of the children may still remain attached to primary ego-centric sources: may, in other words, not have been socialized at all.

Indeed, the material uncovered in the unconscious mental life of adults should make us realize that true socialization is a long and difficult process, and that very few adults can be said completely to achieve it. It appears that most mature persons have not, in their unconscious emotional life, overcome the infantile unsocial demands which hinder a perfect adjustment to society. The socializing process must therefore be looked on as far more prolonged and complex than educational methods in the past have assumed.

Another interesting element in the problem of socialization is the force of the group instinct which is just as deep-rooted in the individual as the ego instinct. This impulse gradually comes into conflict with the strong ego-centric impulses of all the children in the group. It has its effect even upon the youngest, although in ways that may be revealed by unconscious reactions rather than by any active cooperation with the group itself. In this problem as well, the teacher has to deal with a maze of forces below the surface of action. She can therefore not be guided by external acts alone, but must aid in the channeling of all these interacting impulses.

In handling the physical as well as the mental life of the child the teacher must be trained to work back from the external end-symptom to the real underlying causes of the problem. In this field of physical co-ordination, a new and remarkable method of readjusting the child's bodily control has been developed by Mr. F. Matthias Alexander. The technique of his method has a surprising analogy with the new analytic psychology. Both methods insist that physical or mental mistakes cannot be corrected by treatment as isolated problems. Both methods trace back the way by which the individual has arrived at his wrong condition. Just as those trained in analytic psychology know it to be useless to tell a child who lies to stop lying, so those trained in the method of physical co-ordination know it to be useless to tell a child to stand up straight. Both discard the "don't-do-this" principle of teaching; and look for a deeper cause governing the wrong thought or act. For both methods have ascertained that the individual cannot without a fundamental *re-education* know or understand the causes behind his physical and mental processes.

The correlation of these two approaches to the sources of mental and physical activity constitutes a real method of *re-education*. Education in the sense of "leading forth" what is already there, is not enough. The child comes to the school with physical inhibitions and emotional fixations which must be analyzed back to their elementary components, in order that his energies may be released for proper growth. With this true control, the child can now use his powers for expression and creation. This technique of re-education can, moreover, no longer be considered merely hypothetical. Both phases of it are being constantly developed. My own experience during a relatively short time has already led to increasingly real results.

Of great importance in analyzing the child's psychic life is the buried material that comes to light in his spontaneous creative activities. Among these are his first free drawings, his early attempts at dancing, making-up of songs, and the beginnings of play. All of these have more than surface significance. Through them much of the material of primitive thinking is brought forth symbolically by the child, long before language and writing become accessible as means of free expression. In fact, the medium of speech, even when it is mastered as a channel of inquiry and articulation, is often blocked by the false answers of grownups to the child's earliest questionings as to life, birth and death. In consequence, the child is forced back to the expression of these problems in the more primitive language of symbolic form in his drawing, dancing, music, and other activities.

For this reason, I encourage children to draw, dance, and so on, without external plan or suggestion. They find material for their expression freely within themselves and thus, in their abstract designs and their invented dance-figures, are at the threshold of all creative art.

These early artistic enterprises serve to bring into conscious life the buried material of the child's emotional problems. Gradually, his energies are transferred from unconscious, ego-centric attachments, to the wider intercourse of social life. This, indeed, is a function of all art: self-expression in forms that are of social and communicable value. The individual's unconscious energy creates material with meaning to the group. But when I speak of encouraging creative expression as a means of the individual's adjustment to group life, I do not mean that each child must ultimately become a creative artist. Whatever work he may do, if it is to be satisfactory to him and to his fellows, must express himself and become a means toward living in a creative way. All work must serve as a channel whereby the individual's particular life-energy may flow undiminished into the life of the group. This is as true of work in carpentry or mathematics as in music or the dance. So long as work offers a means of true experience it aids the individual to grow and, in turn, enhances the life of the community.

Indeed, no true social adjustment can be hoped for, without the release of the ego impulses brought about through creative work. Expression and experience serve to transfer the childish energies into social consciousness and can alone bring about a deep inner adjustment with the group. The repression or negation of these unconscious elements tends to subvert them into destructive, rather than creative forces.

It is a mistake, moreover, to consider the individual and the group concepts as really antagonistic. The instincts that underlie individual and social life are both inherent in mankind: and the realization of either is impossible without the other. There can be no developed individual without a constructive group-sense. And there can be no developed society that is not integrated and composed of individuals each functioning fully and completely. The true democracy is not an inchoate mass of similar units, but a complex organization of highly differentiated individuals all contributing their particular creative powers to the life of the community.

MARGARET NAUMBURG.

THE CHILDREN'S SCHOOL

Miss Naumburg began her school three years ago with the purpose of helping the children create their own type of environment, as a direct outgrowth of their spontaneous needs and interests. The children in the school range from two and one-quarter to seven years old. Last year there were thirty in the two groups. The school is planned for children as young as two years because this seems the time when their activities and desires are still eager and unwarped by most outside influences. Miss Naumburg, by reaching the children as young as this and allowing them to develop with others of the same age in a free environment, hopes to build upon a fundamental basis for education. Her approach to this work, as she explains in her own statement, is through the technique of the new analytic psychology.

In accordance with this viewpoint the curriculum of the most modern school would have to be subordinated and even sacrificed temporarily if need be to the personal problem of each child. The child's development, his own growth and readjustment day by day as the gradual process of re-education helps to ground him in his own real self—this is held to be the deeply important thing.

To the visitor merely observing the activity the school appears immediately to be one of the group that is putting into practice the newer ideals of education. In the little children's room there are blocks and toys and drawing materials. Part of the Montessori material which fits the need of the children is kept within reach on the shelves. In the yard there are a sand box and apparatus. The little children are allowed to play together if they please. When they do so a large share of the teacher's attention is given to helping the individuals to maintain their places with fairness in the groups. Miss Naumburg has found that at first they isolate themselves and work quite alone, regardless of the others. Then gradually groups of two and three children come together as the need of cooperation arises out of their self-initiated activities, and before the end of the year the entire group of children may be seen together working out a game or story of their own invention

The older children have books and writing materials, as well as blocks and toys, carpentry tools, clay and other constructive materials. Many of them have learned to write and then to read because they wanted to. The method of teaching each child has been adjusted to his particular ability. Some children learned to write by first touching the letters; some learned by sounding and others by seeing them. There has been no attempt to keep the group at the same point of development. In number work it has been the same. The children have learned mostly through the incidental counting and measuring needed in their activity. Miss Naumburg has no particular desire to have the children acquire "the tools" so early, but home surroundings have doubtless stimulated their interest in reading and writing. The children seem to enjoy the learning for its own sake, as an interesting activity.

Much of their work is individual. When they are drawing or making up their note-books they work at individual or group tables. Their air of intentness proves that they are developing thought processes of their own. The teachers answer their questions, whatever they are, with the strictest regard for accuracy, knowing that they are the outcome of attempts at reasoning that are important to the development of the child. It is only in the dancing and various games like "Silence" and "Listening" and story-telling and dramatizing that the class participates as a whole. But no activity is ever forced even in the slightest degree on any of the children. The result is that as the year goes on they grow in spontaneity and expressiveness. The timid little boy who would never join in the dancing is later seen leading little girls by the hand to join in a game of his initiating, and also dancing willingly.

The aim of the teacher in directing the child is to keep him independent and individual so that just as he is free from the repression of the conventional schoolroom he may also be free from the dominating influence of any of his companions in the group. An inspection of the note-books of the children proves that this has been accomplished. Each one is totally different. Some children have gone far with theirs; others have apparently been more interested in something else. It is obvious from seeing these books that they have been allowed to carry out their ideas as they please.

Up to this time the work which shows the largest outward result of any in the school is the drawing. The open shelves in both rooms contain piles of drawing paper and boxes of crayons which the children may use at absolutely any time or as long a time as they choose. The teachers have never suggested that they copy or draw pictures of specific things, and have refrained from asking the leading question, "What is it?" when the child has brought his drawing to show them, because they realize that unless he volunteers the information he is apt to make up an answer to satisfy the grown-up. The result has been that instead of the usual story pictures a great quantity of abstract designs have come from each of the children. Over a period of two years some of the children have evolved strange and remarkable designs, a-symmetrical and symmetrical, strongly colored, and often showing the use of one motif carried over in different ways into many drawings. Some of them suggest the symbols of primitive art, or the naive paintings of some modern artists. The utter absorption with which the children work and the evident satisfaction they take in the results is significant in itself. At almost any time that a visitor comes into the school he may see a child here or there intent on a large drawing, studying it critically from time to time and working apparently oblivious of other activities going on in the room. Sometimes a frail, timid little child will use the boldest contrasts of passionate color, putting the energy he does not dare to express in his relationships with other children into this creative form of work. Very few drawings of people and things have been done up to the present time, but there now seems to be a growing tendency toward representation. All of the children's drawings marked with names and dates are kept at the school. They may form the material of an interesting psychological study later on.

Up to the present time Miss Naumburg has been unable to complete her plan owing to lack of space and the brief hours of the children's attendance at school. But next year "The Children's School" will be established as an open-air school in a house of its own (34 West 68th Street), where each group will have more adequate space. The various school activities, such as carpentry, modeling, music, dancing and science, will each be carried out for the older children in special rooms devoted to these purposes, with special teachers who are in sym-pathy with the spirit of the entire school. The older children will come back in the afternoon. Trips will be taken to link up the life and activities of the city with their own lives and work. The after-noon excursions will include trips to the park and country and museums with a naturalist whose work will be supplemented in the school with pet animals and growing plants. The school will try to create an all-day, all-around life for city children.

LUCILE C. DEMING.

TEACHERS COLLEGE PLAYGROUND

The playground connected with the Horace Mann Kindergarten was started six years ago by Professor Hill. Its purpose was to provide for children from four to eight years of age in some better way than was being done on the usual city playground, where the important play needs of these younger children were largely left out of account. Usually the playground teacher's interest was given chiefly to the organized games which were for the older children, and the younger group spent the play time on see-saws, swings and other apparatus. Except for the sand-pile, things-with-which-to-do had seldom been supplied them, materials which beside making a strong appeal to the children, provide a stimulus for the imaginative play of which the city child has far too little. Miss Hill felt that the possibilities of such simple constructive materials had not been developed.

The small space that was available—a rectangular court-yard of cement about 60 by 150 feet in size, with a narrow strip of ground (which they used for a garden) was less room than that usually afforded by a city school plant. The children were first supplied with sand, clay, wood, and tools. The list of tools includes: No 3 adze hammers, cross-cut saws, rip saws, a keyhole saw, two braces with bits of several sizes, screw driver and claw, nails, screws, hinges, snow shovels, and a spade. Some small wooden boxes that were included in the wood supply immediately attracted them. They furnished them as play houses with little play furniture and brought looms to weave mats of yarn for rugs. When two large packing boxes were brought they suggested to the children the need for larger pieces of wood to make into furniture for the "real houses." Each child now has his own house or store in a large box which he may remodel and decorate and enlarge into several stories with other boxes, as he chooses. Children occasionally bring material from home, such as pieces of carpet, rugs, pictures and dishes. Paints and brushes, door hinges and nails and screws are purchased whenever there is need for them.

In the summer the sand-box is used a great deal even by the older children. Children of eight and nine years built a subway system there last year and also made battle-fields and played war. The strip

INTERIOR DECORATION AT TEACHERS COLLEGE PLAYGROUND

of ground at the side was planted for a garden, and plans are already being made for a garden this spring.

The individual children are chiefly occupied in building and rebuilding their houses and running their "stores". They are satisfied with simple beginnings at first but later are continually improving or "building on," criticizing and making suggestions to each other frequently, and keeping note of each other's progress. One child, seeing his neighbor's superior door-way or window, becomes dissatisfied with his own and sets about improving it. They take keen interest in new projects such as building ladders or chimneys, making lattice-work windows and putting on slanting roofs or second stories. Some children are satisfied with very rough construction and are interested chiefly in the social play, but even left to themselves as they generally are, they gradually discover the need of improving their houses in first this and then that particular. As an example one little girl became known as having the neatest and prettiest house. She had brought cloth for curtains and a rug from home and had put pictures and ornaments on the walls. She locked her house carefully at night and always kept it very neat. One day a boy who had a very rough habitation at the other end of the street announced his intention to make his house over into a nice one like hers, and thereupon set about doing so. The span of interest and also the standard of satisfaction with results increases generally with the ages of the children.

The playground has become a village, with houses and stores facing on a central street, and connected by a telephone system made out of strings and tin cans. With their original allotment of $2.50 of playground paper money the children pretend to rent their houses and sell groceries and other commodities to each other, getting in this way very good experience in handling money. They publish a weekly newspaper, to which the children contribute items. The editor, a precocious child of six and a half, typewrites at home a full sheet with two columns of news every week, and the children are intensely interested in every issue.

The group feeling that quickly developed found expression in the organization of a town government. One child, who had belonged to a Boys' Club, suggested that there be a president of the playground, "so that things will get done better." They now have elections about every two weeks, sometimes a campaign with two opposing parties that draw up platforms and make speeches. Among the elected officers, beside the president, the mayor and the policeman, is the street cleaner who is supposed to sweep the space between the houses every day. For this service he is paid thirty cents a day in playground money by the president. The idea of having taxes on the community to meet this payment was recently suggested by the president himself. It will doubtless come up again and a "law" will be established.

A description of the activity as a whole makes it appear unusually intense and suggests that it must be directed and developed by the teacher. As the play actually goes on from day to day, however, it is crude and spasmodic. The houses are by no means finished products before the interest in building ceases, often for days at a time, and the town organization often drops completely out of sight. For instance, on cold days, when the children like to run and play tag and organized games, the tools are scarcely used at all, but however long abandoned, the interest in the constructive play always revives again. The interests of the children vary greatly. One little boy who came to the playground wanted to do nothing but climb and run. The teachers later found that he had been sitting all the morning in a school where he got only twenty minutes exercise, and they felt that he was simply working out his own needs when he came to the playground. They believe that for children who get very little exercise and for badly co-ordinated children it would be useful to have more apparatus.

Miss Rankin has a student assistant from Teachers College to help her this year. Often they are both so absorbed in the work as to see nothing of each other during the two hours. But the children know that they are entirely free to do whatever they please. As one child observed to Miss Rankin the other day: "Now you are not here to teach us, are you? We are just supposed to practice and learn, ourselves, how to do things." Whenever the children want help in working out a difficult project the teacher enters into it with them, and she often takes part as one of the group in playing house or store or in some organized game. She also talks with them about their houses so that they will feel her interest. She allows the *child's own satisfaction* to be the measure of his achievement. She makes plenty of suggestions but does not urge anything. If a child is interested enough to take up a suggestion, it is because of his own feeling about it, not because of the teacher's attitude. For example, a child who wanted to make a window in his house would perhaps explain his intention and ask how he should finish off the opening when it was made. Lattice work is what he usually decides upon now, as the best houses are finished with it. But if the example were not there to imitate the teacher would make the suggestion, along with others, and the child would doubtless take one of them. If it was something difficult or tedious for him to do she would join in and do part of the actual work for him. The younger children would become discouraged often by the mere amount of work to do in carrying out some idea they have begun, and the teacher should prevent this if possible. When they will persevere without her attention she is ready with appreciation. To an observer the spirit between the teachers and the children is an easy, playful one. There is a mutual confidence and reasonableness. The children are not dependent, and they do not seem to be often inconsiderate or demanding. The teachers have an air of actually sharing the objective interests of the children, and there is rather a give and take of enjoyment than a one-sided interest in only the children's pleasure.

The discipline of the playground is not much of a problem. There are sometimes quarrels over material and disputes as to rights and possessions but it is the policy of the teachers to interfere only when they are consulted as to the fairness of the issue, or when the trouble seems seriously to call for adjustment. The spirit of public opinion is very strong and children criticize one another for wasting materials or leaving their surroundings in an untidy condition. These standards are built by the teacher's suggestions. If a child does persist in offending, excluding him from the playground is always sufficient to make him wish to change his ways and return. A child who was a persistent trouble maker would not be kept on the playround. The teachers definitely prohibit fighting and "bullying." When the children want to throw things, merely because of their desire for activity, the teachers try to turn their interest into some kind of a rivalry game. Target throwing does not have quite the interest of a fight but the children are usually willing to understand and cooperate with the teacher's wishes.

Perhaps the most valuable result of the playground to the children is that they have come to regard it as a center for the expression of all their ideas and interests, a place where they go to talk over the things that have come to their minds and to put their ideas and interests into concrete or active expression.

The result in enthusiasm is also a very important one. The play is real. A child's interest in a project often holds over so that he can be said to be working with perseverance. One little boy, for example, spent an entire afternoon recently wrestling with the problem of removing a big box that was nailed to the top of his house. He had to remove dozens of nails but he finally accomplished what he was after. The children's interest and enthusiasm tends to increase their enjoyment even of the things which they themselves distinguish as work. One little boy recently remarked: "I can always tell the sum of everything on the playground. In school I can't tell how much 3 and 3 make." All parts of the curriculum come into use in their play, in measuring and counting, in publishing the paper, in their buying and selling and in conversations and imaginative play. Miss Rankin believes that the playground interest carries over into their school activities.

The development of individual children has been marked in respect to initiative and physical control. One child who is very superior intellectually, came without the slightest ability to do anything with his hands. He kept an office in a plain box at first and was satisfied with publishing the playground paper. He soon wanted to take part in the building that was going on and he learned to handle the tools sufficiently to make improvements in the construction of his office and to paint the outside walls. Here he used an original idea of his own—to have a red background and black cross lines to represent bricks.

A decided interest in ownership and possession develops in some of the children. Others do not feel the importance of occupying their "own" houses. Sometimes, however, when a child has shown no apparent interest of this kind, after playing in the other houses and in the games he will suddenly wish to possess a building of his own. One boy who has spent most of his time this year helping the others build, or making and selling them things, has recently taken over a neglected house and is putting it into splendid shape.

To modify the individualistic spirit that sometimes grows too strong—the "this is mine" attitude—Miss Rankin not long ago suggested that the children build a slide so that they would have something to own in common. They tried twice to make one without success and she was then going to buy one. Two of the boys wanted to persist, however, and the third attempt was entirely successful. One boy drew the plans at home and brought them to the playground. The tools and supplies are always used in common, and the children are now building a cart which will belong to the playground.

Great progress in the social values is accomplished during a year. First there is a little spontaneous cooperation; then a friendly spirit grows among the children, and one by one little antagonisms, that may even have loomed rather large in the teacher's eyes, disappear. A definite group feeling develops. This community feeling holds over not only throughout the year but from group to group as the children change. It is in this way that so much of the activity is repeated every year.

Traditions have been established and are regularly handed down, as the children always take an interest in what has been done before. There are usually some children who return the second year and they not only pass on the customs, but they take possession as in their own right of whatever property they had before. The group feeling has an effect on all of the children, but particularly modifies the outlook of some who are "only children" at home. To a certain extent the matter of the adjustment to each other is of conscious interest to the children; there is a community "public opinion." They offer criticisms and suggestions to one another and react together against any "bullying."

In Miss Rankin's opinion, even a great deal more might be accomplished on a playground. The space here is too small to accommodate more than twenty-five children, or more equipment. With more resources at their command they might often turn the children's spontaneous curiosity to better advantage. As it is now, the children sometimes go to the carpentry teacher in Horace Mann for advice and suggestions on their building. They often inquire as to the exact workings of something like a telephone system or some other mechanical device for a playground project. They constantly bring ideas and suggestions and questions from school and their home life. If the children were at liberty to go into the college laboratories and work out with the help of scientists the problems that come up in their play, they might find one way in which some of their questions could be adequately answered. Miss Rankin would like to have a house built on the playground where they could keep a typewriter for printing the newspaper, and books of information of all kinds.

One boy suggested the other day that it would be fun to have two villages. This idea suggests many possibilities, such as building a railroad between the towns and having separate industries and exchange of products. Here a great deal of opportunity for elaborate schemes of construction and of government organization might come in.

Miss Rankin keeps a few notes and writes up a record of individual development at the end of the year. She finds in looking back on the year for each child that there is marked individual growth.

This playground has been criticized because one teacher is occupied with so small a group of children. A former student is putting in the same idea with much larger groups of children on the playgrounds in Honolulu. Miss Rankin has found that one teacher can very well give all of her time to twenty-five children. With a larger space, however, and longer time each day, the problems might be worked out differently.

LUCILE C. DEMING.

THE GREGORY SCHOOL

The freedom and activity that have characterized the work in a little school in West Orange, New Jersey, might have caused some people, had they looked in upon it, to wonder if the children could be accomplishing anything there. A little group of eight-year-old children might be playing a game of ring-toss in one corner, while others were working intently over a scheme of block building on the floor. Or if instead they happened to be using books or pencils they would be grouped informally around two tables or sitting in comfortable little individual chairs, talking freely and helping each other in a manner entirely unusual in a public school. Moreover, if one were to watch the activity closely, it would soon be apparent that the spontaneous interest of the children had led them into most of the things they were doing. For the new ideal which conceives of education not as training only but primarily as growth and individual development has been adopted in the school. Its aim is to substitute the power gained through self-control and expression for the inhibitions created by the conventional discipline imposed in the usual school. In an environment specially provided with material that meets the needs of the children, learning becomes largely incidental to the self-activity growing out of their spontaneous impulses to play together, to construct, and to inquire or explore.

When the Gregory School was to open, a woman on the school board who had been impressed with the work in the "organic schools," succeeded in getting cooperation for the establishing of similar methods here. Miss Edith Barnum, who had been connected with a large normal school, consented to take charge of this little five grade school because of her interest in working with the modern point of view. The agreement with the school authorities gave her a free hand; the New Jersey curriculum was not imposed upon her, and she was not concerned with the hard and fast requirements of a conventional course of study. The one provision made was that the children of the fifth grade should leave prepared to enter the sixth grade of an ordinary school.

The kindergarten and first and second grade children play with blocks, sand and toys, and practically all of their learning is incidental to activity. The first and second grades learn to read as much as they can by using story books which the teacher first reads for them. She writes words from the story on the blackboard and the children play a game of guessing them. They play a few games for number work, but do not learn to write before the third grade. The teacher of the fourth and fifth grade is greatly interested in vitalizing the grade work and she is succeeding even with a rather limited equipment and with the necessity of preparing the children for the sixth grade in another school. But a description of the school from the point of view of an experiment must center chiefly around the third grade because this year Miss Barnum has had to give practically all of her time there. The other teachers are quite in sympathy with all that she does, however, and have carried out her ideas as far as they were able.

The school differs from the ordinary public school in the following particulars:

The arrangement of the rooms is informal. The small tables and small green chairs and the chairs with desk attachments for the older children can be moved about as desired. Besides the small tables there are several large low ones for group work.

Play materials, and art and constructive materials are kept on the shelves, to which the children have free access. They may choose whatever they wish to use—clay, drawing materials, wood and tools and patterns for making dolls and toy animals, paper and paste, or sewing and weaving materials. Blocks can be used for houses for which all the other materials can be made up as furniture. Projects can be worked out in the sand table. There are also books and poem leaflets, and prints of great pictures. On window shelves which were made in the school shops there are plants, and each child has had a pot of bulbs of his own. This spring the children have planted a plot of gardens. A large wood behind the building has offered rare opportunity for the study of birds and trees, moss and flowers. Nature study has been part of the most important work of the school.

Freedom of activity has been the rule, and the children group themselves informally for the class work, or arrange their chairs in a circle. They ask questions without raising their hands, and when it would not be an interruption of someone else they converse with each other. When quiet is really necessary it is desired to have them recognize the need and respond to it of their own accord. They are never commanded to be still, but when they are gathering for a group the teacher waits until they show that they are ready to have her begin reading or talking, and when an interruption has occurred she stops and quietly waits for the children to discipline themselves. When a child

WORK THAT IS PLAY

shows no interest at all he is excused from the group and the teacher tries to reach the reason for his inattention later and meet it in the following lessons.   When a class is not in session the children may work in the shop, the play room, the hall or their own class rooms.   They move about freely, with care not to disturb the others, and they help each other.   Miss Barnum believes it is natural for children to cooperate to a much greater extent than they have often been allowed to do before, and that out of their relations with each other they can get information and experience that contribute greatly to their development.

The part of the teacher is to help the children over difficulties in the work they have chosen to do, and to suggest, when it seems necessary, the work she thinks they need and would be interested in.   She directly suggests and arranges for group work in more formal arithmetic and in several types of reading.   She calls the children together for singing, and they sing at their other work when it is possible and they wish to.   She introduces new subject matter through stories and pictures, and in discussions and excursions so as to bring new information to the children and stimulate curiosity and activity.   She organizes the day's work to a certain extent so that several subjects, including some of her planning and some of the children's initiating, are covered.

IN THE GREGORY SCHOOL

The plan of the day's work as prepared in her mind is flexible. It is subject to change on any sign of greater interest of the children in something else. The length of time spent on a subject is partly conditioned by the way in which it develops; a discussion usually continues until it ends naturally. When anything of unusual interest occurs the day's program is swept aside and the time given over to the more vital discussion. A boy brought in a snake and it became the subject of the day. A little Japanese boy joined the kindergarten, and the kindergarten and the whole school spent a good deal of the time every day for a week studying Japan, bringing prints and fans and tea-cups from home and playing Japanese games and reading books of travel and description. One hour of the day is called "free time," during which the children work individually on anything they please. They usually take out some favorite piece of work, or play with the material that most appeals to them. All of the day is comparatively free, but this time the children feel is a little more their very own. The half hour recess in the morning and the quarter hour in the afternoon are given to outdoor play, which is considered an important part of the day's program. There is no apparatus in the yard, as there ought to be, but the teachers often lead the children in games.

The program Miss Barnum has developed in the third grade work is approximately as follows: There is usually a little discussion of the condition and order of the room at nine o'clock. The first work is in reading. If the interest is great this lasts until nearly ten o'clock; if not, it is over at about nine-thirty. The children then go out for half an hour to play, either with or without direction. After this recess those who have brought lunch eat it, and all listen to the teacher reading a story. A twenty or thirty minute period of arithmetic follows the story, and the rest of the time until noon is "free time." Twice a week the first thing in the afternoon is singing; once a week it is rhythm. The other two days it is any special work there is in hand. After this the children are divided into two groups for formal writing, one group writing while the alternate group is at play. The last hour in the afternoon is given to general subject matter, or an excursion through the town or across, country. The periods given to each subject are usually longer than those in public school. This is because the interest of the children, given more spontaneously, lasts longer.

The special work on two afternoons in the week is usually something artistic. The children have poetry note-books made of the Unit Poem sheets. They have decorated covers for them, and also for note books that they have made with Turner prints of great pictures. They study these pictures and write poems about them. They would not have initiated the idea themselves, but after they were given the first picture they asked for more. Some of them also keep note-book records of the growth of their bulbs, made up not in uniform style, but according to their individual taste. There is rhythm and dancing only once a week because there is no one to play the piano more often. A mother of one of the children comes to do it now.

Although drawing is not directed or criticized, children often do the same subjects not from a teacher's suggestion but because they have similar purposes in mind. They all drew Hallowe'en pictures, and a great many of them drew sheep in connection with the study of wool. In some cases where the children wish to accomplish something particular the teacher helps them perfect their work. When they wish to draw a book cover design, and have made several attempts, she helps them choose the best one, and then gives suggestions for improving it. She does not impose her ideas upon the child in his work as a whole, however. After a long struggle to get the drawing supervisor who comes once a week to the older children to cooperate with her, she has finally succeeded in getting her to help the children in working out their own ideas and not to impose her purposes or standards. Since then she has found her very helpful in showing the children the best ways of doing what they were already attempting to do.

A sand table on castors is moved about from one grade room to another as the children wish to use it. They work out geographical forms on it occasionally or illustrate a story they have been reading. The teacher usually has to suggest it and sometimes has to direct them in finishing it. For Robinson Crusoe, as an example, they made a rather crude attempt and were satisfied. She therefore suggested trees for the island and other details which the children were glad to put on but might not have done by themselves.

The blocks used are those devised by Professor Patty Hill. There are only two sets in the school and they have to be divided between three rooms. The children in Miss Barnum's room built the outlines of a house on the floor and furnished it for their dolls. The rooms were large enough for a child to occupy each one while working on it. The house stood intact from Christmas till a week before Easter, and then was taken away only so that the floor might be cleaned. The girls were interested enough to build it again immediately and they often play in it during their free time. Most of the furniture is made of the smaller blocks. The tables hold dishes made of clay and paper, and there are crayon drawings on the wall. The floors are well covered with very nice looking rugs the girls made on the weaving looms. The dolls are dressed in clothes made at the school. The whole house is particularly ingenious in the way it is arranged and furnished. Everything that would be found in a well-filled home is there, even to quantities of art embroidery, in this case made of paper with crayon decoration.

Several of the children made a sheep-fold in connection with the study of wool. They cut sheep from the bristol board with the coping saw, and used a toy man for the shepherd. They built a watering trough and a large barn, and also made a wooden wolf and built a forest off at one side to hide him in.

The first and second grade children built a house similar to that of the girls in Miss Barnum's room, but it was very noticeably more simple and irregular as the undirected work of younger children would be. The kindergarten children have built boats and houses and trains of the blocks, but have not carried out projects as the older children have done. The block play is entirely free. Miss Barnum said that she had not made the slightest suggestion to the children in this particular. Whatever they have done has been genuinely self-initiated. The house and the sheep-fold were cooperative projects. Individual children have built smaller houses of their own, but there are not sufficient blocks for them all to do so.

In reading, a number of different methods have been followed. The children may divide into groups so that those who wish may read to themselves and others may read aloud for each other or for the teacher. Miss Barnum encourages them to read to themselves whenever they will and has succeeded in getting some children to form a habit of reading by themselves who at first had no interest at all. For arithmetic, the children divide into three groups, one working with the teacher while two work at the tables by themselves. She gives simple problems to those that are just learning and works on the board with them. The others get more difficult problems in addition and multiplication and hand in papers to her to be corrected. When the time is up for a lesson they usually ask the teacher to go on. They enjoy their formal work here because free work is the rule.

The general subject matter chosen may be connected with the season, or merely with some general topic introduced for the sake of information by the teacher. The general subjects of interest that have stimulated activity of many different kinds this year were outdoor work in the fall, Hallowe'en, nature study, Thanksgiving, transportation (which merely happened to be started by one boy's questions), Christmas and wool for winter clothing. The study of nature, and of transportation, and of wool has persisted to the present time. The children usually do something for each holiday, and are now making baskets for Easter. Soon they will begin gardening.

The purpose of making these conditions in the school is to teach the children to govern themselves by finding out of their own experiences the need of order and of consideration for others, so that the self-control gained will be inherent and intelligent, and therefore permanent in its effect upon the disposition of the children. Further, by allowing room for individual choice and thus securing genuinely motivated activity the teachers wish to enable each child to find his powers of self-expression and to develop tastes that are his own.

Miss Barnum feels that the most important attitude or quality to develop in the children is honesty—honesty to themselves, to their work, and to each other. Her manner of dealing with them seems one most likely to encourage this quality. It is simple and direct and very considerate and reasonable, so that they feel her respect for their personalities and her sincerity. She has a way of putting things up to them, of calling for their own judgment on things as free, interested individuals, and of showing implicit faith in them as long as possible. She looks for genuinely sincere expressions of opinion from them. She is careful not to impose any influence of hers upon them in such a way as to alter reactions superficially and thus to get merely outward results.

One of the most valuable results of the work is that the children actually do express their opinions freely and sincerely. This is not usual in the public schools, not only because the children's opinions are not solicited, but also because they do not form any individual ones. Here the expression of opinion in general—of public opinion—is beginning to be organized in the little conferences which the children are calling for. During the year the teachers have occasionally called them together for discussion of common matters needing attention. Chalk-marking on the sidewalks all over the neighborhood was a subject brought up by the teachers. The children discussed it, decided it was something that should not be done, and agreed to stop it. Later, they themselves brought up the matter of noise in the halls. There was a brief discussion of it, and the next day the result in self-control was marked, and the noise considerably less. Lately they are asking for these group discussions of their own accord, and have taken up such matters as walking across the flower-beds and keeping the modeling clay off the floor. When one child feels that there is an abuse of some kind about which he would like to protest he knows he can bring it to the attention of the others in this way. Rules that are made during these discussions are enforced by the children themselves.

This growing consciousness of social interest and control is just beginning to be felt in their relations to one another. One child who is troublesome and irritating to the others, is beginning to be recognized by the children as in need of social discipline. Should the matter come up in discussion spontaneously Miss Barnum expects to let them make rules for her. Their criticism might be a little cruel, but would be more helpful than anything her teacher has been able to do.

A problem which may be taken up in conference discussion is the matter of courtesy. Although the children as a whole are not so courteous as seems desirable Miss Barnum does not wish to impose any rules. She feels that there is a limit to what example can accomplish in a school, and that perhaps conscious social opinion among the children, if it arises naturally, might be more effective than conventional training for courtesy.

The children have not covered as much ground in prescribed subjects as they would have in a conventional school. An interesting light upon their accomplishment, however, is thrown by comparison with a number of children, about twice as many as in the original group, who were transferred here from another school. They called this a "baby school," and upset things generally until Miss Barnum took away some of the freedom and gave them some hard lessons to do. When an unexpected examination was recently given by the Superintendent this group of transferred children got lower marks than the others in the school. As the material covered by the questions was new to both groups, the result seems significant of more readiness to deal with unexpected situations on the part of those children who were well accustomed to having freedom and initiative in school.

The work sometimes seems to be proceeding doubtfully and slowly, but a comparison of the children here with what they would be under conventional conditions is always reassuring to the teachers. The progress that is made is undoubtedly more fundamental. One of the largest advantages is.that the native dispositions of the children do come out unmistakably, and can be tempered and rounded out in the social give and take as they could not be where they were more repressed. The spontaneity and enjoyment here are a decided improvement over the usual schoolroom atmosphere, and from time to time individual initiative appears in children who at first seemed to have nothing to contribute at all.

One problem that sometimes occupies the mind of the teacher has to do with determining the degree of organization and direction necessary and desirable. Miss Barnum has observed that the activity goes in waves, periods of absorption in work and of comparative quiet being followed by periods of noticeably lessened concentration. Whether these periods of lessened activity could be avoided by some timely change of program or the stimulus of new materials is one of her present problems. It may be that these waves are to be expected under any conditions, and the more disintegrated mood is part of the sequence of natural growth and development.

The mood variations of the individual child are also a problem. When a child finds work uncongenial that he started the day before, should he meet the discipline that an adult would encounter in a like situation? The habit of humoring himself in his moods would be a handicap in later life, but Miss Barnum feels that it is sometimes doubtful whether encouraging him to continue a piece of work against his inclination would tend to increase his perseverance or merely give him a dislike for that particular kind of work and make him feel that he was being imposed upon. There is also the question of how far the inclination of the children should be permitted to rule. The afternoon the visitor was at the school the children began making Easter baskets and worked eagerly all the afternoon. Sometimes it might be questioned whether or not more direction from the teacher would secure a more useful disposal of the time. But the results of the freedom and self-activity are an undoubted development of initiative, individuality and social adjustment in the children that is not accomplished in the ordinary class-room. The teachers are convinced that however much the equipment of material and the methods of presenting new information need to be improved upon by further experiment the basic principles of individual freedom and of learning through activity must remain.

LUCILE C. DEMING.

NOTE.—Very few public schools have so far ventured to attempt to work on a really experimental basis. This experiment has been a difficult one for the teachers because of the uncertainty of continued support. Recently, because of what appears to be a purely political situation, the report has been that the work will be discontinued and the school made uniform with the others in the town. The large majority of the parents are strongly in favor of its continuing, but the idea is opposed by three of the members of a school board of five. The school will therefore lose Miss Barnum, as only her interest in the new ideas in education induced her to give her time to this little five-grade school.

STONY FORD IS THE HAUNT OF LITTLE NYMPHS AND ELVES

EXPERIMENTAL SCHOOLS

THE STONY FORD SCHOOL

Robert H. and Delia D. Hutchinson
Lucile C. Deming

THE HOME SCHOOL, SPARKILL, N. Y.

Mattie B. Bates
Lucile C. Deming

Bureau of Educational Experiments
1917

THE STONY FORD SCHOOL

The Stony Ford School was founded in September, 1915, as a school based upon new and radical theories of education for children of all ages up to about fourteen, and run upon such terms as to make it accessible to children of all classes. The children and the adults together form a small community and as far as social rights and obligations are concerned, we make as little distinction as possible between the adult and the child.

This is fundamental in the child's education. He is some day to become part of the great community, the world, and he can best be fitted to be a responsible unit in it by first becoming part of a smaller community which he can understand. Responsibility, like other qualities, can best be developed by its exercise. Practically the whole management of the school is shared in by the children; the adults, being more experienced, give suggestions and advice, but none need be followed by the children if it is against their judgment or wish. If they reckon wrongly or neglect their obligations they suffer the natural consequences of their acts as punishment. This does not mean that they are necessarily allowed to endure privations or suffer the results of their own youth and inexperience. But as much as possible we allow them to take their own responsibility in the management of everything.

Education in the past has laid so much emphasis upon the acquisition of knowledge that it has neglected the importance of developing qualities. At Stony Ford it is our plan to develop in the children what we consider the most important qualities for social life and happiness. These qualities may be grouped as the Individual and the Social.

Health is the most important of the individual qualities. Besides fresh air and exercise, of which the children have plenty, we believe that the most important factor is their food. We believe that two meals a day are, with a few exceptions, enough for child and adult. We omit as much as possible from the diet such foods as white bread, cane sugar, tea and coffee, and meat, serving instead whole wheat bread. cocoa and milk, honey and nuts. Fruit and vegetables in season are put on the table. If a child is in a healthy condition and his taste has not been perverted by spiced dishes and like, we believe his natural appetite will, in general, direct him what to eat and how much. Though children are at liberty to buy any kind of food they like provided they keep within a cost limit, they rarely choose to go outside the usual fare, and have little taste for fancy things. We have found that these practices, though not generally accepted elsewhere, do keep children healthy and alert. And without these two qualities in a child very little can be done for him.

Next to health, perhaps the most important individual qualities are a scientific attitude of mind and a desire for perfection. By scientific attitude of mind we do not mean a head full of chemistry and physics, but an ability and tendency to measure the worth of anything one knows or plans to do by using one's judgment and reason, and basing beliefs and acts upon facts which one knows to be true. The desire for perfection is aroused through the imagination. If the direction in which it tends can be found, an idealism and desire to do things well can be developed. The esthetic qualities of the children are appealed to through music, dancing, pictures and the natural beauties of the environment.

Of the social qualities the most desirable are those which will make the child realize himself as part of the group, able to sympathize with others, and shoulder responsibilities—the very qualities which the everyday life of the school with its sharing of responsibilities and pleasures tends to develop.

In the matter of sex relationship, we believe that if things are concealed from children they will develop an unhealthy and secret desire to find them out. When they ask questions we tell them, the very youngest even, what we know about conception and birth. The child's mind is clean and pure, it has no evil association about things, and if these facts come to it in a simple and beautiful way and are referred to perfectly freely, but always with respect and reverence, the child will grow to think of them with respect and reverence.

So far as acquiring knowledge is concerned, we believe that in the actual teaching all work should begin with the inclinations of the child. His interest is the starting point and gives the impetus.

We have no exact catalogue of things the children ought to know, but in a general way our policy is to lead them to become familiar with certain groups of knowledge, those which give them understanding of personal and social life. The subjects may be roughly classified as principles and facts; such principles on the one hand as cause and effect and evolution; and on the other hand such facts as the general history of mankind, geography and natural history, industries and arts, our economic and social structure, and physiology.

The libertarian principle underlies all our methods of teaching. It is a method by which the child is allowed in as many circumstances as possible to choose his own course of action. In other words, with the exception of such circumstances as involve danger or where the direct rights of others are concerned, the child is allowed to do as he likes. This does not mean that he is left to run wild. On the contrary, suggestions are placed before him, always letting him choose, however, that towards which he most naturally tends, and always allowing him to learn by his own experience. Those who believe in this principle feel sure that if intelligently and consistently handled, the child will develop under it a will power, a capacity for discrimination, and in the end gather more knowledge than if taught by the usual restrictive and coercive methods. We make it a point never to force and never to forbid. To forbid means almost always one of two things; punishment or deceitfulness. Punishment is degrading intellectually and morally and deceitfulness is an impossible quality for social life. A child who knows that he will not be punished never hesitates to tell the truth. With the exception of circumstances in which his safety is endangered or where our own personal rights are encroached upon, we find it better to advise than to command. There are no rewards and punishments in the school beside the natural gain and pleasures derived from doing a thing well, or the loss and social depreciation of doing it badly.

A larger aspect of the libertarian idea is that the child is a personality himself, with his own likes and dislikes, hopes and fears, and that his liberty is as much worthy of respect as that of an adult.

We are both Socialists and regard the school as one of the many elements in society which are working to abolish our present economic and social system and to set up a more humane one in its place. For this purpose and for the purpose of human happiness in general, it is necessary to have persons who can think for themselves and play their part in society. On this principle we work, but we do not necessarily teach Socialism. We want every child to work out for itself, as it matures, its own solutions of the problems of life.

The children have no religious instruction. Their ethical philosophy they work out for themselves through their experience in the little community in which they live, and we try to lead them to apply these principles to the larger life into which they will go.

We ourselves are not religious. Our ideal is that of the greatest amount of happiness for the greatest number of human beings, an ideal of great inspiration and beauty, but to be striven for in an intelligent, scientific way. And whatever other ideals the children may have or develop we frankly try to inspire them with this one of our own.

ROBERT H. HUTCHINSON.

DELIA D. HUTCHINSON.

AN ENDURANCE TEST

STONY FORD, A SCHOOL COMMUNITY

The Stony Ford School is on a farm bordering the Wallkill River, a mile and a half from Stony Ford station, New York. The old-fashioned farm-house has been remodelled so that it lends itself to hygienic housekeeping, and an open-air dormitory has been added. In one sunny corner room, with white and blue walls and conservatory-like windows, is the nursery, which is called the "baby garden." The babies also play outdoors in a little, fenced-in inclosure with a floor of heavy canvas. All the rest of the big farm, with the hills and woods, with the swimming pool and the brook that runs to the nearby river, belongs to the older children. The farm buildings have been turned into juvenile workshops, and an equipment that lends itself to the spontaneous interests of children is being collected to complete the environment. The school is regarded as a little community in which each member is to take his own share of the work to be done and then pursue his own interests freely, with opportunity and encouragement to develop them as far as he will.

The school is carrying out consistently the principles which it proclaims. The ideas upon which it is founded are the deep convictions of the teachers, so much a part of their own lives that the practices of the school are their own self-expression. And in every part of the life at Stony Ford they are actually doing what they say they mean to do. The school has an air of robustness, simplicity, sincerity and spirited idealism.

Underlying the school life is the principle that learning is based on activity. In all the practices of the school the emphasis is on the far-reaching, essential value, rather than on any lesser, immediate value. The school does not center about the acquirement of knowledge or accomplishments, but is organized to give the children the fullest opportunity to develop qualities of character and individuality.

In order to emphasize from the first the value of personal independence, self-reliance and individuality, each child is given a room alone or with one other child where he may keep his own things undisturbed. He may keep them in any order he chooses, though he does realize that neatness in his room will be commended by the teachers. He may dress in whatever pleases him, and his mending and his laundry are his own affair. In these particular matters the result has been that the children clean their rooms spasmodically, showing improvement as time goes on, and do learn to take care of their own clothing. It is not uncommon to see a boy sewing a patch on his trousers, or even doing a little washing which he failed to get ready in time for the agent from the laundry. A sewing and laundry teacher is there to give him any suggestions he asks for, but she would not take over the task for him. She has probably taught him in making his own trousers in the first place, so that he needs no further help, anyway. The boys do quite the same kind of things as the girls.

Distinctions between people are as much removed as possible. The teachers are called by their first names, and they dress in simple clothing like the children. They take part in the activities of the children so that sharing their experience they come to have as much of a feeling of common understanding as possible. Doing away with distinctions is an encouragement to self-expression and aids in producing that sincerity which is marked in the treatment by the children and teachers of each other and of the visitors as well. This sincerity consists in directness, in seriousness, and in acting and speaking according to genuine impulses.

Opinions are spoken frankly and no pretense of wishing to do or say a thing that the person does not want to do is made. If one of the teachers asks the child to take a walk and he does not wish to he says so. Teachers and children act very much as they feel provided the act does not obstruct the rights of another person. Even in the class work if a child is not interested in a lesson that is going on it is expected that he will either pay no attention or will leave the room. Another illustration will show what impression has been made upon the children. A teacher recently overheard one of the girls telling, almost with horror in her voice, that she had seen some people last summer who "were false." One of the children asked her how. She answered: "They let on they like you when they don't." And the children seemed to understand and agree with her perfectly.

The teachers do not attempt to give much energy and attention to such things as the children's manners. There are too many other things needing attention first. They do not wish to offer the children a continual stream of suggestions. They accomplish what they can through their own example and manner. The lesson of social consideration is brought home in many ways to them, and the teachers have faith that it will accomplish as good a result in forming their manners as more direct teaching would. No command is ever made to a child, and even a request in the case of table manners might be considered too direct an interference with personal liberty. If the children are careless or disorderly at the table Mr. Hutchinson may leave the table and stay for a while in his study. He says nothing on leaving, but the children notice that he does not return and they invariably feel ashamed of having displeased him.

Personal freedom and a respect for every one as a personality are perhaps the most characteristic ideals of the school. Each one, down to the smallest child, is held to be an individual with a life that belongs very much to him. While he is expected to maintain himself as a unit in the community by contributing equally with the rest in all matters of common necessity, he is at the same time expected to have tastes and wishes of his own, to choose what his individual interests will be, and, above all, to form judgments and opinions for himself.

The seriousness with which the older people treat the children is a sign of the spirit of equality and respect between them. The teachers answer a child's question as they would that of another adult. There is no hint of "talking down" to him, or of effort to be pleasant because he is a child. The effect is unusual and admirable. The children, aware of their contribution to the community life, grow independent, and conscious of their own powers and the respect that is due them. In turn they have confidence and affection for the teachers.

As Socialists, Mr. and Mrs. Hutchinson would be unwilling to have anyone act exclusively as a servant in their house. They believe that activity and experience are the best teachers of most essential things and that a share of the necessary work connected with living should be taken by every one, or at least by all children who have to learn by experience to understand ordinary processes and to realize the meaning of labor.

The children in the Stony Ford School share in all of the necessary work. The smaller ones work with the older ones so as to learn the technique of the different processes, but they do an equal amount with the others. A little child of six and a half will climb up to take dishes from a high shelf and do it with an air of assurance and responsibility. The work is apportioned every week. Two people act as housekeepers and keep the accounts and attend to other single matters. Meals are prepared by two people and cleared away by three. If the little details of finishing up are ever neglected the reaction of the other children is certain and effective. The children seem remarkably contented to carry responsibility. They are doing it by common consent, and it apparently adds an element of reasonableness and seriousness to their lives that many other children lack. It gives them a definite basis for an understanding of other people's rights and feelings and their own independence. They are also independent and slow to ask a favor without attempting to make a return. The smallest child in asking to have a table moved for her, explained that she was preparing the room for a game in which anyone could share and she asked the favor because the visitor was nearest to the table. If the children who have prepared a meal have miscalculated and not prepared enough they leave the table as soon as the fact is discovered and go to the kitchen to remedy the deficiency. They know immediately that it is expected of them and their reaction appears to be against their own mistake rather than against the expectation of the other people.

The children learn to stand up for themselves and to have consideration for other people while they are in the nursery. Even before they can understand language they are definitely taught that some things belong to them and some things belong to other people. When the child has learned to talk, the reason for not allowing him to take away a toy from another child is explained to him. Discussion of fairness in particular cases is very frequent among the children and they usually are open to reason or ready to abide by majority decision. The teachers help by explaining situations impartially when they can. The one standard held up is a social one—the need of regarding other people's reasonable feelings.

The children have cooperated with the teachers to such an extent in the experiment of carrying out the theories of food reformers and other rules that are believed necessary to health, that they seem to share the definite ideal of keeping up the highest possible physical standard. There have been discussions of food values and habits of eating. The children have adopted the conclusions of the others and now abide by them voluntarily. They almost never eat between meals. The food supplies are near at hand—they have put them in the cupboards themselves; but they do not seem to consider even the possibility of taking anything except at meal time. There is not one of the complaints usually heard from children about the food on the table.

The simplicity in eating is paralleled by the simplicity of clothing. The children wear short-sleeved dresses or tunics and summer underwear most of the time. They skate and slide often without wraps and with bare arms and legs. They go wading or swimming after fall and before spring. Although they are allowed freedom in all of these matters, the teachers would not let a sign of danger pass unnoticed. If a child looked blue with cold his attention would be called to the fact. Children who have come recently to the school have to be noticed more than others.

The health of the children has been so remarkable as apparently to justify the teachers' belief in the principles carried out. Every child in school has clear, highly colored skin and clear eyes. There have been cases of grippe and pneumonia almost everywhere in the surrounding country this year but except for a slight epidemic of tonsilitis last spring when each child was sick for a day or two, they have escaped sickness of every kind, even colds.

The children study or work in classes every morning and part of the afternoon. Whatever they do is entirely voluntary. They come and ask for this or that subject that perhaps the other children have been taking. The teachers, however, are using all their powers of invention to make the studies interesting.

The only forms of esthetic self-expression as yet developed in the school are dancing, dramatic play and singing. The girls ask for dancing almost every day. Mr. Hutchinson has been trying to create in them a sense for individual interpretation. He does this by suggesting the mood of the music with a name or a description before he begins to play the piano and then telling them to dance as it makes them feel. They dance spontaneously, as they are never corrected in details of step or position. After seeing Isadora Duncan in New York they put a great deal of spirit and expression into their dancing.

Their interest in dramatizations has been useful in all of the subjects. Some of the plays they write themselves and produce after elaborate preparation. Some the teachers write. Others are spontaneous, simple, worked out at the moment by teachers and children together.

The chief history material the older children have had this year beyond that which has come incidentally into discussions or in story reading, has been a study of Greek life during the Persian War made for the sake of giving a Greek play. The children themselves wrote the play and gave it with charming success before an audience of teachers and neighbors. Several weeks were given to the preliminary reading and to the making of the costumes and scenery. The children often refer to it and they remember vividly what they learned of the events of the history and the characteristics of the people.

Reading is almost always interesting for its own sake, but with the children who are just learning, acting parts helps a great deal. They play school or pretend they are reading to their family in the evening.

The children always insist on giving over an hour to this activity, usually after luncheon every day. The teacher often works into the reading a little arithmetic by noting the number of pages they have read and the number of figures in the pictures in the book. She also *writes* part of the story on the board and gives the children who do not write well the Montessori sand-paper forms to play with. A game of village post-office in which each child keeps a store and one acts as the postman, selling stamps and carrying and delivering orders, teaches the children arithmetic and writing.

Science is the subject of many of the plays. In the beginning of science teaching with the younger children the information is given them only through conversation or in connection with simple experiments. Afterward the subject may be acted out, the children personifying the elements, fire, water and air, and dramatizing their uses. Other methods of science teaching are used. One boy, given pictures of various animals, by noting differences and resemblances, made his own groupings under such headings as "animals that are like cats," "animals that are like horses because they have hoofs," and so on. He was then shown the groups that scientists had worked out. With the aid of pictures and the names of the different orders and families the boy himself has made an evolution chart. In connection with this he reads such books as London's "White Fang," and talks over with the teacher what he has read. One of the chief needs of the school is for laboratory apparatus and for well-written scientific books for children.

The children and teachers working together have made two very large maps, one of Europe and one of the world. They use them to dramatize a study of geography, civics and industry. They spread one of them out on the dining-room floor, distribute products, such as small pieces of rubber, cotton, wool, iron, and so on over the countries that they come from and spend the whole morning trading back and forth. They use paper money and make ships of paper and trains of plasticine. The maps are large enough for one child to occupy each country.

The nursery equipment consists of materials of different kinds, which are kept in the "pen," a space fenced off in the nursery and spread with clean canvas. It contains a little wooden slide with steps up to the platform, made by Mr. Hutchinson and the boys, a rocking horse, and a sand box and three or four boxes of small blocks. The chief toys are kitchen utensils, pails, spoons, pans, and so on. Balls with coverings of different colors and bells of different sounds were furnished to catch the sight and hearing of the children. Every morning the

16

babies are put into the large tub in the nursery bathroom, where they play together with water toys, such as celluloid fish and frogs and little pails. In warm weather they spend most of the day in the outdoor pen where there is another sand box and more equipment. The babies as young as one year or less use the things provided for them continually. Mrs. Hutchinson begins their social training even before they can talk by teaching them not to take things away from each other and to help her pick up their things before bed time.

Among the supplies for the older children there are three large work benches in the shop and the most necessary tools and materials for carpentering. Special material is ordered when needed. Each child has done something in the carpentry shop. There are only a few of the toys that children usually have about the house, and they are encouraged to make their own things as much as possible. They have made two long slides, and the older boys have put up some ingenious arrangements in the barn, a swinging bed-spring and a rope-and-pulley apparatus, by which they can pull themselves mid-air across the barn. They have constructed a large water wheel for the brook and a raft with boards and large empty carbide cans for the pond. In the woods they have built a fairly good sized house. The younger children make blocks by putting a mixture of cement and sand into moulds. At a teacher's suggestion they are planning to make a birds' bath of the same material. All the children were making boxes for the hot bed, and planting seeds to transplant later on. Before long the farm land will be put in charge of a skilled farmer so that the children can have the benefit of observing and helping him.

The school is very young and it has been found impossible to complete the plans yet in full. Mrs. Hutchinson is keeping a detailed and careful record of the development of the three babies. She makes observations on physical development, moral qualities, interests and intelligence, noting under the latter head when and how each one learns to walk and talk. The other teachers are keeping general notes of the activities and of the individual characteristics apparently developing in each child. As they work out more complete systems of records their two chief interests will be in noting the development of important qualities in the child, and making a large general record of the amount of ground covered in information and knowledge.

LUCILE C. DEMING.

IN THE BABY GARDEN AT STONY FORD

THE HOME SCHOOL, SPARKILL, N. Y.

The twenty-four hour Home School has certain real advantages over the day school. In the intimate home life the children reveal intellectual and emotional difficulties or weaknesses that may never be brought to the surface in the social situation of the day school. The well-known phases of entrained egoism and morbid egotism in the young child often constitute the locked door through which healthy demand and expression cannot break.

For instance, a child may often be held back from some activity or self-expression by vanity, expressed through a fear of attempting anything new in which he might not excel. Although the day teacher in this case can diagnose the real cause of the child's unwillingness she could not have the varied positive opportunities of the Home School for helping the child outgrow the weakness. Also, in the hours spent in the home, the day school child often has its psychic weakness actually strengthened through the parents' blindness or their injurious treatment. This opportunity to diagnose the psychic and social nature of the child is one of the distinguishing features of the Home School.

The Home School, conceived to meet this need in one family—this need of the social adjustment of the child—has at the same time successfully met it for other families during the past year. Types of children which have especially benefited by this part of the school work include the only child; the highly nervous child who cannot adjust to the complex conditions of modern home life in a great city; the delicate child who cannot thrive in the city, yet whose family cannot live out of the city; the child lacking in imagination, whose life needs the enrichment that comes from contact with the great out-of-doors; the over-imaginative type that feeds upon itself shut in by the four walls of city life; the child of great force who for lack of proper outlet domineers over all within reach; the timid, shrinking, self-conscious child, who gets pushed to the wall in large groups.

The basic plan of the Home School is to restore the beneficial activities and responsibilities of the big families of the past generation, with the elimination, made possible by modern thought and conditions, of all the sordid and stultifying disadvantages. It is only by holding our own with our equals that we measure up to the best that is in us, and the doing of this through twenty-four hours in each day develops and strengthens character in a way that even the best of day-schools and homes cannot do, because of the unavoidable waste and the conflict, conscious or unconscious, between the day school and the home.

The work of the home school might be divided under three headings:

First—The study and attempted adjustment of the child psychologically. This is the most difficult of tasks, and yet it is the first essential of free school work with little children. A great deal of it is brought about quite naturally by the group life and activities of the school, but when they deem it necessary the teachers themselves undertake to make the child conscious of his strengths and weaknesses through direct or indirect talks and situations. Laziness, greediness, vanity, selfishness, fear, timidity, impatience, enviousness, all are definite psychic states which even very young children can be helped to conquer.

Second—The creation of an environment that will give such a rich mental and imaginative background that the children will be stimulated to attempt creative expression and to make real demands for knowledge.

Third—To provide as many avenues for self-expression and for the first-hand gathering of knowledge as the natural surroundings and financial resources of the school will allow. To this end the school is abundantly supplied with lumber, bricks, blocks, drawing paper and crayons, raffia and other basketry materials, a piano and a victrola for dancing. The test of value of work done by the child is the child's own satisfaction. The children do actually originate; they develop their own product through its stages. To teach crafts is no object of the school; art is given the child as it would be wisely given to a young person engaged in working out an original problem in geometry.

A definite time is taken each day for individual expression, when the children are at liberty to read, to use any of the school or shop materials, climb trees, to use the swing or other apparatus; the sole condition being that the child be alone, a condition made possible by the ample space of the roomy old house, the vast barn, and the "all out-of-doors."

Another part of each day is given to group work. But even in this group work every precaution is taken to keep the more dominating personalities from robbing the other children of creative opportunities. Special note should be made here of the conditions under which the freehand drawing of the school is done. The great beauty of the outdoor surroundings of the school stimulated a few of the children to attempt outdoor landscape work. In these drawings, which were made out of doors entirely without suggestion, comment or direction from the teacher, the children achieved amazing effects, both of decoration and feeling. They were later taken out in groups to draw, but still without any supervision or suggestion from the teacher except the requirement that they draw at sufficient distance from each other so that they should not be affected by each other's work.

For next year I feel a great need of some kind of work in science. I believe that very little children could be helped to discover for themselves some of the dramatic and far-reaching principles of chemistry, physics, astronomy, biology, and botany, and of the organization of the natural world about them. This work should be under the direction of a man, as the other teachers chosen for next year are all women, and I feel strongly the need of children for contact with both men and women.

Parents naturally shrink from placing very young children in a boarding school for fear they will not be surrounded by that atmosphere of love which is so essential, but our parents have so far unanimously agreed that this essential element of love is provided at the Home School. The one indispensable requirement of all who in any way share in the making of the Home School is a capacity to give little children stimulating, uplifting and strengthening love. There are no servants on the place. The household work is carried on by two young girls from the Carolina Mountains, who, in personal dignity, refinement and intelligence, have as much to give the children as the teachers in the school. They have been especially chosen for their love and delight in little children, and the children find in them comrades as well as friends. A third girl of the same type will be brought to the school next year.

While the Home School has all the advantages of a remote country place, it is without the usual disadvantages of remoteness, for not only is it in reach of the great city with its museums and industries, but in the nearby villages are many and varied small industries where the children get the priceless human interest, impossible in visiting the huge plants of the city.

Very little formal school work is done because very little is needed. In the large construction work with lumber, bricks and stone, so much need of arithmetic is felt by the children that they eagerly accept what little help they need in mastering multiplication, division and fractions. Until the children themselves ask for help in reading and writing it is not given, but the example of the older children enjoying stories and books of information has in some instances stimulated the younger children to demand teaching in reading. It has been found that work in groups of two or three for daily periods of twenty minutes has accomplished twice the work of the longer formal school periods.

The school has suffered this first year both from a lack of funds and of children to make up the necessary groups. Many valuable opportunities for work had to be foregone because of a lack of funds to buy material and pay railroad fares and salaries of special teachers.

MATTIE B. BATES.

THE HOME SCHOOL, AN OPEN-AIR EXPERIMENT

The immediate purpose of Mr. and Mrs. Collier and Miss Bates in founding the Home School was to surround the oldest Collier boy with children of his own age and to provide a healthful country environment for him and his two brothers. They hoped also to meet the need of some women who, preferring to work themselves in social and professional fields, wish to find a place where their children can live under conditions based on modern educational principles. The Home School is an experiment in restoring to the children, many of whom are *only* children at home, the benefits, without the disadvantages, of conditions as much as possible like those in the old-fashioned, large-sized family.

The conditions of the school embody the modern educational ideas of freedom and self-expression in activity, and the development of character and culture through occupations that are constructive, artistic and social. The school aims, as Mrs. Collier has said, to bring up children whose emotional expression is so unchecked and spontaneous that they will not need to be psycho-analyzed. The qualities consciously emphasized seem to be first qualities of character and social mindedness, and then imagination, health, courtesy and orderliness.

With children who are fairly well adjusted from training and association with others the teacher relies on absorbing occupation to develop the individuality further in qualities like initiative, self-direction, concentration and perseverance. Material and simple directions are offered them, and their interest in making things carries them through experiences that have all the discipline of purpose, effort and realization of accomplishment. When a child's interest in some activity begins to flag, she sometimes gives him just the needed word of encouragement to carry him over the moment of depression. While her appreciation of work in most cases is measured by the satisfaction of the child, in the case of a child notably lacking in purposefulness and concentration she is particular to call attention to loose ends and uneven places and to ask the reason for this or that uneconomical way of approaching or completing an undertaking. She may rule that he is not to have any new material until the last project that he has begun is accomplished. To a child who is constantly asking for help she gives simple problems and challenges him to help himself.

Social-mindedness is developed in the children unconsciously as they learn to share the material, to wait their turns for the teacher's help, to use the swing or the wagon, and to cooperate in various undertakings and games. They learn to consider each other's rights and feelings by having those rights in particular instances pointed out by the teacher. She always gives the reasons for her decisions in terms that the children can understand and accept. She invariably has a deaf ear for a child who comes to her with anything to say in a whining, complaining tone, and she encourages every child to stand up for himself when he knows his rights are being encroached upon. Miss Bates feels that the children have gained a great deal through helpfulness of each other.

No one in the household is treated as a servant. No class distinctions are recognized and a democratic spirit among the children is encouraged by the manner of living and the spirit of the conversations. When the plan has been developed further, Miss Bates believes that she will have the children share some of the household occupations so that they can have the experience of a common undertaking and of making a contribution to the community; not too much responsibility in the work, however, lest it become a routine and be deadening to the imagination. Certain requirements are now made of them to induce habits of orderliness and to make them appreciate the economy of being able to find things when they want them. Every morning after breakfast they make a general examination of the house and have a simple lesson in the care of some particular part. They have learned to hang their outdoor clothing neatly on their own hooks. The older boys have learned to keep the rest of their clothing in order also, and to clean their bathroom and dressing room every morning. They must put away toys after using them. In the barn each child is responsible for one tool shelf, but all who use the tools are expected to return them to their places immediately after using them.

A few essential table-manners are quietly insisted upon with each individual child as need comes up, and traits of generosity and courtesy encouraged and their opposite discouraged. The method in which this is done of course varies in individual cases, but the teacher attempts to make each appeal on a reasonable basis and also to get the underlying cause of the unsocial trait if possible.

The provisions for health have been an open-air workshop and an open-air sleeping porch, simple meals, warm clothing, and careful attention to any signs of illness. A short nap after luncheon is the regular thing every day. The children are in far better health than when they came from the city. They dress in sweater suits, leggings and mittens for the winter days, and have been kept in the house by the weather only twice—when dampness rather than cold made the outdoors too disagreeable.

The children spend almost all of their time in the open-air workshop in the barn, which is sheltered from the wind by a hay stack piled against the weather side. They get exercise in their activity and play and dancing, and the barn is equipped with a swing, a sailor's climbing rope with knots tied at even distances, two swinging rings, a turning pole, and a ladder on which to climb to the beams of the barn and to the top of the hay stack. The children put up this apparatus for themselves with the direction of the teacher.

Some of their activities they undertake on their own initiative, some at the suggestion of the teacher. As there are eight children of ages from three and a half to eight and ten, Miss Bates has some difficulty in planning for the group as a whole. Next year, with another teacher, she will try to have twelve or sixteen children and separate the older from the younger for the constructive work. As it is now when she shows the older children how to make something the little ones invariably want to do the same thing and it is usually too difficult for them. Some of the things that have been accomplished, however, are bungalow bird-houses made by each child according to his own design, wheelbarrows copied from one which was sent to a child, Knights of the Round Table trappings, and canvas camping utilities. As soon as the ground is ready the children will start gardens, and when the weather is warm they will go for over-night camping trips to the Palisades.

In the open-air nursery, heated with a coal stove, there is a set of blocks like those used in the Play School and a number of simple animal toys and trains. When the children come down before breakfast or when they have been ill they play there. The rest of the time they are outdoors or in the barn.

The smallest children are learning reading simply from looking on as they wish when stories are read to them. The one boy of eight has learned to read in a short time this year. He first learned phonetic spelling and then began reading by himself the stories that he already knew. The ten-year-old boy gives part of each morning to reading by himself and doing arithmetic examples for the teacher. He could not do the latter at all at first, though he could recite the tables easily from having learned to do them at public school. He has been required to do the problems, however, before he can go out to play, and now is learning to do them in an increasingly short time. All the children get the foundations of number work from their calculations with a rule in wood-working.

The attempt throughout the work with the children is to deal with them realistically and sincerely. When the birth of a sister or brother of their own or of one of the other children arouses their interest they are told quite simply of the facts of life. Later they are taught the facts of reproduction in nature. In the opinion of the teacher, the human knowledge has more significance and beauty for them if it comes thus preceding the other.

Miss Bates feels that next to qualities of character, imagination would perhaps be the most valuable asset for the children to have. She encourages them to dramatize their stories and attempts to find in what forms of self-expression they will be most spontaneous and free spirited. She sometimes gets this abandon of spirit in a child for the first time in dancing. One boy who would scarcely enter the dancing at all at first, had his imagination fired when he was allowed to strip off his usual clothing and dance in a tunic made of raffia in imitation of the cave dwellers in a story the teacher read. The Knights of the Round Table have been favorite heroes. The children go off on tourneys with each other, bearing lances made of long inch square poles, with swords and shields of wood, and sticks for horses. They also develop free imaginative plays of their own. Children who at first take a prosaic view of their surroundings, after playing for a while with the unusually imaginative ones seem to develop something of the same quality of imagination.

The children dance with victrola music almost every evening. Their dancing and the choice of the music is left entirely free and all of them respond to the opportunity with enthusiasm. The new teacher who is expected will teach both music and dancing.

The school environment consists of fourteen acres of grounds with an orchard, shade trees, and a brook, and an old Dutch residence furnished with distinct and unusual beauty. The floors are unpainted and worn and kept shining white. The rooms are large, with exposed beams and colonial fire-places, and deep-set, small-paned windows. On each of several window sills in the living room there is a vase or a basket with branches of bitter-sweet or mountain berries, and there are many other interesting suggestions of nature about the room. Rugs and curtains are of raw, unbleached or neutral tone, and here and there in the room there is a patch of beautiful color. The care and taste apparent throughout the house may well catch the imagination and have some influence in forming good taste in the children.

LUCILE C. DEMING

EDUCATION THROUGH EXPERIENCE

A Four Year Experiment
IN
The Ethical Culture School

BY
MABEL R. GOODLANDER

Published by

THE BUREAU OF EDUCATIONAL EXPERIMENTS
16 WEST 8TH STREET, NEW YORK

in co-operation with

THE PARENTS AND TEACHERS ASSOCIATION
ETHICAL CULTURE SCHOOL

CENTRAL PARK WEST & 63RD STREET, NEW YORK

1921

Self-elected Work and Play in the Class Room

Store, Post Office, Marionette Theatre, Weaving, Typewriting and Other Activities

FOREWORD

Four years ago Miss Goodlander, the author of the following article, was invited to conduct what we called at the time an "Experimental Class." The object was to try to work out in class room practice the more recent theories of elementary education under normal conditions, as to number of pupils, class room space, and teaching force. Complete freedom was given in the selection of class room materials, in the use and division of class time, and in the employment of special teachers. Children whose parents approved of the experiment were selected to compose the group. According to intelligence tests, these children were not superior to the average of their classmates in a parallel division. Moreover, on the average, they were younger than the children of the other group. Thus the Experimental Class was started with the prospect of remaining under the guidance of one teacher for at least three years.

The experience of this class and its teachers will be of interest to elementary teachers generally, many of whom will ask: Does the Ethical Culture School look upon the experiment as a success? Answering this question categorically I may say 'yes, undoubtedly.' Miss Goodlander was encouraged to continue with her class for a fourth year and then start with a new group. Her former pupils are now in charge of a fifth grade teacher in sympathy with the aims of the Experimental Class. The term "Experimental Class" has been discontinued. Indeed, many of our Elementary teachers are now conducting their work in the same spirit and according to the same principles that have guided Miss Goodlander in her pioneer undertaking. Furthermore the School has done something toward measuring the results of the so-called Experimental Class as compared with two parallel divisions in the School. The time chosen was the spring of the third year of the experiment. It should be understood that the comparisons given below are the results of a single test. They are naturally far from conclusive and are merely given for what they are worth. In formal work, Miss Goodlander's class met the requirements of the School; in ability to observe and to initiate and carry projects through, the class excelled; in co-operation, it was superior to one group and inferior to another. After observing the course of the experiment in our School for four years, I can state with assurance that the institution endorses and encourages the type of work described in this article.

FRANKLIN C. LEWIS, Superintendent.
Ethical Culture School, New York City.

November 30, 1920.

The Class Post Office. Grade III.
Built in the shop by a small group. The office of postmaster is elective.

EDUCATION THROUGH EXPERIENCE

These discussions of her work by Miss Goodlander are reprinted from "School and Home," the bulletin published by the Parents and Teachers Association of the Ethical Culture School. The first article was written when the experimental group had passed through its first and second grade stages and had entered upon its life as a third year class. The second section was written a year later and emphasizes the more advanced work begun in the fourth grade.—Editor.

I

Doctor Adler has set the aim of our school as that of education for leadership in a democracy, and has emphasized the necessity of the fullest development of the individual, in order that each may render the greatest possible service to society. Looking forward to this end in education, we have endeavored in this class to create a free social environment, where children, in co-operation with others of their own age, may make a beginning in democratic living, under conditions more like life outside of school than those which have commonly been considered appropriate for the school regime. That is, we have tried to make the conduct of the class as informal and unacademic as possible under existing circumstances, with a program sufficiently flexible to allow for individual choice of occupations, for free social intercourse, for pupil organization—either of group activities or of individual undertakings—and for many active experiences of direct interest to the child. These opportunities we consider essential in the experience of the future citizen if, as we assume, the vital functioning of any individual in a democratic society is dependent upon his power to judge and to act independently in new situations, coupled with the ability to appreciate the rights of others and to co-operate intelligently with a group for unselfish ends.

So far as externals of the class room are concerned, we have not made many changes, although we have increased the variety of materials accessible to the children at all times, and have managed to arrange the furniture so that there is room for work and play in groups, free from the desks. The children, as well as the teacher, are at liberty to sit where convenient, to talk and move about as they please, as long as they do not annoy others—and experience proves that noises disturb children much less than we teachers are prone to believe. That the conduct of the class is somewhat unacademic and informal was apparent to the visitor who insisted upon knowing whether she saw a "lesson" or a "recess." It was not a recess—but I could not truthfully say that it was a lesson, although everyone, including the teacher was occupied to some purpose.

The daily program is very flexible. It is divided into few and, for the most part, long periods which allow time for unhurried, thoughtful work and for social intercourse or play, but which may be subdivided by individuals or groups in answer to temporary needs. There are naturally some periods in which the teacher directs the work of the class, either as a whole, or in small groups where she shares the direction with the pupil leaders. However, the greater part of the work and play, especially in the first two years, has consisted of projects originated by the children or elected by them from among the many suggestions received in school. These projects are carried out individually or in small self-organized groups, and the teacher gives her assistance as it is needed to help the children forward in their plans.

The effort to meet individual interests and abilities has resulted in the rapid advancement of some children along special lines where the work could proceed in small groups—notably in the shop—and has made more conspicuous than ever the desirability of small classes.

Rapid advancement in the shop—Desk
made by a second grade child.

Chair for a younger sister.   Grade II.

But I do not wish to over-emphasize the form of our organization; for though mechanical details, such as program and room arrangement, may limit freedom of development, yet, with all the externals of freedom, a teacher may so dominate the situation that the personality of the individual child cannot unfold.   As teachers we must learn to appreciate more sympathetically each child's point of view; and we should be willing to accept his judgments in many things frankly and sincerely, even when they differ from our own.   Children should be able to form judgments and to express opinion on any subject with which they are competent to deal, and I firmly believe that the opportunity for constant choice, even in small matters, is of inestimable importance in the education of children.   It develops responsibility and a self-reliant habit of weighing values, instead of a tendency to accept without thought the decisions of another.

I do not share the fear expressed by some that freedom to follow individual interests will necessarily develop capriciousness and selfishness—that it precludes discipline.   A child cannot escape discipline if he is to live peaceably with twenty-five other free souls—including his teacher—and the less the teacher interferes, often the greater the discipline.   For does not true discipline, of the constructive sort we all receive in life, arise when there is an inherent reason in any social situation for giving up one's own desires?   On the other hand, in individual undertakings it is often necessary to undergo drudgery in order to carry out a self-determined and interesting end. In carrying forward these ideas of individual and social development, the curriculum of the school naturally plays an important part. We have made some changes in our usual course of study but the most important modifications have been in the matter of interpretation and of method. We have held with Dr. Dewey that "more important than the mere piling up of information is an intimate acquaintance with a small number of typical experiences, with a view to learning how to deal with problems of experience." This does not mean that we wish to deprive the children in this class of the control of such tools of learning as the three R's, or of the knowledge resulting from human experiences of the past, as formulated in literature, history, geography, and so on. On the contrary, we hope that ultimately they may have a wider knowledge and a greater control of technique than is common, just because these will have been gained through personal experiences in which knowledge and skill were required. For again to quote Dr. Dewey: "Careful inspection of methods which are permanently successful in formal education, whether in arithmetic, or learning to read, or studying geography, or learning physics or a foreign language, will reveal that they depend for their efficiency upon the fact that they go back to the type of situation which causes reflection out of school in ordinary life. They give the pupil something to do, not something to learn; and the doing is of such a nature as to demand thinking, or the intentional noting of connection; learning naturally results."

As I have said, there is no question of the necessity of learning to read, write, and add; but there is, I believe, a question of where and how this should be done: it is a matter of emphasis and of right relation to individuals. In the experimental class we have tried to shift the *emphasis* of the primary school from formal studies to constructive work and play, to expression in varying art forms, and to first hand knowledge of social and industrial activities related to a child's life. Facility in the use of the tools of knowledge we believe should be acquired to a great extent through their employment in projects which in themselves are of interest to the child.

This means that we have given more time than usual to manual arts, to play, to excursions, and to various social projects, and that we have not demanded that every child begin to use the three R's at the exact age prescribed by tradition; for we believe that children will learn

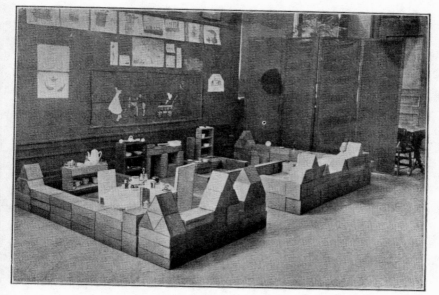

The doll house, center of group play.   Grade I.

more readily and more intelligently if not forced to do so before individual interest, with its accompanying intensity of effort, is naturally aroused.   In this way we hope that we have obviated some of the deadening repetition necessitated by the too early emphasis upon formal subjects.

As for the actual accomplishment of this group at the present time, we expect to finish the formal work required for admission into the regular fourth grade, and to more than cover the content studies scheduled for the primary school.

However, the most important gains made by the class, from my point of view, are in matters difficult to classify, since we have no adequate way to measure them quantitively, but which nevertheless I believe we can record in positive terms.   For example, we note in general the great contentment of the children and their lively interest in real problems of knowledge and experience, their independence in individual undertakings, their ability to cooperate, and their open-minded and intelligent way of meeting new situations and of dealing with ideas.

Of course these claims represent only very small beginnings, for there is no magic formula by which, in a few months or years, the school can make every child responsible and self-reliant. Moreover, we do not consider the present procedure of our class in any sense final; it is subject to constant modification as new problems arise. One of the problems which frequently arises is to provide an experience sufficiently broad in interest to stimulate the whole group and to offer various outlets for individual powers. The account of one such project in the second grade may serve as a concrete illustration of some of the abstract claims I have already made. The work related to foods described below met our needs in many particulars. It provided a variety of active first-hand experiences, it involved new knowledge of some value, and it made use of several of the usual school subjects.

Before school opened I had not planned to take up the subject of food with the children; but the example of the older pupils, who were all preserving foods, led my class to can a few tomatoes which were brought in by one of our members. The success of the first small group in carrying through the various steps of cold-pack canning, led to further work of the same sort, as various vegetables were given us. The children also dried apples and lima beans which they gathered themselves at the school farm.

That the interest in this rather exacting work was sustained for two months was doubtless due to the fact that the children had a genuine purpose in canning a large quantity of vegetables. For early

Washing day at the doll house.

A kitchen sink for the doll house and a truck for home play.

in the work, upon the suggestion of one of the class, it had been decided to have a sale and to use the proceeds to buy milk for a sick baby. Although I had not thought of this plan myself, I was glad to lend it my support.

The final preparation for the sale occupied a large share of the school time for several weeks. The chief consideration from the children's point of view seemed to be who should take charge of the business of selling. They had conducted a play store intermittently during the fall, but, upon testing, it was found that most of the class were ill-prepared to act as salespeople. The children readily recognized this fact and willingly went to work to drill on addition and subtraction. The most successful drill was accomplished by means of a dramatic rehearsal of the forth-coming sale, some children impersonating the visitors and the others the salesmen. Real money, correct prices, and the actual jars of vegetables and fruit were used for this play.

The need of invitations, of price lists, and of bookkeepers the day of the sale, was also recognized and led to much needed practice in written English. The prices were determined by a study of the latest Park and Tilford catalog, a small group with a teacher undertaking this work. It necessitated the use of an alphabetical index, and in some cases the calculation of the price of pints, when only quarts were listed, as we had used both pint and quart jars.

Further preparation consisted in the making of labels for the jars and of posters for the room. The art teacher, when called in to advise, taught the children how to make accurate square letters, which they used in various sizes for the labels and posters. The making of fifty or more small labels with half inch letters proved irksome to the little people, but they showed much persistence in completing the task because of their interest in the sale. The eight children who made the final large posters did a great deal of intelligent, painstaking work. From the artistic point of view the posters were not noteworthy, but they represented the children's own suggestions.

The sale was conducted by the children, who made their own change, kept records of sales and wrapped up purchases. The various duties were agreed upon by the class, in accordance with each one's proved ability to carry them out, and everyone had some share.

Running parallel with the work of canning there was some study of the sources of food and of methods of distribution. This was accomplished by means of talks, pictures, and excursions. Besides the trip to the school garden, the excursions included a visit to Park and Tilford's store, where we saw the retail department and also the large stock of canned goods, a trip to the fruit dock of the Erie Railroad, a visit to Ward's Bakery, and later a day at a farm.

The dock trip was especially interesting. We were shown every activity connected with the handling of fruit, from the unloading of the cars on the floats which brought them from the New Jersey Railroad terminal, until the fruit was carried away in wagons by the market man.

Block construction following trip to the fruit dock. Grade II.

Following this trip, several groups of children constructed from peglock blocks a dock, a float, and a market wagon. One boy brought toy cars from home, and other children made from clay fruit, vegetables, and a tug. Then, for several weeks, the children conducted a self-organized dramatic play which at one time or another involved every member of the class. The play included the play house and store, the newly-made dock, and two other places in the room, respectively called California and New Jersey. The fruit was loaded on the cars at California, brought to New Jersey, and taken across the river on the float to the dock. The storekeeper sent men to the dock to buy fruit, which, in turn, the family in the house bought at the store —toy money being the medium of exchange. This game was of value chiefly because it increased the children's power of initiative and self-direction, and furthered the spirit of social coöperation in the class. But also, the play, in connection with the excursions and talks, helped in some degree to give the children an appreciation of the number of people and of the amount of work involved in providing the food which we obtain so easily.

January, 1919.

II

That the teaching method described in Section I is feasible for young children has been somewhat generally conceded, though its practicability in the middle school is still questioned, chiefly because of the body of formal school studies required here, but in part because of a demand for "discipline" at this period. The development of the plan to meet the needs of fourth grade children should be of particular interest if, as I believe, the experiences of our fourth year point the way for a continuance of the plan further up in the grades. Unless this theory of education can function beyond the primary grades, one may be justified in doubting the truth of its premises.

The apparent incompatibility between the method of learning through problems of experience and the teaching of middle school subject matter arises, I believe, because people associate such terms as occupations, activities and the like, in school, with the manual and play activities of little children. This has resulted in the confusion of particular experiences or situations with the principles which lie back of them. On reflection, it is apparent that a problem in experience, an activity, a project, if you prefer, may lie anywhere along the plane of life experience from the purely material plan of the first grade to a highly intellectual undertaking in the University.   The one point in common between the experience of the six-year-old and of the adult is that the undertaking has a real relation to the life of the projector, that it is in truth his problem, for therein lies the educational value of the experience.

In our "experimental" scheme, as in any method of education, it has been necessary to vary our procedure to meet the changing attitudes and interests of the children as they mature.

In the first grade the mere presence of materials for work or play stimulated unending physical activities.   But now in the second half of the fourth grade, initiative and effort for the most part are determined by undertakings in which some idea appeals to the child, in response to which he seeks and uses either concrete materials or the personal assistance of someone with a larger experience than his own. This change in attitude makes it possible for the teacher, in answer to the child's problem, to introduce him to subject matter which he could not discover for himself.

In the first grade the children drew, modeled or worked in shop with slight regard for perfection of the results and with little desire for aid or approval, and were in great haste to finish what they made. Now they begin to grow critical of their own results; they value the teacher's advice and are glad to defer completion until they have improved their product.   Thus we can give the children control of technique without losing individual initiative and choice.

Doll houses showing slight regard for perfection of results.   Grade I.

In the first grade children to a great extent were individualistic, but now the group plan makes the strongest appeal and individuals are willing to share in processes and in results. This attitude makes possible projects of a constantly widening scope, which bear in their train many educational possibilities. Also through the children's desire to share in group experience it is possible to bring about a more even class attainment in formal studies than seemed desirable in the first years.

The more vital part of the work in the fourth grade, as in the earlier years, goes forward by means of activities, in small groups or individually, rather than through isolated school subjects, in mass teaching. The introduction of a formal study usually comes in response to an immediate need, but later it may be carried on as a special subject. However, all studies do not arise from active undertakings, but some may be introduced directly in response to children's natural interests; for example, history, music and literature.

Certain interests are sometimes pursued intensively for a period of time to the exclusion of some others of equal value, which can receive their due emphasis another time. The consideration of many subjects at once with a limited amount of time is apt to result in scattered attention and very half-hearted thinking. Is it not the efficient method of life to direct one's best energies to carrying forward an undertaking until, in some phase at least, it is completed, and then to return to it later, when we have further leisure for effort?

One of our great difficulties in this fourth year has been the lack of time for the necessary drill on formal studies as well as for those social activities on which we wish to base the acquisition of knowledge and technique. Probably a longer school day or smaller groups are necessary for a thorough-going application of our theories.

To illustrate what has already been said, I will give several concrete examples of fourth grade experiences, selecting these from group problems, which are more far-reaching than individual plans, since they involve both individual expression and coöperative effort.

In the fall, we kept the class until half-past two on playground days, and allowed them to prepare their own luncheons, thus gaining some extra time and providing an undertaking which proved of intense interest to the children, as evidenced by their desire to continue the work through the year. Although this plan consumed much time, to the postponement of some of the academic subjects, it brought many compensating values in its train. The greatest, perhaps, was the practical training gained in meeting a complex and exacting situation, which extended over a considerable period of time and carried with it some drudgery. It was not an easy task for children to prepare and serve on time a luncheon for twenty-five and afterwards to wash the dishes in a given period. That the class met this difficult group problem as they did with intelligence, poise and a co-operative spirit, we believe is largely due to the experience of the last three years. The work was carried forward in three groups, the personnel of which was decided by the class; one group for marketing and preparing the lunch, one for keeping the accounts and one for washing the dishes. These groups changed places every two weeks. As the work got under way many questions in organization arose which the children decided, for example, the confusion in seating led to the institution of hosts, and hostesses, who were responsible for serving and seating at the several tables. The keeping of accounts necessitated much practical work in arithmetic, and furnished the incentive for learning long division since it was needed to find out the cost of the lunches per capita. The planning of the menu brought useful knowledge of relative food values and of the proper food for children, and the marketing led to some knowledge of market prices. A visit to Gansevoort market and one to a Long Island truck farm gave much general information and led to geography lessons, in particular to the use of maps, in tracing the sources of fruit and vegetables seen at the market.

Since the luncheons ended, we have had time to follow up the work with the study of certain other foods, for example cocoa, starch and sugar. This has been done through illustrated talks, through children's reading in the geography text-book and in other references, and by means of visits to a macaroni and a cocoa factory.

A problem of a very different nature from that of the luncheon was met in the making of line drawing designs for Christmas cards to sell for the benefit of our class "orphan"; this means of revenue, though proposed by a teacher, was chosen by the class from a number of suggestions made by both pupils and teachers. The class worked on the designs for several weeks assisted at intervals by the art teacher, and in the end six designs were voted accurate enough to reproduce by means of zinc plates. The printed cards were sold, either uncolored or colored, and for two weeks before the vacation the chief occupation of the class was coloring cards and practicing for their Christmas play. After one or two initial lessons in coloring the designs, the children worked independently, and showed much persistence and self-control in this exacting task, often returning after lunch to work. In several cases, individuals who had never before succeeded in painting neatly, filled in the outlines with good results, their effort stimulated by the interest in this matter which was their own responsibility.

The selling and accounting for the sales was carried on by the children and when it was over and the expenses paid, they were helped to balance their accounts. The formal fourth grade work of making bills followed, with a very live interest, since experience had shown the value of just such work.

As I write this article the class is putting its heart and soul as well as the greater part of its time into the making of a magazine, "The Junior Magazine," which it proposes to send to a hospital. The children have decided upon the following departments: Art, Poems. Stories, Jokes and School News—and have elected an editor for each department as well as an editor-in-chief. The editors choose their own assistants. The designs for cover and fly leaf have been selected by vote from a number submitted by the class, and the art editors are painstakingly reproducing these designs. Everyone is endeavoring to write something worthy of publication, while those who can use the typewriter are copying the accepted manuscripts either at home or in school.

The first number of the magazine is to consist of four copies, and if it is a success we may arrange to have the next number mimeographed, for the children are very desirous of having a large edition so that they may each have a copy.

The acceptance or rejection of contributions, as well as the correction of manuscript, rests with the children, and though this plan will result in a very imperfect magazine, I believe the self criticism which must follow will insure a better result in the next issue than if an adult had corrected all mistakes. Already the increased interest in composition has begun to bear fruit in more thoughtful writing, while some editors, who are poor spellers, are becoming devoted to the dictionary, in an effort to meet the responsibility for which they are so ill prepared. And perhaps even more valuable to the class than the scholastic gain, are the lessons in carrying individual responsibility and in dealing with their fellows in a constructive plan.

The teacher's work lies in carrying forward general class instruction in English composition; in giving advice upon particular points, when asked; in helping some individuals who need special encouragement; and in making school conditions favorable for continued interest in the magazine work.

To further encourage and develop the growing group consciousness at this age, we have given the children as great a share in the class organization as the complexity of our large school will allow. They have elected officers for whom they are building up a set of duties; they have weekly class meetings which they are struggling to conduct harmoniously; and they have, besides regular gymnasium lessons, two free periods each week, in which they usually play competitive team games. It is sometimes difficult to regard with patience the amount of time consumed by the efforts of the group to organize class meetings or other undertakings, but I have faith that these efforts, though only partially successful, are, not a waste of time. For what better work can the school do than to train children to appreciate group responsibility?

That there is a fairly genuine feeling of group solidarity in the class was evidenced in a recent discussion which I overheard. The question before the meeting was how to discipline disturbing members of the class. A suggestion that offenders be disbarred from class meetings was at once met by the objection that it would not be a class meeting unless every child should attend; which democratic statement was unanimously accepted as final. The fact that this class is thoroughly coeducational in character is certainly a great advantage to boys and girls alike. Equal opportunities are open to all, in shop, in preparing luncheons, and in gymnastic games, as well as in learning the three R's.

To recapitulate, in answer to the objections noted in introducing this discussion, I suggest first that the opportunity to introduce the essential subject matter of the middle school lies in our response to the developing interests of children, as they pass from the individualistic to the social point of view, from the play attitude to that of serious work, and from a love of physical activities only, to an interest in abstract subjects. The increase in intellectual curiosity as the child matures furnishes the teacher's opportunity to bring him the accumulated knowledge of the past.

If young people begin with experiences of social value, their natural transfer of interest, from the particular activity to the materials and principles concerned, will call for the assistance of those of wider knowledge than themselves, either through the teacher or through the printed word of authority. When children are ready for abstract studies why should not initiative and independent group effort be aroused by these studies as well as by play activities in the lower grades? It would seem that older pupils should be better prepared than the little ones to use to advantage unacademic methods in the school.

The contention that necessary discipline is incompatible with freedom of choice and with pupil organization, comes, I believe, from a misapprehension of the methods of the class. What better discipline for life can the child have than a situation like the magazine or luncheon experience, where the best powers of each individual are demanded, not for personal glory and attainment, but for the success of the group undertaking. The fact that in so many cases the child's own comrades pass judgment upon his efforts and that he must prove to them his fitness for leadership offers most wholesome discipline.

Again, choice need not mean caprice, but rather personal responsibility for one's actions. Our constant emphasis is on the obligation which comes with freedom of choice—an obligation to prove one's worth by completing a self-imposed task. Moreover, the criticism that the teachers in this class abrogate their authority as educators is without foundation. The final decision in all the larger policies of the school rests with them and they are responsible for providing an environment (of which they themselves are no inconsiderable part) which will offer the necessary stimulus to carry the children forward. They must, as in all classes, encourage the weak, hold up the indolent, and lend their approval to all that is worth making permanent in the children's accomplishments.

One of the greatest difficulties in conducting this type of work lies in the absence of an appropriate technique of teaching. But though the lack of precedent may result in many errors, inexperience has its value, since it forces one to return constantly to basic ideas, as a gauge of results and as a criterion for future plans.

MABEL R. GOODLANDER.

February, 1920.

GREETINGS

THE DAILY PROGRAM

The length of the school day varied with the grade. Sessions for the first grade were from 9 to 12:30, for the second grade from 8:45 to 12:30 and for the third and fourth grades from 8:45 to 1:00. During the play-ground season the fourth grade stayed until 2:30 two days a week and prepared their own lunches.

Of course in a large school like ours where many classes use the same work-rooms, and where the programs of the special teachers are always full, it was necessary to have a daily schedule of periods, although these were always subject to change when need arose. The general plan, varying with the growing development of the children, was as follows:

It was our custom to call the children together for a fifteen or thirty-minute talk every morning, the first period if possible. At this time I brought up matters important for all to share, including interesting information, announcements of various sorts, questions of conduct and plans for future projects, the children joining with the teacher in making the period worth while. At first the children sometimes told stories or poems at this period, but by the middle of the second year there were so many eager volunteers that more time was needed and there grew up spontaneously a daily "story circle" tenaciously clung to by the children for the next two years, though in the fourth grade it was limited to once a week. After a time they instituted a story leader and to make it truly the children's own I often left the room for at least part of the period. The size of this group varied with the offerings. When a good story teller was announced it was large, but less popular speakers had difficulty in gaining an audience. Those not attending were at liberty to engage in any quiet occupation.

Every day a period of from one hour to an hour and a half was set aside for self-elected work, shop, industrial arts or fine arts. A work room was assigned to us at this time. However, only those who had some work in hand which demanded the special equipment went to shop or kitchen on any one day. The rest had the same privilege of choice in the class room. Here the children engaged in social plays such as playing house, store, post-office; they dramatized, played number games, wrote, read, used the typewriter or engaged in various forms of hand work, such as modeling, painting, sewing, weaving. This was also the teacher's opportunity to help individuals over difficulties in the three R's or other subjects, or to start a small group in some worth while occupation which would later be taken up by the others.

Every day there was a gymnasium period—at first largely free with some group games introduced by the teacher. Later, in the third and fourth grades, the gymnasium teacher took the class in regular work twice a week and on the other three days the children conducted self organized team games, the details of which formed a large part of the business transacted by the fourth grade at its weekly class meeting.

The daily period devoted to academic work per se was very short in comparison to the rest of the work, ranging from half an hour only in the first grade to an hour in the third, and in the fourth grade increasing to an hour and a half or sometimes more each day. It was not assigned on the program to any special subject and its use varied with the interest of the class, tempered by the guidance of the teacher along certain lines of accomplishment required for each grade.

There were also two or three music periods each week, two choruses, one ethics lesson and one nature study period. The general school assemblies came every two or three weeks.

Candle making in the school kitchen. Grade III.

Fourth Grade

CLASS MEETINGS

Minutes from the Record Book of the Class Secretary

JANUARY 21, 1920

The meeting was called to order and the class was voting on the inside cover of the magazine. And we voted on Howard's dezine. Then we voted for an "Art" Editor. And he was Moritor and Robert M.

APRIL 7, 1920

The meeting was called to order by President (Leonard). We voted for Leonard & Howard to go on the foreward gard in goleball.

The class decided to enomanate Editors openly. The Class enomanate Editors. We then voted the Editors, the Editors are Editor in Chief (Hilda) Art Editor (Nancy) Story Editor (Sister) Riddel J. S. (R. J.), School News (S. R.) Peom (Nettee).

APRIL 14, 1920

The meeting was called to order by the President (Leonard) Frances said she thought it was not fair for the boys to say they would throw the ball to Frances and they did not throw it once they then voted to setel it themself.

if any one disteb in the class meeting they should keep out for that meeting and the next.

The class decided to put names on mail boxes. Someone suggested that the room committee put the names on the mailbox. The class then decided and voted for the room committee to put on the names on the mailboxes.

APRIL 21, 1920

The Class voted for the locker committee to go in at 15 min. of 9 to see if the light were out.

The Class decided for the children to fight for the ball in gym.

The Class then decided for the children who did not obey the call in gym, to be punished by the leader .

We then decided to choose a person to take an account of all the children in the class meeting that interrupted. That officer is Ruth.

APRIL 28, 1920

The meeting was called to order by the president. The class decided for the leader to add up the score every month. To see who won in Goleball. The class decided for each team to choose a name. The class decided that we should have some new exercides every morning.

The class decided to choose new goal ball leaders. They are Hilda L. & Howard H.

JUNE 2, 1920

The class meeting was called to order by the President and then voted for what we wanted to do with our flag next year and it was voted that we leve it with Miss Goodlander class next year. We then voted to see who wanted to vote for a President for next year, and we decided that we would not vote for President until next year.

CLASS LUNCHEONS
Sample Menus and Pages from the Account Book

Sept. 22, 1919
Tomato with Macaroni
Carrots
Bread and Butter
Peaches (stewed)
Milk

Nov. 17, 1919
Creamed Eggs
Spinach
Bread and Butter
Tapioca

MARKET LIST

2½ eggs	2.25
7 lbs. spinach	1.05
1 Box tapioca	.15
1 lb. butter	.80
3 loaves of Bread...........	.40
3 quarts milk	.60
2 lbs. sugar	.12
	———
	5.37

RECEIPTS

DATE			
April	8	Cash on hand	
"	"	Robert M. Howard, Max	5.47
"	"	Marion, Nancy	6.00
"	"	Ruth, Evelyn, Sylvia	4.00
"	"	Robert L. Nettie, Richard	6.00
"	13	Billy M. Frances, Hilda	6.00
"	"	Mortimer N., Leonard	6.00
"	"	Miss G., Robert J.	4.00
"	19	Charles, Edith B.	4.00
"	19	Auguste	4.00
"	"	Guests, R. S. 22; R. J. 44	2.00
"	26	Mrs. N.	.66
"	29	Hilda L.	.20
May	3	Ruth A.	.19
"	"	Gertrude G.	.40
			2.00
			———
			50.52

EXPENSES

Date	Dry	Milk	Bread	Veg.	Total
April 8	0.19	0.93	0.48	2.50	4.10
" 12		.98	.45	2.89	4.32
" 13	.30	1.86	.45	1.48	4.09
" 19		2.65	.43	2.16	5.24
" 22	.53	2.57	.45	1.43	4.98
" 26	.76	1.39	.45	2.49	5.09
" 29	.06	2.08	.45	1.92	4.51
May 3	.23	1.45	.45	2.80	4.93

	——— $37.26.
Balance	$13.26
Cash on hand	$14.76*

* Accounts did not always balance in spite of conscientious book-keeping.

THE JUNIOR MAGAZINE

The Junior Magazine, whose beginnings have been described, came out for four successive months, that is until the close of the school year, with a change of editors for each issue. The original issue of four copies was increased to thirty-five by the use of the mimeograph, the typewritten stencils being made by a pupil teacher, who, however, made no corrections, even of spelling.

But in spite of this help there remained a very large piece of work for such young editors to carry. The children's contributions were handed directly to the appropriate department, which selected what it considered desirable (there were many rejected manuscripts) corrected the copy, then handed it either in typing or clear long hand to the editor-in-chief. Here further selection took place, with more correction of errors, also the copying of the manuscript on the typewriter, the arrangement of pages and the making of the table of contents. Each number averaged twenty pages of typewriter paper. Perhaps the most interesting point in the experience was the well-sustained interest of the whole class for so long a period. It was a genuine community undertaking.

After each issue was printed I went over the book with the entire class and we all criticized the contents both as to form and matter. The most glaring errors were made the subject of formal English lessons and I think that each number showed some gain in the control of written English.

The selections given below are from various numbers of the magazine, chosen chiefly because they reflect the life of the school. There were also a great many stories and verses, with about as much merit as such efforts ordinarily have when composed without help. The jokes, as might be expected, were very crude, but happily assumed diminishing importance as the interest in other forms of writing increased.

M. R. G.

To Our Readers

This magazine is for your benefit and we hope you will enjoy it. If it is a success you will receive it monthly.

It contains stories and poems which were composed by our class, but the riddles, jokes and sayings are not all original.

Grade four (2)
Ethical Culture School

Our French Friend

Class four two Ethical Culture School, had a French orphon in France. Her father was killed in the war, her mother had to work all day. She had a brother that was not old enough to work, so you see that they couldn't have been very comfortable. So the class decided to support the little girl, as the class could not support the whole family.

We had several sales, which I will tell you about. In the year of

1917 we had a sale of food. We sold such things as pickles, popcorn balls, apple sauce, and candy and many other things. We cooked the food ourselves, with the help of our domestic science teacher.

In the year of 1918 we had a sale of needlebooks, clay bowls, and other things.

In the year of 1919 we decided to have a sale of Christmas cards, for Christmas was quite near. I am sure you would like to know how we made the cards, and so I will tell you.

First of all the children in the class made any kind of a card the people would like to buy, then with the help of our art teacher we improved our cards. Then the children in the class chose the cards they wanted to be printed. After we had chosen the card we liked best, we sent a copy of each card to the printers, and he made zinc plates. A zinc plate is a wood block, the block is the design of the card in zinc.

We then sent the zinc plate down to the printing office in our school for the high school boys to print, which they so kindly did. That is how our cards were made.

After our bills were paid, for the zinc plate, paper, envelopes, our profit was $30.65. We then sent the money to the orphon, who, you may be sure was glad to get it.

H. L.

Our Experience in Cooking

Our class cook their own luncheons on Monday and Thursday. But the whole class cannot cook all at once, so we divided the class into different committees. We have a cooking committee, an account committee to keep account of the luncheons. We also have a cleaningup committee.

I am going to tell you what we had to eat. Sometimes we had soup and bread and butter, vegetables and pudding. We very seldom had meat.

First, the cooking committee goes into the cooking room, and talk about what kind of lunch they are going to have. When they have planned it, the cooking committee begins to cook. At one o'clock lunch is ready and the whole class comes into lunch. After lunch the cleaning up committee cleans up the dishes.

We found that our luncheon costs sixteen or seventeen cents each time, unless we had meat then we payed over twenty. By G. G.

One of Our Excursions

In our cooking class we found out many things. One of the things was we found out how cheaply we could get things in large quantities. So we went down to Gansvoort Market, which is on 14th Street and 10th Avenue. There we saw many kinds of vegetables, meats and fruit.

One of the things that interested me very much was when they smoked the ham. The ham was put into a closet where there were shelves. When night came they would shut the door and fill the closet with smoke. Then they would keep the door shut for two days. At the end of this time the ham was smoked.

Another thing that interested me very much was to watch the men unload the meats. First one man in the street would take the meat from a man in the truck. The man on the street would take the meat and put it into a box with wheels on it. Then another man would come and take the box, after it was full, and bring it into the store.

Testing Vegetables

Our class had been making luncheon every Monday and Thursday, and we learned from the luncheons, that we should have a certain amount of protein and starch in our food. We also wanted to be sure certain foods had starch in them.

First of all our teacher made a solution of iodine. She took some rice, which of course, we know has starch in it, boiled the rice a few minutes, then put it into a dish and put a few drops of iodine on the rice. It emediately turned purple, which meant that rice had starch in it.

I will not tell you all of the vegetables that had starch in them, but I will tell you that our teacher tried to test sugar, and she found that sugar and salt have no starch in them. Because they turned brown.

By H. L.

Macaroni

Macaroni is an important product of the United States. There is also speghetti and noodles.

Macaroni is a typical Italian food. Maybe you think that macaroni is a plant but you are quite wrong if you do.

One day we went to Mueller's factory and I am going to tell you how they make Macaroni.

First we saw the workmen putting farina into a roller to be carried downstairs.

Farina is a wheat product and is very fine like sand.

Next we saw them mixing flour and farina together after which they mixed the combination with water.

Some dough must be kneaded for the macaroni. This dough is put in big iron boxes with sort of paddles, these paddles which turn around knead the dough.

Then they rolled the dough under heavy steel rollers.

Then they were put in a machine that rolled the dough and after that they are shaped, and the macaroni fell down in long strings from the floor above. Then it is put on a big board and is cut by a sharp machine.

After they were cut and then they were put into a drier.

The warm air pressed out the dampness from the soft dough.

Now it is ready for packing. The boxes are cut and a lady puts the cardboard with wax paper on a machine which folds the cardboard into the right shape of a box.

The big boxes are cut the same way and are put through a machine that glues the cardboard. The cardboard then goes on rollers, then two ladies take the cardboard off the rollers and put the glued sides together, then they would wait for another piece and would put the next piece in the first piece and packed more securely.

These boxes are again put on the slide which brings it down to the wagon.

The End.

By B. M., H. H., N. N., and S. R.

The Chocolate Factory

At the beginning of this year the class made their own luncheons, and so became a good friend of chocolate and cocoa. We also had a play about cocoa. But we did not have a very clear idea of a real factory.

Our class was taken to the cocoa factory, and, so, I will tell you what we saw there. When our class went to Runkle's chocolate factory, Mr. Runkle showed us around.

The first machine Mr. Runkle showed us was the cacao (cocoa) bean roaster. The cacao bean roaster looks like a big iron drum. Underneath the drum is the fire, which roasts the beans. The roasted cacao beans, are then taken to the next floor by means of a slide.

The beans are then ground. The beans must be ground a certain size, if they, by chance, are ground too large, the machine will grind the bean over again.

The next process is to melt the ground cacao. This is done by mills. When the cacao comes out of the mills it is a very thick liquid.

The next process is to make melted cacao into hard chocolate. This is done by putting the melted cacao into moulds then the moulds with the melted cacao in them, are put on a moving belt, which brings them to a very cold room. After the liquid has hardened into chocolate, it is taken down stairs to be packed.

We think that men or women pack the chocolate, but if you do you are mistaken, the packing is done by machine too, then it is put in boxes by women.

Mr. Runkle told us that the factory produces six tons of chocolate a day.

By H. L. and L. P.

Our Trip to the Museum of Natural History

Our class went to the Museum of Natural History to see some moving pictures taken by Mr. Finley.

Mr. Finley was a naturalist, he went camping with his family to take pictures for the "Audubon Society." The Audubon Society is a society for the protection of birds and animals.

Mr. Finley saw the chickadee. The chickadee is a brownish bird and is rather small in size. The chickadee's chief food is worms. He eats mostly cut-worms.

Mr. Finley also saw the white heron and the blue heron. People take the feathers of the heron to decorate their hats with. It is a pity to kill the heron just for its plumage.

E. B.

Something About Nuthatches

The nuthatch is the best acrobat of the birds, for he can go down a tree with his head towards the ground, and do many other things that other birds cannot do.

He feeds his young by dashing up to him, putting the food in the young one's mouth and dashing away again as if he had to catch a train.

If you should take the roof of a nuthatche's home off, you would either see eggs or young nuthatches huddled up in a corner.

Nuthatches like a certain kind of caterpillar. They are also trained very easily.

M. N.

Baby Bear

Baby Bear was found under an old log. He was a tiny fellow, only about a foot and a half in length.

Bears live in the forest in an old hollow log or under stumps. They live on smaller animals that they can catch. The bear is a very good climber and he is pretty quick, although not so awfully.

Baby's first meal out of a bottle was a queer one, but he soon caught on to the way of getting it.

Although Baby bear was not half as big as Peter the dog, he was always ready for a scrap. As he grew older he got stronger and so he most always got the best of it.

As baby got older he climbed about in the trees and he seemed to like it all right.

Once when he was out rambling along in the woods a careless boy with a rifle shot at him and he rolled over and pretended to have gotten hit, but he was just playing.

Baby was carried for miles and miles in a knapsack and he did look so cute and sweet.

When the children went out into the woods Baby went too. No matter where they went he was always there. He seemed to love the children well enough. Baby lived a very happy life.

B. M.

A Lesson in Astronomy

The Carpet with the Yellow Dots

We all call those little objects that twinkle "Stars." But they are not really stars, they are "Suns."

Some of these Suns are larger than our particular Sun, and some are smaller, but those suns are so many trillions of miles away that they just look like tiny dots in the sky.

But now we will go to something far different than those suns, and their names are "Planets."

Then you will ask me what the difference between stars, or suns, and planets, is, and I will say that planets shine with a steady light and suns twinkle.

I will give you the names of the planets, they were named after the Greek Gods, and the Greeks named them.

Mercury	Mars	Neptune
Venus	Saturn	Jupiter
The Earth	Uranus	

I named the earth among the planets because the earth is a planet.

And the earth goes around the sun too, and so you see the earth is a planet, because all the planets go around the sun.

Mercury goes around the sun in 88 of our days. Venus goes around the sun in 225 of our days. The earth goes around the sun in 365 days. Mars goes around the sun in 687 of our days. Jupiter goes around the sun in 12 of our years. Saturn goes around the sun in 29 of our years. Uranus goes around the sun in 84 of our years. Neptune goes around the sun in 165 of our years.

Now I wonder, wouldn't you like to know whether the planets are inhabited?

Well, astronomers have studied the surfaces of the planets, but they are not sure. But astronomers have thought that if there are any human beings on the planets, most likely there are human beings on Mars.

It is pretty certain that Venus, Jupiter, Saturn, Mars and Neptune have air of some kind around them, it is not by any means certain that their air is of a kind fit for human beings.

Now let us look at our pretty blue carpet, and we will see a very big design which we called the "Moon."

The moon is a dead world. Those marks that we see on the moon's surface are really dead volcanoes, and dead craters.

The moon has no air, and if we visited the moon and asked a question, our voice could not be heard. Because the moon is a dead world.

Now we will go to something far different from planets or suns.

"Comets" is the name of the new design in our blue carpet. People who do not know the correct name for comets call them flying stars, but that is not the correct name for comets, and so we should call them by their correct name.

If you were up at night you would see a comet flying in the sky. It is true that a comet looks like a flying star, but we must use the correct name for every design in our blue carpet.

Now we will go back to the largest planet "Jupiter." I will tell you something about Jupiter that is very true.

Jupiter has four moons and Saturn has nine moons. Uranus has five, Neptune nine, the earth has one, and Mars has nine moons. But we cannot see the moons with the naked eye, but we can only see the planet alone.

I will tell you something very funny. Do you know that Mars' nine moons are not half as good as the earth's one moon.

If we lived on Mercury or Venus, we would scorch to death in the winter, because they are so much nearer to the sun than our earth. But if we lived on the moon (our nearest neighbor) we should freeze to death, because the moon is so far away from the sun.   H. L.

Some Curious Things About the World

The world, like most of the planets was thrown off the sun many thousands of years ago. It was just a hot whirling mass of hot liquid rock (it seems funny to think of rock being liquid which after many years cooled down). Of course, turning round and round, made its shape become round. The world though it quickly cooled on the outside, isn't cool inside yet.

The continual shifting of the melted rock caused great mountains to rise up and great valleys to be made.

In some places the melted rock got out and made volcanoes and the melted rock was called lava.

The Aleutian Islands between Alaska and the north eastern part of Asia, are volcanic or have volcanoes on them. Most of the volcanoes are dead, but there are some that are active. These are continually making changes in the Islands.

By R. J.

The author traced a map showing the Aleutian Islands, to go with this article.

Spring

The Spring is like the morning
In which the sun gets up:
'Tis quite like early dawning
For yellow buttercup.

A Riddle

It is an animal that is very small, it's tail fluffs up when it's frightened. Sometimes it's striped, sometimes it's not, it likes to catch something that runs in the bread box, and spoils the bread. What is it?

Ans. It's only a kitty,
What a pity.

Our Bird Tommy

My sister, when she was three years old, got a bird for a birthday present, and I was born that day so I was a birthday present too.

Now I am going to tell you about the bird. My sister got the bird on September 22, which is her birthday and mine too, when she got the bird it was about six months old, so first thing to do was to name him, and my sister named him Tommy. When Tommy was a year old he began to sing and he would sing beautifully.

When Tommy would get a cold and not be able to sing, we used to give him bird tonic.

It grew nearer to summer and we wondered what we should do with Tommy when we went to the country, but at last we decided to give him into our cousin's care, for it was too far to take him to the country. When we got back from the country we took Tommy back from our cousin's house. Every winter he stayed with us and every summer he stayed at our cousin's house.

At last, on March 30, 1917, a Saturday, our Tommy died. When my sister and I came home Saturday morning (from a walk) we found that Tommy had died. In the afternoon we had a funeral but I do not remember much about it. It was so long ago. On Tommy's grave we put a stick, and on the stick was a piece of paper on which was written "Here lies our Tommy, eight years old on March 18, 1917, loved and mourned by all his friends."

A true story, By R. A.

Rover—A Collie's Life

PART ONE—MY EARLY ADVENTURES

I am Rover, a big collie now, but at one time I was a cute little collie. But now I'm full grown.

When I was a cute little baby collie I used to gambol around with my brothers and sisters, and many visitors came to look at us. (I did not know then, but now I know they were looking to see if they would like to buy one of us.)

We lived in a place called a dog kennel. There were thousands of dogs there of all kinds, but my family lived in a large cage all by itself. Right across the way from us was a big bulldog. One day the bulldog bit the keeper. He was very ugly.

Behind our cage was a big horse stable. (For you must know that the owner of the dog kennel was also a horse dealer.)

One day I wandered out of the cage and into the horse stable, where I made friends with a nice mare whose stall had a window in it, which overlooked our cage. After a while a man came and took the horse out, but a stable boy found me and put me back in our cage.

A month and a half passed by uneventfully without my having any more adventures, although several times I nearly got out.

At last one day when I was quite a good-sized puppy a man came and put me in a wagon, and by peeping over the front I found out that the mare that I made friends with when I went into the stable was pulling the wagon.

The owner of the wagon drove off. He was a young man of about nineteen or twenty. His name was Charles, and he was very jolly.

At last when the mare had gone along at a good stiff trot for about an hour, she suddenly turned in at a nice driveway and went up it past a small horse stable. Immediately after that she stopped in front of a carriage house.

I was very glad when Charles lifted me out, and I barked at a chicken, and the chicken ran away with squawks of fear. Then I ran back to watch with interest the way Charles unhooked the mare. Soon he led the mare, whom he called Lady, down to the horse barn and put her in a stall, taking off the harness as he did so.

(To be continued)

R. J.

Bobby's Adventures in Europe

CHAPTER I. PREPARATION

Once there was a boy named Bobby. Bobby did good work at school. He took French, German and Spanish.

Bobby's father belonged to a club that lent people money if they would pay it back in a certain number of days, weeks, months or years, according to the amount of the man's salary.

One day Bobby's father came home and said to his wife: "In a month I shall go to France and Germany on business and I will take Bobby, and you, too." "Well! Well! What do you think of that Bobby?" said his mother. "Oh, really, papa?" "Yes, darling." "Yes, but, father, such a little boy like me would be too young," said Bobby. "No 'yes buts.'" "Should we have our picture taken?" asked his mother. "Yes," said his father. "Why should we have our pictures taken?" asked Bobby. "To put on our passport." "Go to bed now, Bobby."

CHAPTER II. THE START

One month later the bell rang and Bobby answered it. "Expressman," called a loud voice. "Right here," said Bobby, and led the expressman to the cellar, up through the coal bin, upstairs to the nursery, where his trunk was, and said: "Take this trunk downstairs and then come back for another, while I get my mother."

Bobby found his mother just as the expressman came in. After Bobby's mother had signed the paper, Bobby showed the man his parent's room. Then the expressman left.

The next morning Bobby had his best suit on.

Again the doorbell rang. This time, "Taxi, taxi," was called. "Just a minute," said Mrs. White.

An hour later all were standing on board the ship.

The ship sailed out to sea.

CHAPTER III. JAKE

The next morning Bobby awoke and found little round windows instead of oblong ones.

Just as he was about to get out of bed his father said, "Stop! Get back!"

"Why should I get back?" asked Bobby.

"Because you will fall," said his father.

"I often fall out of bed," said Bobby.

"All right you can have your own way," said his father.

—THUMP!—

"Ouch!"

"That's what happens when you have your own way," said his father.

By M. G.

(To be continued)

The Tempest in the Teacup

Once upon a time which was neither in your time nor in mine, there lived a rather grumpy little girl of about seven years of age.

She lived in a quaint little hut near the silver rippling brook. Her name was Kitty.

One morning Kitty came down to breakfast in a little blue hoop-skirt with a tiny lace collar and a black bodice.

She spied a little china plate before her, filled with strawberries and cream. Beside her stood a bowl of porridge and a brand-new teacup blue as the sea. "Good heavens," she cried.

I forgot to tell you that Kitty was very curious and so she peeped into the teacup to see whether there was any tea in it. But alas for poor Kitty the cup was empty. Her anger rose and she hid her face on the tablecloth. The tears came rolling down her little dimpled cheeks.

When Kitty sat up she was still wanting to pour her marmee's tea, but still we know she'd spill it, for many a time the hot thin tea would go a burning down her knee.

What in the world did she do, the naughty little thing? She went to the pantry and took the teapot to the teacup. Then the teacup cried:

> "Little girl, little girl,
> Do not spill tea,
> Into the inside,
> Of brand-new me."

"I will" Kitty said, and so grumpily. So thumb and finger went to work to move the heavy thing. And all at once, with a mighty jerk, Kitty the mischief did. The tea came pouring down her dress. Too bad, too bad! "So you didn't pour tea, into brand-new me!" cried the teacup. "No, but I wanted to control your angry mood!" shouted Kitty. "Well, anyway, I have the power to speak and I have the power to talk to you," said the teacup.

"Yes, yes; please do," replied Kitty.

"Well, to begin with," said the teacup, "I am a brand-new teacup with blue edges, and I would like to tell you a little about my brothers and sisters. I have four sisters and two brothers.

"My oldest brother is so very nice, oh very nice, and we call him leaky, because he has a hole in his bottom. We all have blue edges except my youngest sister Annie. She is spoilt and she has gold edges and a gold handle," said the teacup.

"Here comes mother now" cried Kitty.

The teacup was so frightened that it tumbled off the table, for it was just at the edge.

It broke in ten pieces and then Kitty screamed so hard and then quieted down again and thought. "If I am ever a teacup I hope never to break."

And so ends this story.

N. N.

Our Carpenter Shop

I think our school is one of the best in the United States because it gives the children in the lower grades a chance to learn a trade before they go to college.

The trade I am talking to you about is the carpenter's trade. We learn this trade in a large room which we call a workshop. It has all the tools one needs.

I made a boat in the shop and I'm going to tell you how I did it.

I went into the lumber room and found a piece of lumber three inches thick. I first marked out the shape of my boat. Then I took a rip saw and sawed straight down the lines. I then took a spokeshave (which is a tool similar to a knife) and shaved the wood down to the lines and also shaved the corners of the bottom, which I made round. Then I sandpapered it until it was smooth. I took a gouge (which is a knife, round at the bottom) and made the boat hollow. Then I sandpapered it in the inside. I then went into the lumber room again and took a very thin piece of wood, and cut it in the same shape as the boat, and nailed it to the top of the boat. I then drilled holes in the piece of wood which is called the deck and put sticks of wood in them. The sticks are called masts, and my mother put cloth on the masts. The cloth is called a sail. After I did that I painted the boat white on the deck and green on the bottom, and then I let it dry.

And it is now ready to sail at any time.

L. F.

The Owl and the Oregon

The Owl and the Oregon went to sea,
With Billy and Robert and Howard and me.
The Owl and the Oregon are two sail boats,
And when the wind blows they surely will float.

By L. F.

A NURSERY SCHOOL EXPERIMENT

Descriptive Report by
HARRIET M. JOHNSON

with a Section on Music by
MAUDE STEWART

Second Edition—Revised

BUREAU OF EDUCATIONAL EXPERIMENTS
144 West 13th Street, New York
1924

INTRODUCTION

Why do we want such young children? The question has been asked us oftener than any other since our Nursery School was started some three years ago. We have two answers and neither is that of the Day Nursery or the English type of Nursery School. Unlike these other organizations we did not set about our task of caring for children from fifteen months to three years of age because of the economic situation of working or professional mothers,—though this situation is distinctly a part of our problem. Our answers are not in terms of social or economic need. Our first answer is in terms of educational need: we feel that the educational factors in the environment for babies need study and planning as much as and perhaps more than those in the environment of older children. Our second answer is in terms of research: we feel the need of fuller scientific data concerning children's growth,—growth of every sort that is measurable or observable.

Now what "educational need" do we feel for babies under three? The following reports by Miss Johnson and Miss Stewart should answer this question. They give a picture as far as we have worked it out of an environment designed for babies; designed to give them rich sense and motor experiences; designed to give them scope for learning through experimentation; designed to give them adventure without danger to life or limb; designed to give them contacts with others without demanding inappropriate adjustments; in short, an environment planned with educational needs in mind. Of course the physical needs are rigorously attended to. The babies are not only under constant expert surveillance but recommendations given by family physicians for individual children are scrupulously adhered to. All the physical side is thoroughly incorporated into the Nursery procedure and thoroughly recorded. But this is not the field where experimenting is taking place. We are not experimenting in diets nor in the amount of clothing nor in the countless physical details to which we attend. We are experimenting in the equipment and situations which lead to muscular coordination, to experimentation, to purposeful activities, to emotional stability. We are noting, for instance, the amount and kind of climbing a two-year-old can do, the degree and kind of response he makes to various sense stimuli, the amount and kind of contact with other children and with adults that he can bear without strain, and the kind of use he makes of his body and of all his surroundings. Miss Johnson's report is a description of the set-up in which the children find themselves and the use they make of it. It is our first answer to the question of why we wish young children.

Our second answer,—that we feel the need of scientific data concerning children's growth,—is not as evident in the report. Nevertheless it is the point of view from which we started and is still the center of our attention. Some six years ago the Bureau began its attempt to study children's growth, to measure and record growth from many angles and in many ways. Our laboratory has been always in schools,—some public and some private. The aim underlying all the Bureau work has been to get specialists and schools together for their mutual benefit. We have wanted schools, which are providing "an environment" for children, to know whatever there is of accurate thinking and information regarding children and their growth; and we have wanted research into children's growth conducted in close connection with their activities (both of play and of work),—not in isolated laboratories. We found, however, that this connection between the children's activities and our research was more nominal than real in the public schools. Indeed, it needed a very special kind of private school (and also a very special kind of research staff!) to make this connection either vital or significant. Such a school we think we have in the City and Country School. Caroline Pratt, Director of this school and also a member of the Bureau, early offered her school as a laboratory. From the beginning we have felt this offered unique opportunities for research, for the study of the complex interaction of children and their environments. For this school regards as the "environment" all the factors which influence a child's growth,—the school equipment, the general set-up, the curriculum in the narrow sense, the teacher, the children in the class, the child's home, the city streets,—and regards its own function as essentially that of adapting all these factors, so far as it is able, so that the child is released to normal functioning, physical, mental, and social. Such a school is not only the best place for children to grow in but also a real laboratory in which to study growth.

But Miss Pratt's children do not go below three years of age. The overwhelmingly significant early years of growth have passed. She receives children with clearly defined sets or habits. Had they as babies these different action patterns from the beginning? Or what environmental influences have brought them about? To study growth of children in the first three years the Bureau opened the Nursery School in 1919. These two schools with the children from eighteen months through the eleventh year afford the Bureau its present laboratory.

Our study of growth has been in the charge of a research staff. From the beginning this staff has included a physician, a psychologist and a social worker to gather home histories. Other members added for special experiments and for varying numbers of years have been a recorder, who worked on the technique of school records, a health worker, and nutrition workers. These members of our research staff have, to a certain extent, worked with Miss

Johnson either on the procedure or the records in the Nursery. The more technical laboratory data, in particular those gathered by physician and psychologist, accumulate slowly. They cover a range from the general clinical picture of the children gained in an hour's examination, to X-rays of chests and cardiagram measurements, and to schematograph records of posture; from a study of blood sugar under fatigue, to the records of the Stanford revision and performance tests. Already they give growth records of some individual children over a succession of five years; already the numbers of some age groups amounts to 65 and 70. Slowly they are filling gaps in our knowledge; slowly they are building a conception of growth. To get this continuous sequence of records and measurements on growth is our second answer to the question of why we wish such young children.

It is obvious that the problems open to our experiment with babies are extremely big and our experience and our results are extremely small. In fact, we do not feel like talking about "results" at all. This first report of our Nursery School represents not our final thinking but "our thinking up to date." We believe that experimenters should share their thinking as they work,—their aims, their programs, their methods of attack, their current findings, and even their hopes for the future. At the present moment many are groping their way towards a new conception in the treatment and study of babies. We are among them. This report aims only to show how we are making the effort to study the educational factors in the environment of small children and to gather scientific data concerning their growth.

Lucy Sprague Mitchell,
Bureau of Educational Experiments,
New York City.

July, 1922.

THE PLAY ROOM—ADULT FURNISHINGS ARE ELIMINATED AS FAR AS POSSIBLE

THE NURSERY SCHOOL

The Nursery School is completing its fourth year as an undertaking of the Bureau of Educational Experiments. The initial steps toward the organization of this experiment were taken five years ago when the parents of six small children between the ages of nine months and two and a half years with a Director, carried on a Nursery School, giving the children all day care and a program approximating in many ways the one we have attempted.

The set-up for a Nursery School is of necessity more complicated than that of any other similar school group. Ideally the arrangement should be that of a home in its intimate unity and in its equipment for physical care; but it must besides be planned for children, not for adults, in its space and furnishings. These requirements differentiate it from the day nursery on one hand, and the school on the other. The problem has been further complicated in our case by the fact that we are considering the research aspects and possibilities as well as the educational features. In other words our first aim has been to provide for our children an environment favorable to their fullest development, and this of necessity includes provisions for physical care as efficient as those of a well-ordered home. Our second aim has been to work out through our records a method of checking up our educational procedure and of gathering data which could be used for research purposes.

In a discussion of our experiment a statement regarding the space provided and its arrangement, the age and number of children, the equipment chosen, the staff and its duties and the program would seem the best method to make clear our aims in setting up the Nursery School and whatever contribution we may have to make to better knowledge of the pre-school child.

PLANT

We believe that space indoors and out, is the first essential for children of this age, especially since their city homes are usually apartment houses with no out-of-door playgrounds. The great adventure of children of a year and a half is that of locomotion and balance, learning to use their legs in walking and climbing, and up to three and beyond vigorous full-body activities characterize their play. Moreover true cooperative play which would hold a group together has not yet developed. There is, therefore, much more tendency to interfere with each other if they are in restricted quarters.

During the first two years our quarters were the two lower floors of old houses, with outside porches for sleeping. The house arrangement was for the most part very satisfactory. It gave a very spacious indoor play-room which could be divided when the children needed to be separated; it also gave us extra sleeping space since half the big room was adequate for either play or sleep, and an additional room on the lower floor could be used either for dining room or for an overflow play-room.

Aside from the additional space and the ease of caring for babies on a first floor nursery our present quarters are much more suitable and it is this set-up which I shall describe. The essentials remain constant and can be met under a variety of conditions. They are briefly: a generous indoor and outdoor play space, sleeping quarters isolated from the sound of voices and capable of being divided so that sleepers will not disturb each other, an isolation room, a good sized kitchen and dressing room with toilet.

1. PLAY ROOMS: Indoors children need to carry on vigorous running and jumping as well as quieter floor play. The two activities must not interfere with each other. Our play room faces south and contains about five hundred square feet of floor space. A balcony with steps at one end and a slide extending into the room occupies one side. Our aim is to eliminate adult furnishings as far as is possible in order, first to free as much space for the children's activities as possible, and second to limit as much as we can forbidden pursuits and the incessant correction that an adult environment entails.

2. SLEEPING QUARTERS: In a group like ours there are likely to be children sleeping in the morning and in the afternoon. We find that in order to assure the best results we must have rooms removed from the sound of children's voices, the possibility of complete isolation for certain children and a method of separating all cribs so that there is little or no consciousness among the children of each other's presence. At first we tried to keep the sleeping quarters entirely separated from the play space. We found, however, that it was an advantage, measured by quality and quantity of sleeping to isolate

the children, so we have a crib in each room, including the shelter. We have slat cribs, fitted with awnings, carioles and two window cribs which make possible out of door sleeping for the smallest babies. The ideal arrangement would be a properly ventilated cubicle for each child but that is practically impossible in the limited space of a city environment.

3. KITCHEN: We conceived a child's entering the Nursery School as his taking his first step out from his home into a more generously spaced environment, less personal, but essentially that of a home, differing from his own in that it is planned for children not for adults, but where certain adult activities like the preparation and serving of meals, go on in a place which is open for his investigation.

This means that the kitchen is large enough so that the presence there of a child or two does not seriously impede operations. It has the usual kitchen furnishings, and since laundry has to be done every day, a tub as well as the

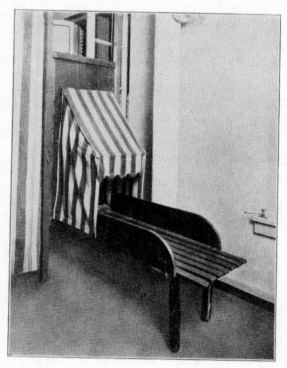

SLAT CRIB WITH INDIVIDUAL AWNING

sink. We use for the cooking a Toledo Steam Cooker which economizes fuel and attention, and also conserves full food value and vitamine content.

4. DRESSING ROOM :   Taking children to the toilet, washing and dressing them form a large part of the Nursery School program.   It is more convenient not to have the toilet enclosed and we have a good sized room where all these operations can be carried on at once.

We find it better to have wash bowls set at normal heights so that experiments with the taps will be carried on only under adult supervision.   A broad shelf or table where the children can sit to be washed and dressed is convenient. It should be about table height but five feet long and broad enough so that a child feels no insecurity in standing on it.   We have used a bath tub with a fitted cover as a very satisfactory substitute for the shelf.   There are cupboards and shelves for first aid materials and for supplies, and fixtures for towels and face cloths.   A wide shelf holds the wire filing cases which we use for individual clothing.   Rubber-lined bags in which soiled articles are returned home and fresh clothing brought back hang in the dressing-room. The scale is set on a fixed platform and is to have a screen fastened around it to protect it from small marauders whose investigating impulses tend to invalidate our weight figures.

ADVENTURE

THE ROOF PLAY-GROUND AFFORDS A MAXIMUM OF SUN

5. STAIRS: Climbing and walking up and down stairs are so necessary a part of a runabout's experience that there must be provision for this activity. If the nursery occupies two floors this essential is simply met, but on one floor an extension of the play space by a balcony will give an opportunity for the stair climbing experience. We climb a wide flight to the roof play ground and the indoor slide besides has open steps leading to a balcony.

6. OUTDOOR PLAY SPACE: One of the advantages offered by the Nursery School is that the children are kept out of doors for the greater part of the day whenever the weather is suitable. Outside as indoors the larger the area the better. A yard as large as those back of the old city houses is probably as small a space as eight children ought to have if they are to play all together, and if they are to be allowed a maximum of free activities. Much has been said of the value of dirt beds, but they cannot be used during the winter, and children under three have not the strength to spade up the soil alone, so that they really get little from the contact that they can not get more fully from sand.

The advantages of a roof playground are a maximum of sun with the consequent rapid drying after snow or rain, clear air, removal from the confusion of noise and from the presence of other children, which is especially important in a school plant, and a new range of visual and auditory experiences which has proved of unexpected value.

Our present plant has a playground extending over the roofs of two houses. The hall and stair-well break the space and an area of about 17 feet by 13 feet is glass enclosed. A space about 17 feet by 18 feet is filled with rounded quartz pebbles to a depth of 8 inches, with thorough drainage, and there the apparatus is placed. The remainder of the roof is tiled. In the center the dumb waiter shaft rises and about it we have built a seat which the children use in various activities. A cement sand box with a water-proof cover is built against a chimney that divides the roof near the shelter.

A NEW RANGE OF VISUAL AND AUDITORY EXPERIENCES

STAFF—NUMBER OF CHILDREN—AGE RANGE

We believe that there is no process in the care of a child that is not educational to him and illuminating to the adults who are trying to learn from him. Therefore, we as teachers assume the entire care of the children. We include no maids on our staff except one for cleaning and laundry work. Since the first year the cooking and serving of meals has been in the hands of a teacher.

We planned originally for ten children but we thought it best to enter them by degrees, taking first three or four who were already acquainted with one of us at least, so that each new entrant should find a somewhat integrated group. As the year progressed we found that two teachers were necessary for eight children. It must be remembered in justification of this staff that besides the physical care of the children, which we aim to make as efficient as that of a well organized home, we are keeping very careful and detailed records. Neither of these pieces of work can be neglected at the expense of the other, both are very exacting in point of time and in the amount and sequence of attention. Moreover we must work over the records we take, and prepare to vary procedure and to supplement our materials or change our environment if the need of such change is shown.

Once since the first year we attempted a registry of ten, adding the new children late in the year when the group was well established and when we were assured of a third assistant. Again we are convinced that eight is a more satisfactory number. A social group of two-year-olds is quite different from one of "fours." It is a group of individuals, playing individually. Too close contact results in interference and in a disturbance of the serenity which is essential for success. If the group grows there must be an increase in space as well as in attendants so that an individual or a few children can be removed for play elsewhere.

It must be remembered also that the occupations of our children are not dictated. The materials lie open to them and we encourage their impulse to explore their environment and to investigate and experiment with whatever they find there. They must be assured safety in their explorations if the spirit of inquiry is to be fostered. This means the constant presence of an adult and a degree of attention that would be unnecessary in a more formal program.

After the first year we decided to limit the age range to from about eighteen months to three years. We are more and more convinced that the homogenous group is desirable. Advocates of a mixed group always refer back to the family unit as a model. We believe that the extension of the family grouping into the school is unwise. The older children have either to submit to continual interference by the younger ones or they adopt the role of mother or nurse, in which case the younger tend to become passive and lose their impulse to independence and initiative. The constructive and purposeful functioning which we expect from the older group is turned into artificial channels.

At three, after a Nursery School experience children seem more ready for a more closely organized program and our children are then sent on to the first group of the City and Country School. Children younger than eighteen months usually do not walk with entire facility and we are not equipped to protect them enough from floor draughts and other exposure to cold. The adventure that the set-up for run-abouts must provide is also more elaborate than is necessary for creepers, so we do not plan to take children younger than a year and a half. We hope eventually, however, to be able to admit children each year at the lower end of the scale so that we shall have two years' observation of each child.

MID-MORNING LUNCH ON THE ROOF

PLAY EQUIPMENT

Our general aim has been to provide the children with play material which they would use to further their impulses toward activity. The chief interests of children of the age we have under consideration can be stated as concerned with play that gives them facility in locomotion, and that allows them to put out a maximum of physical energy, and play that gives them an opportunity for sense experience. That is, they seek occupations that will give them vigorous physical activities with no defined purpose toward which they are putting out their energy, doing normally the thing which is physiologically most important at this age.

We may illustrate this classification by citing the following activities: first, running and climbing; second, jumping, throwing, pulling, dragging, hauling carts about and shifting materials in and out of boxes, chests and other receptacles; and third, manipulating all sorts of materials of varying forms, colors, sounds, textures, weights and consistencies.

These activities are in themselves useful, and moreover through them children are progressing toward more constructive purposes. Our interest is in growth and in the attack children make on their environment through dramatic play, through the development of skill in their chosen pursuits and through an inventive use of the materials at hand. We see the beginnings of these interests in the play of the youngest children, and when a free opportunity is provided development comes, not only with age, but also with the accumulation of a background of experience and associations which a child taps for his play activities. If he is not stimulated to inquiry and encouraged to use materials freely and to adapt them to purposes of his own, his background is less rich and his development is to that degree retarded. Experimentation on the part of our babies is not elaborate but it is no less real.

We conceive our problem to be building up an environment, and developing a procedure which will not only give children an opportunity for the full exercise of their physical powers and for real adventure, but which will also look toward the growth of these impulses into directed and organized activities. Beyond this we are opening up to them the world of social contacts and social relationships, and it must be remembered that this is the feature of our experiment most needing careful consideration. Taking children under three from their homes and placing them in a group of their peers demands from them fundamental adjustments. Whether or not those adjustments are wholesome and contribute to the health of their emotional life, depends in part at least upon the way they are introduced into the activities of the group. We believe that at first children must be protected from too close social contacts,

THE APPARATUS STANDS IN A PEBBLE-FILLED SPACE

that their individual interests must be allowed full scope, and that little by little their participation in activities that are common to all the children will integrate them with the least possible amount of strain and friction. If we accept the thesis that early sets determine or affect a child's later emotional life, we can not fail to realize how fundamental and far-reaching must be the readjustments he makes in building up new relationships and in cutting home ties, in finding himself one of a group instead of the center of an adult family. If we did not believe that these adjustments were essentially wholesome, even more if we did not feel assured that the early social experience makes for a more healthy and normal emotional life, we should not feel justified in our undertaking. We find even in so small a group that many of the children have already set up patterns of behavior that make social relationships difficult for them. In most cases, I should say the individual home situation has been responsible for these habits, such as for instance, reluctance to make social contacts on the part of an only child who has never known children, dependence upon adult companionship in the case of a child under constant care of a nurse, or an emotional drive toward his mother with resulting "tantrums" on the part of a child whose mother has been his constant and sole adult companion. In all cases cited the nursery environment, that is a world of his own inhabited by his peers, cleared up or entirely removed the difficulties. We believe that the contacts and relationships made possible in the Nursery School will do much toward bringing about in our children an increased freedom in their social and emotional life.

In our choice of equipment, activities with the larger muscles govern us largely. We attempt to duplicate certain things like sand toys, small carts, drawing material, etc., so that the gregarious impulse which causes children to choose the same occupation at the same time may be satisfied. On the other hand in order that individual choice may play a part and that the children may learn to consider individual rights, there are certain single pieces of apparatus or play material.

Occasionally we try out special toys or other material but the following list gives our regular, permanent equipment:

LOW SWINGS CAN BE USED STANDING

SHOWING YARD BLOCKS AND PACKING BOX, THE FLOOR OF TILES,
AND CEMENT BORDER OF PEBBLE-FILLED SPACE

THE SAND BOX IN USE—LID RAISED

APPARATUS—PLAY MATERIAL

Out of Doors

Slide.

2 low swings.

See-saw plank, 12 feet long by 1 foot wide.

2 saw horses.

2 large packing boxes: 23½ x 42½ x 29½ inches, 48 x 38 x 30 inches.

3 dozen yard blocks, hollow blocks, 4 x 10 x 10 inches.

Boards. This was odd shelving material, about ⅞ inches thick, some shorter and some longer pieces.

Painter's ladder, steps.

Sand box.

Pails.

Spoons.

Trowels.

Shovels.

Perforated sink shovels.

Small pans and cups.

Skylight peak, 27 inches high, and skylight seat, 15 inches high.

Three movable steps, 18 inches high.

2 kiddy cars, small, low.

Large express wagons.

Small "Trailer" cart.

Brooms.

Rubber balls, various sizes.

Basket ball.

Hammers.

Nails.

Odd bits of heavy lumber for nails.

Work bench.

INDOOR SLIDE SHOWING SETTLE-TABLE AND CHAIR USED BY BEGINNERS AS A HALF-WAY STATION

144

APPARATUS—PLAY MATERIAL

In Doors

Small tables, chairs and benches in play rooms.

Adult chairs and table.

Large ironing table settle.

Indoor slide.

Gymnasium mat.

Block chest.

Blocks: unpainted bricks, half bricks and multiples of that size up to three feet in length, triangles of two sizes; Montessori Pink Tower: turned pillars.

Montessori Brown Stair, Milton Bradley cubes: purple, blue, green, yellow, orange, and red.

Nested boxes, largest about 12 x 12 x 10 inches.

Montessori cylinders—three sets.

Wooden dolls—11½ inches—Schoenhut.

Large doll's bedstead, with mattress and pillows and covers.

Flatirons.

Covered boxes—about 8 by 14 inches.

Above boxes converted into carts.

Extra wheels and axles.

Rubber balls, various sizes.

Plasticene.

Drawing paper and crayons, large size.

Swiss tuned bells, key of E flat.

Musical bells, set at either end of a handle, dumb-bell fashion.

Wooden tone bars.

Sand bar, sand paper covered boards, shaped like board erasers, with handles on one side.

Piano.

Wooden paving blocks.

There are other incidental things, which have been rarely used, or which would not constitute a part of our intentional equipment. Much of this play material is on shelves behind closed doors; any of it can be had on request but it is not all exposed at all times.

PROGRAM

We attempt no stipulated program in the activities of our children. That is, there is no prescribed activity for any special time of day, except for the music period, which will be described hereafter. Certain details of their physical care, however, have definite place in the day and make divisions which might be called a program.

On arrival the children go at once out of doors if the weather is suitable. They stay there until mid-morning lunch at 10:30. Immediately thereafter the forenoon nappers are undressed and put to bed. The others return to the yard and play there until time to wash up for dinner. After the meal the afternoon sleepers are put to bed and adult lunch is served. The children who sleep in the forenoon come to dinner as they wake, and there are often toilet duties to attend to after the meal, so there is a period of indoor play of varying length. Sometimes the children are dressed early and put into the yard, where they are joined by the afternoon sleepers as they wake. Sometimes the indoor period extends so late that the group does not get yard play at all in the afternoon.

After the nappers are all up and dressed, about 3 or 3:30,* comes fifteen minutes or so of music. During this time the activities go on freely, but we definitely go in from the roof for music, and the period is not a casual happening, but is planned for and announced. As can be seen, these stations in the day divide it and make the framework of a program.

If we are indoors all day there are certain materials that we present to the children, such as plasticene and crayons. Sometimes we are asked for these materials, but they differ from most of the equipment in that they are kept out of sight and out of the reach of the children. Musical bells, stringed instruments, sand bars and tone bars we deliberately choose for the children, and we usually supervise their use and set them before the children for definite and limited periods.

Out of doors we frequently arrange the apparatus for special experimenting, and after a period of play with it we re-set the stage. The sand box, too, is opened for a limited time, generally after the mid-morning lunch. All such intentional changes in the presentation of materials constitute our program. In the usually accepted meaning of the term, however, we have none.

---

*The music hour varies from year to year.

RECORDS

We have attempted to develop a system of note-taking which will record the use of the environment in terms of the children's activities, the progress of the group toward social integration, and the growth of individuals in control and in facility and purpose in their use of the equipment. Along with these records we state our procedure with the children, our method of handling this or that situation, and our intention regarding the set-up and the experiences that we offer the group or individuals.

Many persons think of a Nursery School as a place where children can be given the same sort of physical care that the home provides, and can have the advantages as well of association with others of their own ages. This is all true, but what is less often recognized is that while we attempt to keep our attitude, our relationship with the children casual and unstudied, the environment is an intentional one, and we are trying constantly to test it and our methods in the light of the behavior and development of individuals and of the group.

We are, moreover, concerned with the research aspects of the experiment, and, together with the physician and psychologist, are trying to develop a technique of observing and recording children's responses in an environment where there are as few restrictions as the welfare of the group will permit. There have been many studies of individual children, but we have at hand little collected evidence about the reactions of children in groups, their ability to make social adjustments, the degree of muscular co-ordination and facility in handling their own bodies which they develop at different ages, and the methods they build up in learning the various processes which the use of the equipment and the social situation present to them. We have as yet done little more than state the problems tentatively. We are, however, attempting in our various types of records to meet two problems, first, that of keeping our environment, including teachers' methods, under scrutiny in order that it shall be as favorable for normal development as we can make it, and, second, that of amassing accurate data which can be used in establishing standards of growth.

We have an accumulation of two years' records which we regard as very incomplete. In a later section there are given quotations from them in order to illustrate our method of note-taking and the use of records to check up the progress of the children and the procedure of the teachers.

Our current records follow two forms: The individual daily chart on which we check in brief certain significant items and which also shows the height-weight figures, and a weekly summary gathered from a running diary account.

INDIVIDUAL DAILY RECORD   BG

June 1922

Date	NAP				URINATION			DEFECATION	APPETITE AND GENERAL BEHAVIOR AT TABLE	SOCIAL CONTACTS CHILDREN – ADULTS	CRYING ATTACKS CAUSES	NOTES ON PHYSICAL CONDITION RECTAL TEMPERATURE
	In bed	Asleep	Awake	Length	Vol.	Irreg.	Nap	Time–Qual.				
1	12.40	12.55	3.40	2.45	9.25 10.30 11.15 12.15		✓	0	Much less messy than usual. Not very fond of asparagus. Threw toast away. Received another and larger piece.	A curious drive toward adult. Not very find of adult after nap. Seemed a response to attention	0	
2	12.45	1.15	2.30	1.15	9.30 10.05 11.40 2.30		Dry	0	Ate very well. Toast again muddled on floor.	None with children. Tends to stick to adults if noticed	Woke crying—rather tremulous—murmuring something which I could not understand.	
5	12.30	12.40	3	2.20	9.35 10.55 12.30		✓	0	Good appetite and technique. Warned about toast—did not drop it.	Social with L and J (see notes)	0	
6	12.30	12.40	3.30	2.50	9.30 10.15 11.30 12.30		✓	0	"	Affectionate to adult tho' not clinging as on the first.	Cried hard when J dropped stuffer from top shelf of closet– on his head	Weight 28.5 9.10 A.M. Height 36. (voided) Mother reports him very irritable at home.
7	12.25	12.40	3	2.20	10.30 11.40 12.30		✓	0	"	See notes.	Cried hard when he tipped himself over in wheelbarrow	
8	12.40 Waked by L	12.45	2.30 by L	1.50	9.30 11.00 12.30 3.00		Dry	0	No spilling at all. Very good form. Expeditious	Affectionate but not dependent. Frequently came up for a friendly embrace, not staying long.	0	
9	12.30	12.41	3	2.15	10.00 11.30 12.30 3.00		✓	0	Messier than for last few days.		Cried hard when J. bit finger. (B had abstracted J's property)	
12	12.40	1.20	3.15	1.55	9.10 11.05 11.45 12.35		✓	0	Good appetite. Was helped a bit.	Very gay and social. Very responsive to advances of children or adults	0	Weight 28.5 9.10 A M (voided)
13	12.30	12.45	2.35	1.50	9.15 10.44 11.40 12.40		✓	0	Fed self largely	"	Cried twice for actual hurt.	Today and yesterday I have noticed fingers in mouth only, just as he went to sleep.
14	12.30	12.45	3.35	1.55	9.30 10.35 11.30 12.35 3.05		✓	0	"	"	Cried once when he fell.	Fingers not in mouth at all. Teeth' nearly all thru'.

EXAMPLE OF INDIVIDUAL DAILY RECORD (reduced in size)

INDIVIDUAL DAILY RECORD.

We built up the form of this record on the supposition that by it we could check up a child's degree of social and emotional adjustment to the environment at a given time and follow his integration in the group. Early in our experience as we worked on the problem with our children, these factors seemed outstanding: control of bodily functions, especially urination; length and regularity of nap; the attitude of the child toward his food, his ability to handle his implements, his appetite and readiness to accept new articles of diet; contacts, whether friendly or quarrelsome, made with other children and with adults; and the amount of crying and its causes. His physical condition, if there are unusual or significant manifestations is also recorded.

We have not yet evaluated the material from our notes and cannot say how significant they are except for current use, but we are convinced that these particular factors are affected, if not conditioned, by a child's degree of at-homeness with us. They also indicate his maturity in some instances, and deviations in them sometimes herald physical disturbances.

To a certain degree a child's development in these functions is dependent upon his age; that is, there is probably an approximate norm, and we can say, for instance, that by and large, children attain a fair control of the function of urination at about three, that by the second year they ought to be able to feed themselves with a certain degree of skill and efficiency, and that between five and six naps will be taken less regularly. We doubtless have some such general average in mind in making our judgments. We wish to verify these judgments, to note variations, and to find if possible what causes a generally slow development or sporadic slumps.

At the end of each month we summarize on the back of the chart the daily record. In this way the months can be easily compared and progress or change noted.

M. M. (21 Months) INDIVIDUAL RECORD—MONTHLY SUMMARY.

October, 1921.

Present 13 days. Absent 3 days.

Nap:
Average time awake .... 12 hours
Average length of nap .... 1.8 hours

Urination:
Average number of times daily 4
Accidents 2
During nap, wet 12 times, dry 1.

Defecation:
Number, 6 times at school. Quality, normal.
Quality, normal.

Appetite:
No appetite. Slow and unwilling to eat. Cried over dinner on 7 days. Did not feed herself.

Social Contacts:
Very affectionate to adults, bidding for their attention, especially during first few days. Made occasional advances to children but till the last few days of the month they were in the main controversial.

Crying Attacks:
Crying recorded on 12 days.

Causes:
Going home in taxi, till last few days. Being put to bed. Injuries whether slight or serious. Being given dinner.

Physical:
Examined on entrance. Has been in town all summer and has had a bad attack of whooping cough. Seems in poor physical condition.

M. M. (22 Months) INDIVIDUAL RECORD—MONTHLY SUMMARY.

November, 1921. Present 18 days. Absent 1 day.

Nap:	Average time awake .... 13 hours
	Average length of nap .... 1.9 hours
	Still sucks thumb and has to be gloved.
Urination:	Average number of times daily 4
	Wet in nap 18 times, dry none.
	Accidents 4
	Can go longer period than any other child without having to urinate.
Defecation:	Number, 7 times; 2 in one day. 1 involuntary, in nap.
	Quality, normal except the involuntary one which was soft and ill-digested.
Appetite:	First record: resisted feeding but was taken to kitchen where under pressure she finished more than half dinner. After an absence appetite improved and she fed herself till last three days when she was very slow and needed constant prodding. Fed herself a part of every meal.
Social Contacts:	Records inadequate but showing progressive good humor. Very snappish if opposed. More affectionate to adults than to children but some friendly advances to children recorded.
Crying Attacks:	Crying recorded on 6 days. Did not cry in taxi nor for parents' departure.
Causes:	Injuries, no matter how small.
	Prodding or forcing at dinner.
	Interferences or advances from children.
Physical:	Cough bad all through month.

PHYSICAL GROWTH CHARTS.

Shortly after entrance, Dr. Lincoln, the physician of the Bureau staff, gives each child a thorough examination, preceded by a laboratory analysis of a specimen of stool and urine. Following the examination, recommendations are made to parents and to the nursery as well. The charts remain on file in the physician's office, where they are available for reference.

We consider the physician a member of the Nursery staff, and she is consulted on questions of arrangement of quarters, activities, diet and records. The current contribution which she makes in the physical examination is an essential part of our work of caring for children, and her research program is one in which we are sharing.

Our own physical program is a modest one. Stripped weights are taken on the first day of each week between nine and ten-thirty. The weight is taken directly after the bladder is emptied and also after the bowels are evacuated in the case of those children who have a morning stool, which is usual. Every four weeks the children are also measured. At first we attempted heights, but it was manifestly impossible to get accurate measurements of children who

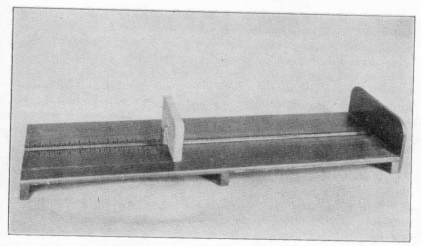

BOARD FOR TAKING HEIGHT MEASUREMENTS

were just beginning to stand without support. Miss Forbes, the Bureau health worker, devised a measuring board to be used with the child in a recumbent position.*

We have also been experimenting with photographs of the children stripped, against a background ruled in inch and a half squares, in order to get a measure by inspection of proportionate length of legs, arms, head and trunk.

As is well known, the proportions of the new born are quite different from those of the adult, and the relative part taken in the total length by head, trunk and legs at different age periods is quite different.† Studies have been made which seem to show that increment in length and in girth of various parts of the body is gained by an alternating process.‡ We all note differences in proportional development as children begin learning to walk. We comment on the extraordinary size of the head in proportion to the rest of the

---

* Miss Forbes' instrument is very similar to that devised by Dr. Bird T. Baldwin and illustrated in his study "The Physical Growth of Children," Studies in Child Welfare, Vol. 1, No. 1, Uvs. of Iowa, 1922 and also one made by Mr. Gilbert Tucker of the New York State Board of Health. Neither of these instruments was known to us at the time.

We are planning to experiment with the apparatus used by Dr. Charles A. Wilson in the Merrill-Palmer School, Detroit, Michigan, which we have been permitted to duplicate.

† Bardeen, C. R., *The Height-Weight Index of Build*, Pub. 272, Carnegie Inst. of Wash., pp. 483-554.

‡ Godin, P., *Growth During School Age*, Richard G. Badger, 1920.

body, or we generalize by saying that one child seems much more of a baby in his physical development than another. Whether or not these biological differences result in appreciable differences in behavior has not been the subject of investigation, as far as I know, nor has any study been made of them from the educational point of view.

We are now working tentatively on the thesis that there is a relationship between proportional development and types of activity. We find, for instance, that certain of our children whose muscle co-ordination, as shown in posture and facility in maintaining balance in walking, is less advanced than others of the same age, show also a proportional development approaching more nearly that of the new-born child. Is this only a coincidence, and what relationship has it to the types of activity offered to children? Are such children able to protect themselves in a free environment? Will they choose appropriate activities and avoid overtaxing themselves? In other words, is it enough to keeps hands off? From our observations we suspect that it is, but we believe that the natural tendency of teachers to increase the stimuli if a child seems physically inert in comparison with others of his age must be rigorously controlled. We are now working with our physician upon a methodology for taking proportional measurements of the nursery children. Up to this time we have used our findings only as a check on our study of individuals.

The accumulation of these measures of growth is, of course, essential to our program and is valuable research material. We are asking various questions regarding seasonal variation in growth, rhythmic alternation in increase of different parts of the body and, as has been said, of proportional development to types of activities.

Porter's* figures on seasonal variation are based on work with school children. There are very few studies of groups of pre-school age.† Our numbers are small, but as our data accumulate we hope to make our contribution to the questions raised.

DIARY RECORD—WEEKLY SUMMARY.

Our current notes are taken in diary form, jotted down in small books as we can during the day while the activities are going on, and summarized weekly. The summaries are verbatim copies of the diaries, but the material is organized under the following headings, which indicate the line of inquiries we have raised regarding the children and the environment:

---

* Porter, Wm. T.: *Seasonal Variation in the Growth of Boston School Children*, Amer. Jour. of Physiology, 1920, (52), 121-131.
† Bleyer, A.: *Periodic Variations in the Rate of Growth of Infants*, Arch. of Pediat., 1917, (34), 366-371.

1. Activities—indoors and out.
2. Social Contacts.
3. Emotional Reactions.
4. Language.
5. Music.

1. ACTIVITIES.—Under this head we indicate how the play material is used, to what extent and to what purpose, and whether or not it meets the needs of the children as they develop. We list the various pieces of equipment, the slide, cart, shovels, etc., out of doors; dolls, boxes, balls and blocks, indoors, and record the part taken by each child. In this way, as time goes on, and our evidence accumulates, we learn how actively the material is used, whether it lends itself to varied and progressive uses, and what techniques and what purposes the children develop in the use of it. Upon this record we base our procedure.

2. SOCIAL CONTACTS.—We wish to know in greater detail than the individual daily record chart furnishes, what contacts the children are making with each other, how their consciousness of each other and their relationship in the group to each other and to the adults is developing, how their play impulses are affected, and whether or not there emerges any tendency to co-operative activity.

3. EMOTIONAL REACTIONS.—We are trying to study the effect on the child of bringing him into the group, how he adjusts emotionally to it, and how, in consequence the group becomes a unit. We note whatever we can of the affective life of the children, around what centers it revolves, how it affects the other children, and what causes emotional strain in the individuals or in the group as a whole. The second and third topics are closely related, often merge, and in the definition we give of them at least are frankly experimental. How significant they are we shall know only as we use and relate the material.

4. LANGUAGE.—The subject of language development is one of our main interests, because we feel that it is one of the main channels of social and emotional expression. This is true whether one regards language in its technical and utilitarian sense, as a vehicle for the conveyance of thought or in its art or play sense, as a rhythmic instrument by which thought can be enriched and enlivened or arranged in pleasing forms or patterns.

The first words are probably attempted as other activities are, because of the urge toward sense or muscle experience. Babbling is in itself pleasant. As the range of tone and the control of the vocal organs increase, the pleasurable sensation grows. Bellowings for the sake of brute noise hold increased possibilities of pleasure as they increase their range and form and take on content. We believe, however, that the social element, the desire to communicate, to share, enters early into the speech beginnings if attention is given early to conversation; and by conversation I do not mean making wants known, but sharing experience, the give and take of social intercourse.

In our diary notes we make no thoroughgoing attempt to collect vocabularies, though we do try to get occasional samples. At regular intervals through the year and over a two-days' period, we note all words or expressions used by a child as we can in the course of our work with him. We are trying to follow the progress of the children's effort to communicate, to understand and to respond to the communication of others. We note the differences in the children in the need of a motor accompaniment to speech, in clearness of enunciation, in their method of acquiring speech and in their interest in words— their attention to language. This slips into our second inquiry regarding language as play or as a pleasurable instrument, whether as a rhythmic accompaniment or as a means of intensifying an experience. We note originality and facility in verbal expression and pleasure in the rhythmic use of language. (See "Intentional Procedure" for further account of language.)

5.   MUSIC.—The whole subject of rhythm in language, or of language as an art, very closely approaches music. This is the fifth heading under which we arrange our notes. The music program and the methods we use in our work with the children in music will be stated in detail in a further section of this report. It is the social significance of music that we are trying to trace, the interest shown by the children in it, and their use of it in their play, rather than the reproduction by the children of songs. Our records show what the children do during the music period, and how they react to the songs and phrases that we use as accompaniments to certain of their activities. We note their rhythmic play or accompaniments to the music, and their attitude toward the singing voice as it differs from uncontrolled shouts or bellowings. We also record musical or rhythmic responses made throughout the day. The general feeling which we are trying to pass on to the children is that music, its enjoyment and use, is not a thing apart, to be reserved for the exceptionally gifted, but is theirs to the extent of their desire and ability to make it part of their social equipment.

RECORDS OF INTENTIONAL PROCEDURE.

Besides using the diaries as a general check, we have tried to segregate from them the record of individuals in order to see whether, as they stand, they can be used to indicate a child's progress toward social and mental maturity. We have taken very generalized topics representing abilities present from the first, but fundamentally modified by experience and by contacts as well as by time alone, namely: Bodily Control, Social Control, Associative Memory,—power to bring past experience to bear on a new situation, and Use of Language,—as a social tool and as play material.

As we began defining these abilities we realized that we had a very definite and intentional attitude toward them and that it might be valuable to record the procedure that we are developing. Taking then, the above heads, I have tried to state the impulses and intentions that govern our attitude and our method of approach.

We believe that there is more rather than less danger in correctional work with little children. We are more afraid of imposing our wills than of letting the children go too far along their own paths. We desire above all to know where they are; to set up no barriers to a freely flowing emotional life. As far as we can we aim to make our environment and the social group the corrective material. We are constantly going beyond this standard, but we feel that it is altogether safer to set it for ourselves. I am now referring to such activities as those governing play interests and social reactions, rather than to such bodily habits as attending to eating at food time, to sleeping at nap time, etc. We believe that those habits easily become automatic if no emotional conflict has been set up, and the sooner they do the better, so we do bring the children into line on these details as soon as possible. Even here the establishment of a routine program with a group has more effect than any coercion on our part.

1. BODILY CONTROL.

a. *Control of or voluntary attention to bodily functions.*—Our effort at training is confined to seating on the chamber at regular intervals which we attempt to make frequent enough so that the child will have little experience of remaining wet. After a child has control we exhort him not to forget to ask for the toilet, and we reprove him mildly when he gets wet. We express enthusiastic approval of dryness. We also attempt to accustom the children to casual treatment so that they will sit interchangeably on a nursery chair, the toilet or a chamber without fear or agitation.

We believe that too much stress has been laid upon acquiring the dry habit. Probably the habit of control can be acquired very young, but we do not know at what expense to a child nervously, nor at the sacrifice of what more important and dynamic interests. In the first place, it is surely done at a big emotional expense for adult and child. It fills the conversational horizon when there are many more absorbing subjects at hand that the child is ready for, and we cannot yet estimate the sex connotations which the emphasis upon aversion to the excreta may later contain. After the age (about three years) at which control is usually established it is largely a question of attention with normal children, and we are much more energetic in our effort to impress them with its importance.

b. *Interest in feeding self; ability to handle implements.*—We try to stimulate the child's interest in feeding himself, or rather, we cultivate it, as it is usually present. We put the spoon into his hand and make sure that the attempt at getting food into his mouth is successful enough to ensure further trials We do not entirely refuse to feed the older children if they wish it, often helping them with the last few spoonfulls which are difficult to scrape from the plate, and sometimes even starting a child off if he seems to want it. We should try not to do this often enough to make a child dependent upon us, but the hand co-ordinations involved are fine enough so that we do not dare insist upon a complete performance on the part of an unwilling child.

Our general atittude during meals is to set up the habit of quiet and attention to the business at hand. We make little conversation, seating the children so that they will be as little disturbed by each other as possible, and discouraging play. We make no effort to teach the children good table manners as such, but we try to improve their postures by pulling them back in their chairs, and we discourage messing with their food or handling it. We encourage their clearing off their dishes after they have finished, but we do not require it.

Caprices in appetite or vehement dislikes and reluctance to try new articles of food have made family feeding difficult and idiosyncracies in appetite rather than in digestion have given rise to the saying, "One man's meat is another man's poison." An emotional connotation attaches itself to mealtime in many instances because of the method used to introduce unfamiliar articles, and the attitude assumed by the adult of an expectation of reluctance or refusal on the part of a child. We are sure that there are fewer idiosyncracies of appetite than mothers of "unusual" children would lead us to believe, but we are noting persistent reluctances, disinclination for milk and our success in cultivating a taste for it, and the way children react to the introduction of new foods. We do not call a child's attention to a new food, nor persuade him to try it. We decrease portions of an objectionable article, but we present it again and again with other well-liked varieties. When there is persistent refusal of it we try methods of diverting the attention from the food till it is taken and swallowed.

We watch the children's chewing habits and see that fluids are withheld till the mouth is empty. We give them a sort of homemade zwiebach in order to cultivate the taste for hard bread, and with the little ones we often use some sort of refrain like, "Crunch, crunch, munch, munch," or "Chew it and grind it and mince it very fine." Other refrains are, "Sippety-sip and down again," "Up cup, down milk, a long, long, long, drink," "The bottom of the cup, drink it up," "A long, long drink for daddy," which we use instead of urging a child in so many words.

c. *Interest and ability to share in the dressing processes.*—We wash and dress the children on a table usually, so that we can stand at the process and be more free than if we held them. Also we believe that they become accustomed to standing or sitting on a height by that method. Another advantage is that we can leave them for a second and find them in the same place when we turn back to them. This only till they learn to let themselves off.

In dressing the babies we try to call attention to the various articles as we put them on and to get their co-operation in the way of arms and legs. We found as the children came to us that there was a marked difference in their reaction to the dressing process. Some of them are entirely passive and lumpish, accustomed apparently to being stowed away into their clothing, while others find armholes and legs, hold up their hands and poke their heads through, taking some responsibility for the performance. We get their attention to the armholes and legs by games or songs like, "First one hand and then another," "Peek-a-boo, peek-a-boo, Richard's hand is coming through," or "Bobbie's hand goes in, Bobbie's hand comes out," making the child look into the hole and calling his attention to the way the hand comes out.

With the older ones we follow their interest in doing for themselves as far as it will go. Unlacing shoes and removing them is generally the first step. We get their interest in the lacing process as early as we can after the first glimmer of it appears, using the criss-cross song, or poking the laces up and letting the children pull them.

> "Jane-O puts on her stockings,
> Jane-O puts on her shoes,
> Jane-O laces criss-cross,   criss-cross,
> Jane-O laces her shoes."

The same thing is true of the outdoor clothing. We do not try to teach the children to hang up their hats and coats. We found during the first year that they were physically so inadequate to these processes that they gained nothing from their attempts. Each child now has a stout wire waste basket into which all the outside clothing is put and which is then placed on a shelf. Practically all the children bring their baskets to us and drop in certain articles. They can all remove their hats, and whenever a child shows any interest in struggling out of a garment we give him that opportunity. As long as he has not acquired the technique we do not expect that he will do more than play at it. Even then we occasionally help him if he wishes it.

We carry on a good deal of play and much conversation with the children when we are putting on and taking off their outside clothing. We maul them and swing them, especially if the garments are restricting so that dressing is an unwelcome process. We can generally hold the play in hand enough so that we get their attention when it is necessary to hurry through. We take various occasions for this kind of rough-housing with the children, for we believe that they gain in poise if they become accustomed to such play. There is an element of good sportsmanship in it which makes them, when they are older, take hard knocks in various games with a better will. Furthermore, most

children enjoy play of this sort intensely, and get a valuable muscle sense satisfaction from it.   It seems to us wholesome for children to get accustomed to
rough handling, for the child who feels that he is not to be touched or even
approached in an informal way has much discomfort in store for him.

d. *Ability   in use of the stairs and apparatus.*—When we opened the
Nursery School in 1919 we had gates fixed at the head of our stairs.   Before
many weeks had passed these gates were never closed, and since then our stairs
have been unprotected.   We find the stairs a real adventure for the younger
children, and though they have occasional falls, as a general rule they learn
caution and get more freedom then they lose.   We begin walking the children
down as soon as they get their legs, and encourage them to hold on by the
banisters whenever they go down accompanied by an adult.

We have put no limit on their climbing.   This means that they require
constant supervision, for we feel that it would be disastrous to let them get
the experience of a serious fall, which might set up inhibitions and fears.   We

WE PUT NO LIMIT ON THEIR CLIMBING

try to insure them safety in their experiments with the apparatus. We find as a matter of fact that it takes very little encouragement to send children back at once to a piece of apparatus from which they have taken a tumble. When they are engaged in an experiment pretty sure to result in a slight fall, we make a game of it, chanting something appropriate, like "Tippity-top, there goes Michael; Tippity-top, there goes Jimmie," etc., to the tune of "One little, two little, three little Indians," and so prepare them for falling and making light of it.

We try to urge the older children to take care of themselves in any situation, that is, to jump, to climb on the boxes and to go up and down the ladder without an appeal for adult help. On the other hand, we do not refuse to give it in most instances, even after a child has done his stunt alone. We think there is little danger of our children becoming passive and dependent, and we know so little of the reasons for appeals that unless they persist and unless a bad habit seems likely to result, we pay little attention to them. We make suggestions to the children as to methods; for instance, telling a child to get a box if he has asked for help in climbing, and we always try to make him do his share if play material is to be changed or carried to a different part of the yard at his direction. Our general attitude, however, is one of expectation that each child will work with the material as he likes and that he will devise ways to reach desired ends.

We make changes in the arrangement of outdoor apparatus in order to stimulate the children to activities, if, as sometimes happens, they seem to be going stale. I do not mean that we demand from them incessant use of the pieces of play material, but that we have found that they go to old things with fresh joy if new combinations or varied positions are made.

2. SOCIAL CONTROL.—Our method with regard to social contacts differs with the individual, though in general we proceed much as we do with the materials, giving the child an opportunity to experiment and watching in order to avoid disastrous consequences. For instance, we let the children's interference with each other go on to a certain degree, but our general effort is to turn a vicious attack into a friendly one. In other words, we encourage the children to settle their own troubles, but we interfere if strain seems resulting. We try to avoid the thing which is done so constantly in families, making the older child give up his plans for play or his actual play material to the younger one. On the other hand, we do make a very definite effort to smooth the way for a child socially. We do this because assembling children at this age is such an unusual social procedure that it may well demand of them an emotional strain which will prove too taxing. We try to give the individual an opportunity to carry on his activities without reference to the group, unless they are distinctly anti-social, believing that a gradual evolution of co-operative play

will follow as the social adjustment comes. In individual instances we deliberately let a child suffer from the results of an anti-social impulse. There are certain Nursery rules necessitated by circumstances, the justice of which is obvious or becomes so, even to the babies: "All the toys belong to everyone," but as long as a child has one it is his. When an individual leaves a toy anyone else may take it. "Take turns and don't push" on slide or on top of boxes or on the springboard. These are examples, and before the end of the year the children have made them their own even to the extent of quoting them against us when we have not understood a situation, or if they wish to convince us against our judgment that their cause is just.

We try to avoid giving the children the feeling of dependence upon us. In most cases there is little impulse to come to us for any but social reasons, in order that we may share their interests. It is not a part of our program to join in the play of the children in the yard or playroom except in a game like ball, or on a piece of apparatus that demands constant supervision. Occasionally we vary our procedure in order to introduce them to new material or to new uses of old.

We have had only one child with whom it was necessary to set up positive corrective measures. We had to teach him to play and to thrust him out among the children and persuade him to make contacts with them.

3. ASSOCIATIVE MEMORY.—*Ability to bring past experience to bear on a new situation.*

Our aim under this head is to indicate development and the definite usable information that a child has on various subjects. We want to show instances of a definite looking back and making judgments, or of showing foresight in avoiding the repetition of a disagreeable experience. Discriminating reactions and ideas of relationships are very clearly shown even with little children, and our children differ in the degree to which this ability is developed. The question of maturity enters into the reckoning so much that our records are not easy to evaluate, and it is difficult to define our procedure. We try to make the children see the significance of events as they occur, by their own share in the occurrence. When they are balked by a piece of apparatus, we try to persuade them to investigate instead of tugging or screaming. We call their attention to the relationship of things in which they are interested, we watch for the first signs of experimenting, we do not avert disasters if the results are not too severe and are illuminating to the victims, and we help the children put through a plan to something like a successful finish. We call their attention to the simple phenomena of their small world, and encourage them to observe through all their senses and by the social attitude which is developing, to talk with us about their observations.

4. USE OF LANGUAGE.—*As a social tool, as play material.*

I have already described what we include under this head. We try from the first to converse with the children as rational human beings. Anything to which we expect a direct response either by words or acts we make clear and simple. We try to put our requests into ordinary words and to give reasons for restrictions which we put up to them. We mean to give our directions and our responses to them in simple, short, clear-cut phrases, repeating them till they get over. I do not mean by this that we rationalize over every process that we are carrying out with the children. We have come to feel strongly as we have watched our children, and have seen the results of the various kinds of treatment that their various homes have given, that detailed explanations about the simpler "musts" of life are mistakes in that, in the last analysis, a child has no choice. He *is* put to bed, he *is* washed and dressed, and his best efforts to take part in the discussion that a well-meaning, reasonable grown-up initiates, result only in deferring the act at the expense of time and temper. We try not to seize and hurry a youngster head on for larger exploits, but we do not give opportunity for argument. We do not put upon a child responsibility for choice in these details.

We try to encourage conversation. We respond to the first monosyllables by giving back something which is in the nature of social give and take. We talk about situations as they arise, and ask the children questions so that they will voice their thoughts. We try never to show amusement at their attempts, but to take them seriously and give them time. On the other hand, we try not to talk down to them, nor to simplify our general conversation. As a rule, simplifying language means robbing it of all its spontaneity and reducing it to generalizations. We try to take into consideration in our conversation with the children the fact that their interests and their reactions are in sense and motor terms. We try to adopt for current use and give back to them rhythmic phrases or expressions that they invent. We also use devices, sing-song phrases or actual songs to call the children's attention to certain processes, as already cited, and we introduce into our speech reiterated refrains, associations of certain words with certain activities which seem to be pleasurable.* "Down, down, down, down," "Cloppety, clop, goes Old Dan," "Climb up the slide; slide-down," etc. Children differ very much in the way they attend and enjoy these patterns and use and adapt them.

We use no baby talk, of course, and we pay no attention to it except to pronounce all words correctly if we repeat a child's remark. We have had children in our group, however, whose speech was not normally developed for their age. We have given special emphasis to enunciation with these children, calling their attention to the sounds of words, giving the syllables their full value, and asking them to imitate the position of our lips, tongue, etc. We believe that even definite speech training must be done as play and in the course

---

* Mitchell, Lucy Sprague: *Here and Now Story-Book,* E. P. Dutton, 1921.

of normal activities, and our very inadequate experiments have accompanied ordinary conversation at times when we are carrying on the feeding or dressing processes which bring us into close contact with the individual children.

As we subject our notes to closer and more critical examination our procedure improves, we cover the topics we have chosen more adequately. We are still convinced that for current use, for following the group and checking up on our own methods, the diary is essential, and will be more valuable as we become more skilled.

For the purposes of research we need to make sure that we have full and consistent records of the activities of each individual over a fixed and regular period. We are now taking such a record for one full day each month. In the course of a year we ought to have in these records a progressive series of pictures of each child's interests and responses. Whether or not we shall accumulate valuable and reliable data in this way remains to be seen. It will at least point the way toward the type of record we need.

SWING, SWING!

EXCERPTS FROM THE RECORDS

In taking excerpts from our records I have tried to choose citations that would illustrate, first, the use children make of our play material, the muscular power, bodily control, which they acquire and the part adults play in the situation; second, those that would show the sort of social contacts that are made by the children, how such an activity as dramatic play develops, and again, adult sharing or intervention; third and fourth, the way children learn to use their experiences and the part language plays in intensifying those experiences and in building up relationships.

It is impossible entirely to segregate the topics so that each record illustrates but one, but we hope that they will help complete the picture of the environment and the program.

ACTIVITIES: OUT OF DOORS.

SPRING BOARD, PACKING BOXES.

January, 1921.—Spring board, 12 feet long by 1 foot wide very popular in any situation. Edward (2 years, 9 months), Jane and Arnold (each 2 years, 11 months), ran down it from the packing box, 31½ inches high, a big stunt because of the springiness of the board. Michael (19 months), started up it once alone, and with hand held by adult finished performance. As I was changing position of packing boxes one morning I laid the plank over on a long box, 14 inches high, leaving one end out about three or four feet. Arnold climbed up and began walking on the plank out into space. I went to hold the free end and he began objecting and saying something which I could not understand. (See "Language" for statement of his difficulties.) I thought he wanted something placed under the free end of the plank so I moved up three-steps. This further annoyed him. He gesticulated wildly and I finally moved everything out of the way which was what he desired. He then set off walking toward the free end of the plank. I offered him my hand which he refused. He held his body ready for the thump which he seemed to be anticipating and when the board finally tipped down he was ready for it and made the rest of the descent with a broad smile. It seemed amazing that he understood just what the board would do and was able to hold his body in equilibrium so skilfully. Later I made a small see-saw by putting the plank across the low slide support, about 15 inches high, so that both ends were free. George (2 years, 7 months), and Arnold got on. George laughed loudly when the board flew up with Arnold's weight. Arnold was not content with a commonplace see-saw game but got off to let the board fly up, climbed on the lower half and started off, creeping toward the elevated end waiting for the board to tip. It did not begin to tip as soon as he expected. He looked toward me. I said, "Crawl up nearer the end and it will go down." This he did immediately.

October 17-24, 1921.—One morning the children found a packing box standing open side up. Richard (2 years, 3 months), asked to get in. He was lifted and then three steps were put up against the side of the box. Richard immediately made signs to get out but could not pull himself up. Two yard blocks were put in upon which he stood and promptly climbed out. He then climbed in again. Jimmie (2 years, 2 months), later climbed in and out though with less facility in handling his body.

HE HELD HIS BODY READY FOR THE THUMP

Moya (21 months), has ventured to walk across the plank from one box to the other (about 30 inches high). Loud squeals accompany her progress but she seems very sure and shows no reluctance. Enjoys being jumped down. Repeated four times on one occasion. Jimmie and Richard climbed to opposite ends and bounced with great vigor, standing. Jimmie's side of the board extended back over his box and he did not venture out beyond. Richard stood well away from his box and kept a skilful balance. Neither child would walk across at adult suggestion though both can do it. Michael (2 years, 3 months), crawled over on his hands and knees. Later Jimmie, David (19 months), Michael, Richard and Sonia (19 months), walked across plank from packing box to box.

HAMMER, NAILS.

October 24-31, 1921.—David (1 year, 7 months), and Jimmie (2 years, 2 months), are entranced with hammers. I set seven nails in a thick board and gave Jimmie the hammer. He held it near the head and struck well, generally hitting the heads. We chanted, "Bang it on the head." He drove them all in to the head, then I showed him

AFTER THE THUMP—FINISHING THE DESCENT

how to draw them out. He tried to pull the hammer toward him. I placed the claws under the nail so that if he pushed up on the hammer handle the nails would come up. He was soon able to claw them all out. David set them again in the same holes with his fingers and Jimmie again pounded them in. We then gave hammer to David who pounded well, hammer held close to head. He has used one at home.

November 21-28, 1921.—Jimmie climbed the shelves and got a hammer. Asked for nails and finished driving them in after they had been set for him. Used claw end with no hesitation. He chose old holes when pounding nails in but pounded well, varying direction of stroke if nail did not go in straight. Left work after he had driven in about a dozen one inch nails. Jimmie holds hammer at narrowest place and drives well and strongly. David (1 year, 8 months), sets his own nails, does not use ready-made holes, usually does not drive them all the way in and refuses to attempt it till coerced. Tries to claw them out but this is too difficult for him. He holds hammer at its narrowest portion. First pounds are straight but most of the nails are at an angle before he leaves them. For the fifteen or twenty minutes that Jimmie and David were pounding Michael (2 years, 3 months), did not achieve a single nail. No interest in process though he objected if anyone took his board or nails.

March 13-20, 1922.—David (2 years), pounding one forenoon. David set nails anywhere in board, not necessarily in holes or cracks. He gave a strong bang to set nail then drove it in to the head with strong strokes. Held hammer close to its head. He pulls nails out by worrying them with the claw end. Has not yet the trick of pushing back the handle. The following day he lay on his tummy and drove into a very small piece of wood. Was very careful to get hand out of the way before he struck. Tried to straighten a bent nail. Struck it gently at side. On another day David very deliberately went to work to fill up a crack between the bottom and sides of a wooden box. Hammered in at least two dozen nails side by side, little or no real effort or strength needed. Very proud of his achievement.

CLIMBING TO THE TOP OF THE SKYLIGHT

SKYLIGHT.

October 24-Nov. 1, 1921.—Laddie (21 months), climbed up on skylight, stood on top which is sloping, 27 inches high, and balanced, holding arms up, then climbed down on the other side.

November 28-Dec. 5, 1921.—Moya (1 year, 11 months), ran off from a ball game to climb on skylight. After a futile pull she got down, went off to the shelter, got one of the small benches and came staggering out. She put it down and spent some seconds arranging it to her satisfaction at side of skylight. Then she climbed up. Sonia (1 year, 9 months), in the meantime was attempting it from opposite side standing on a yard block. Both got up on it but at this time neither could stand erect on it.

March 27-Apr. 3, 1922.—Michael (2 years, 9 months), is very fond of climbing to the top of the skylight and standing poised. On one afternoon Sonia (2 years, 1 month), followed his example, repeating the stunt with no apparent difficulty. She sprang out to meet me as I held my arms out.

ACTIVITIES: INDOORS.

BLOCKS.

November 8-15, 1921.—An impulse toward a constructive use of the blocks seems to have started. On Wednesday Richard (2 years, 4 months), built a "train," four bricks laid end to end, and pushed it about singing "chu, chu." C. R., a teacher, joined in the singing and his interest and pleasure were marked. He bumped his train against the leg of a chair and it was suggested that he use chair for a tunnel. He fell in cordially and pushed back and forth till he discovered the possibilities of running the train under the door into the room where one of the children was asleep. To

AND STANDING POISED

divert him a bridge was built, several brick blocks on edge in two lines, roofed with double unit blocks. His interest in pushing blocks under held altogether for more than 35 minutes. Some of the other children were attracted but no one persisted in the play as long as Richard. Michael (also 2 years, 4 months), built a train like Richard's but played with it only a few moments. Laddie (21 months), made a large pile of blocks, large and small bricks and triangles. His use of them reminded us that he rarely does his feat of pulling all of them off the shelves as he did quite persistently at first. David (20 months), also piled up several only to knock them down again. Moya (23 months), joined in the building group with delight but after a very minor achievement went to Richard offering him her quota, which he used to top his bridge. She returned to building later and after she had piled up a few blocks she came to call my attention to them. She used five in her first pile and seven in the second, topped by large triangles. Each time she would run smiling to me, putting her arms about my neck, squeeze with her face pressed against me, then run back to building.

November 29-December 6, 1921.—In the afternoon Laddie was found absorbed with the cubes, one red and one purple set side by side, one yellow and one purple near it. Rearranged them in line on the window ledge where he pushed them about. As he pushed he chanted monotonously. It suggested the Chu, Chu of the older children. Repeatedly went back to the cubes, placing them in different "designs" and crowing each time he achieved a new pattern.

December 26-January 2, 1922.—Sonia (22 months), took the pink blocks. The first time she made an unfortunate attack, leaving the large blocks till the last. They were placed irregularly too and fell with a gratifying bang when she laid the last and largest. She tried again and began with a large one. No actual but approximate discrimination and a very good tower as a result. She started the third with one of the small ones, laid a fairly large one on it, then a tiny one with larger ones on that. Joyfully demolished as soon as it was done. Deserted after fourth one was built.

January 9-16, 1922.—Michael began his building with a "tower," actually a line of blocks, running north and south. Moya (2 years), joined in and twice she brought up a block, saying, "Ee, ee, ee?" as she prepared to lay it. Michael said "Yes" both times, laid his east and west with a four-brick-high tower on the second block. After Michael had laid ten blocks he began pushing it like a train. Deserted it to build a real tower on the edge of the chest. Made it four bricks high, each block set on end. As it fell he rebuilt it five times before deserting it. On another day Jimmie laid all his blocks on end and as he chose units of varying heights and placed them close against each other the effect was very suggestive of the New York skyline. It followed an irregular course and contained 40 blocks in all. The line was interrupted by a tower, a charming decorative structure.

January 16-23, 1922.—Michael built a structure which he called a boat. He and Jimmie now open the chest on their arrival. Jimmie lays long lines always, usually with a more or less pretentious tower somewhere on the line. On one occasion when Michael joined him he laid a second story along the line, all sorts of blocks laid flat. Midway the tower rose on a big cube. Michael added to it and topped it by a triangle. At the base of the tower a third story of two bricks was added. They took posts out of chest but discarded them, seeing no possibilities in them. There was about 20 minutes of consecutive building. Outside the long line they put up four bricks on edge close together. This is also a usual "remark." Michael chanted all the time a charming and varied phrase.

April 24-May 1, 1922.—Michael went downstairs to play by himself one forenoon. The blocks were suggested to him and he said he would build a boat. He built with absorption till one structure was finished. A post in the middle he called a smokestack. A second attempt was named the train to Atlantic Highlands, and the third was a lighthouse. Very excellent and fine adjustments to set the small blocks, narrow end down on the third. He commented, "See the train turning round and going to the country?" "This is the water," indicating space about lighthouse.

May 22-29, 1922.—Jimmie went to the closet and got out the Montessori brown stair. I had previously suggested it to him as a diversion from teasing and he had then refused. Returned to it later, and placed the blocks, tower fashion, as far as he could reach. Got a small chair and placed two more. He was asked as he reached vainly with another: "What are you going to do now?" Jimmie: "Get a bigger chair," bringing a grown-up chair. Placed two more, leaving only the smallest. Was asked again what he could do and he replied, looking about vaguely, "A bench." I then said, "Look about and see if you can find something higher." Almost at once his eye roved over the room, he ran to a small high table, and he pushed it over, saying, "Is this what you meant?" Moya and he had a controversy about the last block which she had appropriated, but when she understood what he wanted it for she was appreciative and gave it up, saying, "I not going to knock down Jimmie's tower."

Bobbie (2 years, 2 months) entered and ran to it with a gleam in his eye, but we were able to get his attention and, after we had explained that Jimmie had built the tower and we were all letting it stand, he kept away. It stood unmolested through the afternoon during getting up from naps and music. Everyone except Joan (17 months) and Mollie (18 months) appears to realize the sanctity of a building.

INDOOR SLIDE, BALCONY, STAIRS.

November 7-14, 1921.—The indoor slide was brought into requisition this week though the light pipe railing has not yet been put on the steps, so we had to supervise very carefully. It consists of a platform in two heights, the upper 2 feet, 6 inches wide, 6 feet, 2 inches long and 6 feet, 4 inches from the floor, with a step down to another 5 feet 5 inches square and 5 feet 5 inches from the floor. The slide is 9 feet 9 inches long and 14 inches wide.

The stairway measures 6 feet 7 inches, and the treads are 9½ inches apart. We rest the end of the slide on the gym mat to make the landing easier, for the momentum is really great and a child is likely to lose his balance and roll over at the foot.

Richard (2 years, 4 months), went down at once with no real hesitation, though he went through the business of "falling" as he had done before out of doors, calling "help me" with great relish. We did not go to his assistance but laughed at him and with him for he seemed to appreciate his joke.

David (1 year, 8 months), turned a complete somersault at the foot the first time down. He does not lose control on the descent but sits with a straight back. He was entirely undisturbed by the sudden overturning and went down repeatedly. He shows less excitement over it than Michael and Laddie (2 years, 4 months and 1 year, 9 months), who are fairly lyric over the experience. They show eagerness and excitement not only over the climb but over the sensation of being high. They trot about on the platform, climbing up to the higher level, laughing and shouting and holding their arms raised and their heads thrown back.

Moya (1 year, 10 months), went up the steps but did not venture a descent. Insisted upon backing down the stairs.

Jimmie (2 years, 3 months), could at first be urged to it if we stood near and assured him that we would catch him. Once he went down alone but thereafter shied at it and gradually came to a refusal to descend. Before the end of the week he had devised a method of grading the descent. We had pushed the settle table under the slide. (See cut page 20.) He climbed on it which brought him about half way down the slide and from this height he ventured to descend.

November 14-21, 1921.—The settle was left under the slide all week. One of

POUND, POUND, WITH MY HAMMER POUND!

the three older children pushed an adult chair against it, climbed up, as Jimmie had done and slid. Richard, Jimmie and Michael did this over and over. Jimmie found this a feat scaled to his courage. Once he slid on Michael but after a few tears serenity was restored and as a result the children began to get the idea of watching out to see if anyone was in the way.

The next day Moya devised a way of using the slide. Standing at the side she stretched her arms across, climbed up and slid down, only two feet or so. A big chair was placed for her against the slide but she removed it at once. Laddie pushed it against the table, climbed up and went down from the half-way station as the Olders had done. The climb over the back of the chair was almost more than Moya could accomplish but she persisted, reaching over the slide to grasp the sides and went down successfully.

November 21-28, 1921.—Popularity of this piece of apparatus remains constant. The children are not as excited about it as they were and the first ecstastic thrill over the height seems less manifest. All except Jane (1 year, 5 months), and Moya have now had the self-initiated experience of a descent from the top. Moya goes up the steps rather less since she has found a way of going down from the table.

Moya and Jimmie sliding from the half-way station, a chair at either end of the table. (See cut page 20.) Jimmie ventured a new method and slid sitting three times while Moya was climbing into the chair and getting ready. She began her usual squawk of protest. We are trying to give her an appropriate remark for a substitute. This time I said, "Jimmie's turn," and as Moya slid she called "Muya, turn." One afternoon she pushed up the chair herself so that she could slide.

After some practice with the half-way station Jimmie experimented with a slide from the top when he was in the room all alone. He raised his arms as he started, opened his eyes very wide, sat very straight and zipped down. Went down four times.

Sonia (1 year, 8 months), went to the foot of the slide as Moya climbed on the chair, but regarding Moya, followed her up on the table and down. She was very careless about her off leg, letting it trail so that we had to be on hand to load it on the slide. At first she did not know how to stretch her arms across to seize further edge of slide, but after I had put her arms across three times she voluntarily adopted that method, though she continued to trail her leg. This was on Monday. On Wednesday she was entirely self sufficient, handling herself adequately as to arms and legs.

Tuesday she climbed the stairs, which she had not done before, went to top of slide and instead of sitting down like a cautious child, she stepped on the slope which of course threw her and she whizzed down. The track held her but it was a disconcerting experience for the adults. We had to watch her at the steps, too, because she tended to slip through and we feared she might fall between the rail and the platform at the top. She is so debonair about it and so mischievous that it adds to our concern. After reaching the platform she dashes for the slide so she has to dash too in readiness for her plunge. She refused at first to accede to our demands that she sit before going down but on the second day she did slip down to sitting position at the top of the slide. Shows no reluctance or aversion to the sudden descent as Jimmie did. She is insecure on her feet and not at all cautious. She is the only child who has fallen on the step from lower to upper level of the platform. She walked off twice.

November 28-December 5, 1921.—Sonia has little control of her body though she hangs on well if she slips on the stairs. We do not yet let her slide from the top without breaking the force of the descent for she sways and tips as she goes and rolls over at the bottom even without our help. Jane also is sliding this week. Jane often lies on her back and Sonia sways and swings like a train on a curve but so far they have both kept on the rails.

December 12-19, 1921.—There was great activity on the slide on a rainy morning. Michael, Jimmie, Jane and David followed one another up and over rapidly and with an excellent appreciation of taking turns. A call for a child to wait for some one else to go up or down would bring instant response. David varied his method by

EXPERIMENTATION IS SIMPLE BUT NO LESS REAL

climbing on the block chest and under the railing to the steps. Michael has taken up sliding feet first on his stomach as has also David. Sonia added a new element of risk by placing a small high-backed chair in front of the steps and climbing over it to the stairs. Jimmie is going down from the top quite fearlessly though he does not always choose this route. He goes on his stomach, feet first.

January 30-February 5, 1922.—Moya went up stairs and down slide sitting for first time this week. Also went lying on stomach, feet first.

April 17-24, 1922.—Bobbie (entered March 1st, 2 years), ventured down the slide this week. He sat and I held him so that he went slowly. He has not gone down alone and we do not encourage it.

April 24-May 1st, 1922.—Bobbie now goes down outdoor and indoor slides, sitting, with no help or restraint.

Mollie (entered March 13th, 17 months), adventured the indoor slide on the afternoon of April 26th. She climbed to the platform and was helped down. Later she went up again. At the top of the slide she attempted to go down as Sonia did, by stepping off into space. I repeated over and over "No, no, sit down, Mollie Anne." She followed directions, sitting and then "hitching" forward to go over the edge. Up and down again eight times. Then we elevated steps to keep her away as we could no longer watch her. On the afternoon of the 28th I tried to teach her to lie down and go down on her stomach as being a less dangerous method. We have not dared

A FIRST PASSAGE

let her coast alone because of the danger of her bouncing off. Also she shows the excitement of the descent by fully dilated pupils. Once I went up on the platform and turned her over and over and once I indicated by my pokes and gestures what was desired. After that I said each time, "Lie down and turn over, Mollie Anne," and each time she complied. It is not yet her habit so we have to remind her each time.

SELF HELP IN PRACTICAL MATTERS.

AT MEALS.

November, 1920.—Michael (17 months), shows interest in feeding himself, but still has considerable lack of understanding of the process and also of the muscular control necessary. We frequently allow experimentation with a few spoonfuls which are inserted in his mouth upside down. He still does not close his mouth after taking a sip of milk from a cup and so we are still spooning his liquids. Has a few very decided dislikes—rice, spinach. At first would take these articles when pressed, but lately has fought hard, spitting out the offending articles and including the rest of the meal in his displeasure. We are going to try isolating the rice and spinach and giving them after the rest of the meal has been taken.

December, 1920.—Has entirely adjusted to novelties in diet, even rice and spinach which he did not like at first. Except when he has colds, eats with good appetite. Has occasionally used spoon himself for a teaspoon or so, and feeds self dessert fairly well. Is learning not to put spoon in mouth on edge. As a whole, however, except for rare occasions, does not feed himself nor has he yet learned to drink from a cup though we offer him the cup at each feeding. Still holds mouth open.

January, 1921.—Has been drinking from a cup which he holds alone. Is feeding himself dessert.

February, 1921.—Fed himself and drank milk with very little help on every day but one, when he was fed most of dinner.

EXPERIENCE

PRACTICE

March, 1921.—His appetite has not been keen and his interest in food has been less as our records stand. Absent from 21st through 25th with German measles. Just before that we noted less interest in feeding himself and during the last week he has done very little himself. Ate entire dinner, if fed.

April, 1921.—Up to the last week of April the lack of interest in food noted in March was very apparent. He stalled, refused to feed himself and was cross if urged. We removed him from the table twice with no effect. On April 20th he was forced to take up his cup of milk, that is, his hand was held on the cup while he drank. He cried and resisted at first, but succumbed and fed himself a good part of every meal. From then on to the end of the month he showed improvement.

IN GETTING PLAY MATERIAL.

November 29-December 6, 1921.—Jimmie (2 years, 4 months), and Richard (2 years, 5 months), are quite fond of climbing up the shelves in the cupboard where toys are kept, in order to get what they want. Jimmie got up on the third shelf, took some tin dishes in one hand and could not get down. He called for help. C. R. took the dishes and showed him how to bring one hand down to the shelf below. It took just one direction for him to get the idea and to apply it, coming down quite safely. Later he climbed up and got out two dumbbells. He clung there for a second or so but did not call and after a space laid his bells on a lower shelf and got down as he had been directed, lowering the bells shelf by shelf.

In the roof shelter he also climbs for the hammer and has hung, calling us to help him down. He has been put through the process of lowering himself and his trophies, and now he scrambles down without demur.

January 9-16, 1922.—Moya pulled up a chair to the left door of the cupboard, the door which does not open, and pulled at the latch till it was loosened, then got down, opened the door, and got a doll, her declared desire.

January 16-23, 1922.—Michael opened door from hall into shelter not previously opened by him or others. Sonia (23 months), put chair against right side of closet door, unlatched door, pushed chair back and opened door.

IN DRESSING.

January 9-16, 1922.—Moya (2 years), unlaced her shoes and pulled them off after they had been untied and loosened at the heel for her. She pulled off her stockings after they had been pushed down. Took off waist and drawers. Very sure and deft.

Jimmie (2 years, 5 months), unlaces and takes off his shoes and makes a stab at buttons though his method is to pull the two parts of a garment apart. Pulls off his stockings.

Michael (2 years, 6 months), is oblivious to dressing and undressing unless his attention is forcibly called to the business in hand. He can unbutton his gaiters because the button and buttonholes part company at a touch. He has seemed interested in trying to unbutton his coat and with help does quite a good job. He pulls off his shoes and stockings.

January 16-23, 1922.—Moya (2 years), wipes off drops of milk on table or her own face with great nicety, taking a corner or small portion of the bib and hitting the spot. Very careful to wipe face often. On the 17th she unfastened her garters and took off stockings and drawers with waist attached with no help except on buttons. She pushed her stockings down about her ankles and then pulled them off by the toes. Put on stockings and shoes with help. Has put on stockings alone. Reached for them and put them on with no suggestion, then took shoes and called for help.

She reached behind her in bathroom, pulled up the chamber and sat down. No suggestion.

At suggestion Michael took off his shoes, laces untied, then his stockings, (instructed to pull heel first, then toe) and then put up his arms to be de-sweatered and bloused. Later when told to climb up on the bath tub cover alone he pushed up small toilet seat and did so. Climbed down when asked.

March 20-27, 1922.—Jane (1 year, 9 months), got down her basket, as we began dressing children one P. M. It tipped over and she brought the leggins to us. Did the same the night before when taxi was announced, except that she toted basket to an adult.

April 10-14, 1922.—Sonia (2 years, 1 month), opened door from hall to shelter. Jimmie (2 years, 8 months), and Richard (2 years, 9 months), also do it.

SOCIAL AND EMOTIONAL CONTROL.

Accepting the Rules of the Game.

Arnold is adjusting to the requirement that he share the horses. As the new ones are brought in he lays claim to each for the day, but yields to the rule and does not insist. Arnold's appeals for help distinguish his technique from that of the others. As yet he calls for help from adults only, and usually resents help from children. On October 21st, in attempting to get the horses into the rabbit hutch, it was necessary to turn the heads of the animals after they were partly in. Arnold was very irritated at his failure and called for help. He was not willing to be shown how to do the work, nor to do a part of it himself, and repeatedly cast himself on the ground, growled and threw pebbles at H. J. who had gone to his help. Each time the difficulty arose as he was putting the three horses in, he finally yielded and helped. When he took them out he went through the same performance.

Adjustment to Parent's Departure.

October 24—November 1, 1921.—Richard continues extravagant attacks of woe at mother's departure. He spends himself at these times and is quite inactive after them.

November 7-14, 1921.—C. R. has been calling for Richard at his home all the week. She reports: He comes to me from whoever brings him down stairs with the happiest smile. He talks on his way to school of going to see John, Michael and the rest. He says at intervals, "Munnie gone to work. We're going to work," but otherwise there is no sign of disturbance.

November 14-21, 1921.—C. R. is still bringing Richard to school, and he seems quite happy about coming to us. On Friday his mother brought him and he began the usual tantrum as she deposited him in the Nursery. I took him up and told him he must stop. He gulped down a roar and then allowed me to divert him by asking him to put away a patty-pan which he had borrowed the night before. We then went up to the roof in great content.

January 16-23, 1922.—Richard returned on Monday after a long absence. He greeted us cheerfully. Held out his hand to show his mittens. Mother left us and he went up on roof smiling. Stayed there in entire content. His mother came up once or twice during the day. He ran to her and asked her to stay, but made no demur when she actually went. He was very affectionate. Stood backed up against V. M. C. watching her feed Moya. Asked to sit in my lap and tended to slow up in activities and give attention to adults.

Adjustment to Details of Nursery Program.

November 14-21, 1921.—Again Richard remonstrated over the weighing. (Daily record shows that weighing has been up to this time the signal for tears.) He filled the air with his wails calling upon the absent "Munnie" and "Nene," and· writhing so that it was quite impossible to get correct weight. Rather than force the issue I took him in my arms and we were weighed together. He made no objection and recovered cheerfulness at once.

December 5-12, 1921.—Richard began to cry as soon as weighing preparations began and we started to undress him. We reassured him and explained that it wasn't going-to-bed time, but he persisted in his crying. Then I said if he cried it was because he was sick and that he would have to be put to bed. This also was unavailing and he began to scream and kick. H. J. picked him up then and removed him to the bathroom. As she undressed him in spite of his struggles she kept saying that he was going to be a fine big boy and that he didn't cry when he was weighed. When his clothes were off she took him up in her arms, put her head down to his and said something to the effect that he was a dear little Richard and a fine boy and that we were going into the other room to get weighed. As soon as she took him up he put his arms about her neck and nestled up to her, more responsive than often in this way. He had stopped crying and there was a little general conversation. As soon as she had assured him that he was going in without crying she took him in. He stood on the scales with no outcry and all alone.

THE PROGRESSIVE ADJUSTMENT OF AN UNUSUALLY RESERVED AND SHY CHILD.

From Record of November 15, 1920: George, a new child (2 years, 4 months), entered today. He has been a week to the Little People's Home School. Mother says the association with other children has helped his shyness, which was very marked. He shows it even with her, if she asks for any social demonstration like shaking hands and saying goodbye when he leaves her. His interest in the play material gradually overcame his reluctance, so that he used shovel and pail and dragged a cart about before the end of the first day.

November 21.—George welcomed his mother when she came to visit. Was not excited and "introduced" her to each child. He called her and put each child's hand in hers, grunting something in explanation as he did so. He went the rounds in this fashion while children were having lunch at 10:30. In a music period during the same week he entered into active uproarious relation with the others. He and Jane crawled gleefully around the block chest, and he was heard to laugh loudly more than once. Seemed more at home the last two days of his second week.

November 22-29.—George followed me up on porch where I was working with paper and rule. "Wha doon?" he inquired. Threw himself across my lap, over my paper. Laughed and seized rule and tried to run off with it. I took it and attempted to rule the paper. George reached around me, grabbing at the rule in great glee. Followed me to yard, where he seized rule again and beat me joyously. We are glad to see this easy familiarity.

December, 1920.—George makes relatively few contacts with other children, but seems to enjoy being with them if they do not approach him intimately. Objects even to friendly demonstrations. Joins children, however, more frequently than before. Is rather dependent upon adults. Tends to become less active when alone with the children, sometimes standing by the window or door waiting for adults to return to the yard.

January, 1921.—George and Jane attempted a co-operative play of loading one of the big wagons. Jane finally mounted the horse which they had put on top of their load, and George dragged her about the yard. He is very friendly, has joined the group very much more actively. Has begun very definite contacts, chasing the children, pulling off their caps, etc. Occasionally seems to have hard feelings, but generally is very gay about it. He has thrown himself into group activities like running and sliding almost with boisterousness and certainly with hilarity. Of course this is only a comparative statement. A good deal of his time is still spent by himself.

February, 1921.—Increasingly active and aggressive as the month progressed. He has made attacks on the babies, Michael and Richard, several times this week. It is very easy to turn his unfriendliness to affection and concern. Once he seized a chair that Richard was seated in and pulled it out from under him so that Richard got a bad fall. Reproved, he was at once contrite. He put his arms about Richard and petted him, solicitude written on his face. He gets excited in play, and we warn him if we see disaster coming. On one such time when he rushed at Michael he stopped and turned his attack into an embrace, and then went to Jimmie and then to Richard, putting his arms about them with great tenderness. One morning Arnold and George seemed to have some sort of hostile feeling, making occasion to interfere with each other. Arnold took George's wagon. He was asked to give it up, and did so with reluctance, keeping his foot on the handle. George pushed him, and he returned it with interest, knocking George over. George yapped and bounced up again, shaking his head. Arnold, standing very close facing him, also shook his. Then Arnold bobbed his up and down. George continued to shake his. Arnold imitated, and then the humor of it struck them both and they grinned broadly in perfect good humor.

When we take George up from his nap we hold him up to look over the porch rail at the children in the yard. The first time or two he acted very shy, turning his head away if anyone noticed him. The third day and regularly thereafter he asked to be held up and called an answer to a greeting.

March, 1921.—George is probably "loosened up" enough so that he feels no more need of violent contacts. These have ceased and he is very affectionate to children and adults alike, though he can and does defend himself when affronted.

DEVELOPMENT OF DRAMATIC PLAY.

November 28-December 5, 1921.—C. R. sang "Old Dan" to children on roof. Michael (2 years, 5 months), Richard (2 years, 5 months) and Jimmie (2 years, 4 months), and got them much interested in rhythmic changes in walking and running. Michael and Jimmie felt the change between the slow and fast rhythm. They held hands and went round the roof twice, changing speed off and on. Michael tried to chant with C. R. Richard ran by himself and registered the changes well.

> "Old Dan can walk, walk,
> Old Dan can trot, trot, trot,
> Old Dan can run, run, run, run,
> Many, many, many, many miles."

We dropped out the second line, using only "walk" sung very slowly, and "run."

December 12-19, 1921.—In order to attract Jane (17 months) and Jimmie (2 years, 4 months) out of the shelter V. M. C. took a hand of each and played "Old Dan." Pretty soon Moya (2 years) came up with hand outstretched. V. M. C. told her to take hold of Jane's hand. She did so with no further direction. Soon Michael (2 years, 5 months) approached with outstretched hand and took Jimmie's hand at suggestion. Next Sonia (21 months) and last David (21 months) joined the throng. David was slower in getting the idea of taking Moya's hand, perhaps because the line had grown long and unwieldy. All the children laughed as we walked and trotted and ran together. All change tempo with the song.

April 17-24, 1922.—Michael (2 years, 9 months) very frequently does not join the group, but seeks solitude. One A. M. he took kiddie kar and set off, calling "Goodbye, John." I answered and asked where he was going. Michael: "I going far, far away." . . . Michael held his empty hand out to C. R. "Here, Carmen, take it." She accepted his gift. He said: "It's a hammer." She thanked him and pretended to drive a nail vigorously into the table. He smiled appreciatively, and said, "I want my hammer." C. R. gave it to him and he pounded a nail. Then, with appropriate action, said, "I throw my hammer away."

April 24-May 1, 1922.—Richard (2 years, 10 months), sitting in packing box. Hat fell off. C. R. said, "Come over here and let me put it on." Richard: "But the car is going. How can I get out?" C. R.: "Ask the conductor to stop a moment." Richard: "Will he wait?" C. R.: "I think so." Richard (turning to address the interior of the box): "Stop the car, Mr. Man. I have to put my hat on." Later he said he was going to visit Dr. Lincoln. Invited Jimmie to go along. Said "But first we must telephone to find if she's at home." Again said, "Jimmie and I are playing. Jimmie is the father and I am the little mother." Apparently they did nothing but sit in the packing-box.

ASSOCIATIVE MEMORY.

December, 1920.—Edward (2 years, 7 months) tried to raise ladder against the wall alone. I helped him lift it and he landed it upright, flat against the wall. I held it so that it would not fall and he began to climb. I let his weight tip it slightly. He instantly pulled out the lower end of the ladder, and began again to climb. Experiments of this sort repeated again and again are laying the foundation for the process we call reasoning, whether or not we accept the behaviorists' definition of reasoning as the organization and co-operation of habits.

March 13-20, 1922.—A good deal of play this week with *wagons, kiddie kars* and *wheelbarrows*. Our equipment has been enriched by a new wagon, a low light though well-constructed cart with a hook on the shaft, making it possible to couple it with other vehicles. It runs more easily than anything we have and is lighter. One morning early in the week Michael (2 years, 8 months) had the cart, and David (1 year, 1 month) wanted it. David went to the old express wagon, patted it, and called "Cart, cart," at Michael. Ran after Michael, an arm extended toward the coveted novelty, calling again "Cart," and pointing back at the old wagon. Michael was shown the new cart hitched to a kiddie kar. He rode half a minute, then dismounted because David got into the wagon. After Michael had discarded the small trailer, we looked up to see David riding kiddie kar, trailer fastened on behind. David again repeated this performance.

October 10-17, 1921.—Richard (2 years, 3 months) was much interested in sounds made by thumping or throwing pebbles against iron pipe. Threw stones of varying size against it and thumped with increased or decreased vigor. He experimented with several different materials, going from one thing to another and hitting them with small sticks, then listening to the sound. While Richard was calling Jimmie's attention to the "big pipe," Jimmie appropriated the wagon. Richard made an attempt to regain it, failed, said "wheelbarry," and went off for one. Brought it to pebbles, filled it, then dumped them out.

David (20 months) discovered that the shovel would tip back. Adjusted it, slipping the catch down the handle out of the way, and went about picking at boxes and brick wall.

October 24-November 1, 1921.—As usual children are eager to shovel pebbles out on the cement. I put a board into one of the packing boxes, coal chute fashion, and shoveled some pebbles in letting them run down the board. I called the children to put coal into the house. David and Richard shoveled for several minutes. I also diverted Richard's throwing by singing "Drop, drop, drop," etc., down the scale as I let pebbles slip through my hand one by one. Richard, seated on a packing box, was delighted and dropped to my chanting.

The pebbles and shovels made their appeal to Jane (15 months), and she spent much of her first two days there. She would take up one of the larger stones, bring it up so close to her eyes that they crossed horribly, utter a shriek of delight and then approach it to her wide open mouth. At that point adult supervision would come into play. The first word would bring a response and she soon began to pause before the act. After about six repetitions she ceased her attempt to make a meal.

December 12-19, 1921.—Jimmie has discovered a general law the application of which will make him take the slide with more assurance. He finds that he can regulate his speed by pushing his feet against the sides. When he wants to move a little he lets up on the pressure. Then he eases himself down a little further, then stops again. This is done with a very conscious, pleased expression.

January 9-16, 1922.—I was singing my old ditty, "Ha, ha, Moya; Ho, ho, Jimmie Jo," etc. Michael listened, Jimmie also, and then piped up "Many, many, many, many miles." Interval identical and rhythm also.

January 23-31, 1922.—The room was disorderly one P. M.—blocks scattered over the floor. C. R. sang "Who will help me pick up blocks?" Jimmie instantly sang back on a very similar melody "I will help you pick up blocks." Then C. R. sang "Thank you, thank you, very much," a phrase similar to the first line of London Bridge. Richard, who was walking about, took it up instantly—sang "Very much, very much, thank you, thank you, very much, my fair lady." Then he went through another verse, "Build it up with sticks and stones." Jimmie repeated "Thank you very much" in a chant over and over as we worked till all the blocks were put away.

March 20-27, 1922.—Michael building said, "Smoke's coming out there," pointing to a single block set on end. Later held it up said, "Do you see that? It's the chimney."

April 3-7, 1922.—

Jimmie: "Who put this on?" (grating over dumbwaiter shaft on roof).

H. J.: "A big man."

Jimmie: "Was it Frank?"

H. J.: "Yes or Big Jimmie."

Jimmie: "Frank had a white hat on." (Foreman of building work last Autumn wore white cap).

April 17-24, 1922.—Moya (2 years, 3 months), asked to have the sandbox opened. Was told that it was too cold, said "Have dinner, open sandbox?" It is usually opened directly after lunch.

May 1-8, 1922.—One P. M. on the roof Mollie Anne (18 months), picked up a hammer, took it over to the pipe and began beating. At the first stroke she sang "pown" and on three successive strokes thereafter. The rhythm was excellent. Moya (2 years, 4 months), from the sandbox sang with her. C. R. started the song, "Pound, pound." Mollie kept with me for six beats, a delighted grin on her face.

"Pound, pound, with my hammer pound,
Whanging, banging, whanging, banging, whanging banging, pound."

May 8-15, 1922.—All the sweaters were hanging in the shelter window. David (2 years, 2 months), who was pulling Joan in the small wagon, caught sight of his, stopped, chuckled, pointed and said, "Boy—coat." Then named "Jimmie sweater— David coat—Laddie coat— Joan sweater—Mac sweater"— when V. M. C. pointed to each one and asked him. Hesitated long over Laddie's, looking at him, then at the coat, trying to get the name.

Sonia spied Bobby, her brother, in the school yard. She commented on it with enthusiasm. David "*I* see Bobby—*Where* Dindy," his sister.

May 15-22, 1922.—After digging for a few moments in pebbles Mollie got up and pounded on the tin ventilator pipe. Exchanged for sand shovel which makes more noise than a small shovel which she had. Beat first on tin shaft, then on iron pipe, then on end of board. Off to pick up hammer and holding it claw end down, tried to break pebbles on the curb as Olders do. The whole performance seems like a cross-section reproduction of older children's activities.

USE OF LANGUAGE.

CORRECTION OF DEFECT.

December 20-27, 1920.—Arnold (2 years, 10 months), calls for "Hot wapper" when injured, or when his face is being washed. One day at this request we said, "Oh Arnold, not hot wapper, hot water," enunciating very clearly and emphasizing with dramatic fervor. Arnold looked mischevous for a moment, then said, "Hot water" very distinctly, repeating it several times, amid the plaudits of grown-ups. The next day when he was being washed for dinner he made his usual demand. I pointed my finger at him and said accusingly, "Why Arnold Mitchell 'Hot wapper?' " He stopped and looked at me for a moment then said, "Hot water" with a chuckle.

March, 1921.—Arnold's speech has improved both in pronunciation and facility of expression (this report comes from home also) since we arrived at the conclusion

PROGRESS TOWARD CONSTRUCTIVE PURPOSES

COMES WITH THE ACCUMULATION OF EXPERIENCE

AND WITH ASSOCIATIONS WHICH A CHILD TAPS FOR HIS PLAY ACTIVITIES

toward the end of March that he was not hearing everything that was said, as a result of an ear infection. We have been at great pains to make ourselves clear,—bending down and speaking slowly and incisively and the consequent effect on Arnold's language has been startling. His speech is clearer and he uses words with greater confidence as though he were surer of being understood. His sentences are longer and more complicated and his whole impulse to speech stronger.

April 11-18, 1921.—While I was dressing Arnold on Monday morning, he got my attention by poking and said very distinctly, "Ford, Ford"—blowing out the initial letter with much energy. This was carried over from three weeks before. He had said "Pord" and had been corrected and shown position of lips for the F sound.

April, 1921.—Arnold's advance in language continues. He is distinctly interested in the "exercises" in pronunciation which we give him—correcting mistakes that are pretty well established. (See notes April 11-18 for illustrations). A report from home notes that he objects to Mary's using gestures—nods or shakes of head—when talking to him, and he apparently reproduces our directions to him and to Edward: "You musn't do that—you must talk." He carries on long and rather elaborate conversations often with quite an imaginative quality and very dramatic.

January 9-16, 1922.—Michael (2 years, 6 months), is wrestling with the aspirate, which up to this time has been a negligible quantity in his vocabulary. We breathe out forcibly in pronouncing *hat* or *here* and he imitates us at once, showing evident interest in the effort. He blows out, "Huh, huh, house." "Where Michael going? In 'ere?" "Here, Michael." "Huh, here." After a conversation about ice we heard him practicing, "Hi, hi, hice"!

VOCABULARIES.

December 5-12, 1921.—David (22 months), found a pebble imbedded in ice on the roof after a snow storm. Brought it to me saying, "Ice." Put it into his mouth at once. The day before at lunch he had said that his soup was hot.

Vocabulary recorded this week:

stockings

up

iron

hot

boh (broken)

au (automobile)

cart

ice

He brought up a small tin automobile and said, "Hoo, hoo." The horn? January 9-16, 1922.—David (23 months), vocabulary recorded this week:

More

David

pocket

John

'ammer—'ammer

Gone—Michael

Look—look

No, no, no (Jimmie interrupting him)

bucky (buckle)

That nose (pointing to nose of cow)

piano

Nail (repeated after grown-up)

Nanykee (Thank you)

I am

iron (i-en)

bang

hatty (hat)

ice

boy

Uh—Moo-oo (Cow)

Engine (presenting one to adult)

Aw-gawn

N'aw—gwan

Lon' lon' (long long drink)

Calls birds on cretonne apron "Gackies" (ducks).

Pointed to eye of an adult feeding him and said, "Eye." Poked it shut, said "Aw gone" and chuckled. Very much interested in features. Eating dinner pointed to bird on V. M. C.'s apron which had been decapitated by a seam. Remarked, "Gawn" and turned the apron over, ostensibly to find the head and back again, repeating "Gawn?"

"Big Jimmie" (carpenter) took David in his arms to show him the little ventilating door in bathroom. David banged it shut with a "Boom." Later when he was being undressed in the bathroom, he continued pointing at the little door, saying "Door-boom" and laughing.

Michael standing on packing box facing out, talking to himself, "Men on the house, men on the house, men on the house."

V. M. C.: "What are they doing?"

Michael, promptly, "Fixing the pipe. I don't know how they fix it. How they fix the pipe, Mac?" Then regarding her as she stood on some planks which brought her head level with his, "Mac is a very big boy." After the storm he mounted to top of packing box which V. M. C. was clearing. She apologized for sending a fine spray of snow into his face. Michael: "I like it. I like it. Do it again." He continued to stand there chanting in his customary fashion. Impossible to catch his remarks except occasionally one refrain, "It is nice, nice, nice." A visitor came in and I stood talking to her. Michael came up and said, "Hello" cordially, then to me, "Who is that, John?" I introduced him. At my suggestion he shook hands then turned to E. B. who was standing near and said, "This is Millie."

Michael's language flows like a stream, accompanying all his activities directed to anyone who is near but not lessening apparently when he is alone. Thought and language certainly seem identical with him.

INDIVIDUAL LANGUAGE RECORD: EDWARD.

I have segregated all the notes taken on the language development of one child as an illustration of the facts we are gathering and of the possibility of tracing individual progress within group records. The degree to which the teachers' methods are recorded and changed in accord with the findings is indicated. It is here especially that our technique must be developed. We have an exacting program and we do not often enough go back and scrutinize our records to get objective evidence of the failure or success of our methods. Oftentimes we are probably not sufficiently aware of them to get them adequately recorded.

Edward came to us with a serious speech limitation and we believe that very definite and concentrated work was needed to give him an impulse toward the acquisition of language. There was a question in his case whether there might be a permanent defect.

Edward was born on April 15th, 1918, and was two years, six months old when he came to us on October 13th, 1920. He remained till June 1st, 1921, and so spent seven months in the Nursery School.

His mother is German and his father Dutch. Both speak English with a marked foreign accent. German and English are the languages used at home chiefly, though with friends and relatives French and occasionally Dutch are spoken.

Edward gives an impression of unusual sturdiness and has stupendous physical energy and strength. Has a very sweet, merry and affectionate disposition, shows no inhibitions, is social and suggestible. This makes it easy to divert him from an undesirable activity, but difficult to develop in him a self control or self direction of which he has control. He was found to have diseased and much enlarged tonsils which were operated upon in November. Seemed to be very susceptible to colds and infections. Had an abcess and a small boil during the winter, colds and a mild attack of bronchial pneumonia. Was overweight and overheight on entrance and even more so at the end of the year, in spite of his various illnesses. Out of a school year of 154 days he was present 116½, absent 37½.

OCTOBER.

No speech; no attempt at imitation of the speech of others. Voice peculiarly strained and unmusical.

Has no formulated speech and little technique for communication. He grunts and points with thumb and forefinger and gibbers remonstrance, but he shows much less persistence in his endeavor to make one understand than Arnold did before he acquired words. Edward may make his wants known better in a familiar environment, but it seems to us that the dissipation of his energies shown in his play activities is characteristic of his method of communication. He carries on long dissertations with himself and at other persons, for there is no return from adults or children, varying his tone and inflection slightly and gesticulating. At home his wants are anticipated, his parents have learned the desired responses to his calls and gestures, and he has not yet been forced by a situation to break into speech nor to feel the need of so doing. There is a peculiarity in his enunciation, as far as anything he does can be be called enunciation, which suggests a defect in the speech mechanism but no defect is discoverable. There is also a curious strained note in his voice which reminds one of the voices of deaf mutes. His efforts toward speech are fearful, for he makes strange and uncanny growls, squeals and mutterings which have no suggestion of actual words. He directs these efforts toward adults and children, but they seem more generalized, less directed than his "questions." He comes to us when he wants something, points to it and grunts, and occasionally, whether accidental or not, the grunt resembles the appropriate word. His mother says that there are certain sounds which he makes or expressions which he uses to indicate certain desires or questions and that they are always the same and quite clearly spoken.

His understanding of simple directions is adequate. Since arrival he has said several words which we could understand but he has never repeated them as far as we know. These words were dirt, throw ball, no, in there, read, down.

Edward does not imitate other children, that is he does not do what they are doing as they do it, but he does still at the end of the month, leap to any activity that they initiate or seize any toy or piece of apparatus in their possession.

He makes no attempt to repeat words used to him, whether or not we try to interest him in saying them. If he is asked to say a word he often says. "Na" and shakes his head. Our method with him is to enunciate clearly, to use simple, abbreviated phrases and to try to get him to repeat, for instance, the name of the toy he is asking for or the article of clothing we are putting on for him. He asked one day by gestures, about the picture of a cat on one of the boxes and seemed to make an effort to say, "Pussy" after me, the only time, however, when an attempt to imitate was made.

The following illustrates his general method: He climbed into one of the packing boxes but could not get out. He emitted grunts of distress till we went to his assistance. We put a small box in for him to stand on and he climbed out with evidence of joy. Then he threw all the small boxes in, leaving himself outside with nothing to stand on. He tried to climb and we took out one of the small boxes. He instantly hurled it in again, grunted, looked about him and then seized a wheelbarrow, turned it upside down and got in. The following day he repeated the play, showing much concern when he was unable to follow the small boxes into the large one. We suggested that he find a small box to stand on but instead he took a small cart which was not high enough. Again he appealed for help with groans and yelps but paid no attention to suggestions from adults. He suddenly seized the cart and turned it over which raised it just high enough for his purpose. Radiant smiles indicated his pleasure in the accomplishment.

NOVEMBER.

Interest in speech aroused. A conception of language as communication evident. Words and short phrases attempted.

We have been trying to tempt Edward to speech and have repeated clearly the names of things he was using but he makes no attempt to imitate us. This week, (November 1-8), we have begun giving simply the initial consonant sound of words, greatly exaggerated, followed by the word. This has arrested his attention and he has made the K sound in coat, the H sound in hat, the T sound in table and various others. He is much more responsive to this method than any other so far tried.

Later in the month, (November 15-22), we record: Edward seems to have passed a stage in his language development and to be making real progress. He now tries to ejaculate words instead of what have seemed to us before only sounds. This is obvious to outsiders for Miss K. passing through our yard, caught words from him which she understood. One day he said, as we looked out of the front window, "Whurse," pointing to a horse. It was a breathing, whistling sibilant, the "wh" very prominent. Perhaps the new method of getting him to make the initial consonant sound of a word is bearing fruit. Later the same day he said, "Out of the way," which we instantly understood but cannot approximate. Then climbing on a table he said, "Si dow'." He has also said, "Down there," and "John."

He still resorts to his own method in an emotional situation. Once he grew angry at the exclusiveness of two other children of his age and gibbered painfully at them.

At the end of the month we summarize the situation thus: Edward has waked to the difference between making noises and saying words. His vocabulary is not large but he is making a definite effort at the names of things.

DECEMBER.

Beginning to ask the names of things. Enunciation still sketchy. Voice production better. Shows appreciation of the distinction between singing and shouting.

Edward was absent a good deal this month. The last week he seemed sick on arrival and was isolated till we could get his parents to take him home. He was allowed to play indoors and no restrictions were put on his use of the equipment. It is interesting to note that for the hour he spent alone with an adult, during which time detailed notes were taken of his activities and reactions there is no record of communication in language.

The monthly summary notes definite advance: Edward is making slow progress and puts it up to himself consistently, asking the name of everything and repeating after us the initial sound. He is talking in his own gibberish much less and occasionally will come out with short phrases which we can understand. Asked several times, "What is that?" Still uses a much abbreviated form of speech.

Edward is singing a good deal lately. He recognizes the difference between singing and shouting. When he is particularly boisterous we ask him if he cannot sing instead. He then changes pitch and tone.

JANUARY AND FEBRUARY.

Beginning of the use of short sentences but sentence word still the chief reliance. Voice tone improving.

Edward improves steadily. He uses short sentences now: "What is that?" "That's a horse," etc., and his vocabulary is beginning to show variety. His gibberish is almost entirely a thing of the past, though we notice that he goes back to it after an absence from the Nursery. His voice quality has improved and he sings a good deal with a very sweet tone. We can always divert him from gibbering by asking him if he can make a pleasant noise or sing us a song.

He understands practically everything that is said to him and his responses are rapid. The physician says that he will carry out all her directions at an examination better than any of the three-year-olds. This is the more remarkable considering the unhappy experiences he has had with doctors in the course of his many accidents and illnesses.

Edward said, "What are you doing?" clearly enough so that several of us understood. He is using phrases and short sentences but the sentence word is still his medium for the communication of ideas. The notes on "Emotional Attitudes" suggest that he has reached a plateau or that his advance has been affected by his physical condition. Perhaps because of absences, nine days in the month, his disorganized attack on the environment and his excited manner have returned. His effect on the group is notably disturbing, his contribution being almost inevitably a destructive one. That is especially true during indoor play.

MARCH.

First attempt at social use of language.

As has been stated Edward has shown a good deal of disorganization and the first of the week (February 28-March 7), he disturbed us very much by his return to grunts and shrill cries and chattering. There are numerous curious calls that he makes and he has revived these unpleasant and animal-like cries. He has, however, during the same period carried on quite consecutive conversation. After we went down to luncheon one afternoon, Edward pointed up stairs and said, "Up—play?" We said, "No. We are going out of doors after milk." Edward asked, "Tomorrow?"

He speaks of Jane, a child who has left us, almost every day, either asking where she is or saying, "That's Jane's bed." One day he said her name several times and then said, "Back?" We said, "No, Jane isn't coming back. Jane is in the country." He repeated the word, then thumped himself on the chest and said, "Ma—country." (I am going to the country.)

One day during the last week of March, Edward got a flatiron to play with. He brought it to me saying, "Hot!" There followed a play of burning me with the hot iron. Children enjoyed it hugely. Finally I showed Edward the scar of a real burn on my arm and asked him if his iron had made it. He looked sober, shook his head and pointed up to the part of the house where my apartment was, saying, "Up stairs." These are the first records of conversation for the purpose of sharing experience.

Monthly Summary: Edward's use of phrases and short sentences has increased. He has become much more fluent and clear in his speech. It is an activity which he seems to enjoy. Early in the month we were much disturbed to find that he had returned to grunts and gibberings. It was after quite a long period of time at home, but the situation righted itself and although he tries us much by shouts and howls we feel that it is now his way of getting rid of energy, rather than a substitute for speech. He gets over to us all that he needs to say and understands us perfectly.

APRIL.

Original use of language to describe experiences.

Edward is very fond of a boot-black game of his own devising. He approaches, says, "Shine, shine?" and goes through a very dramatic and realistic game of polishing our shoes. He called one of us to play with him. Taking up the ball, he took an appropriate position, calling, "P'ay ball!" He has changed the form of his requests. Formerly, in March, he said, "P'ay?" if he saw a child with a toy which he desired. Now he names the article and puts it into sentence form. "I want hammer—me."

For a time during the month difficulties again arose. Edward has become very obstreperous. We wonder sometimes whether there may be an emotional blocking because of inadequate language expression. When he came to us he had a large range of sounds and calls which represented language to him. As he has learned the possibilities of communication through speech it may be that his powers have not kept pace with his desires for adequate expression. He reverts to his original gibberings less but he gets much excited and spins around, a purposeless zigzagging about the yard, and his behavior is at times a very demoralizing influence. It has made it difficult to work out anything with the other two older children, who seem ready for more regular and organized occupation.

Edward is much interested in coal carts and recognizes them as far as he can see them. He points them out with great excitement, saying "Coal, coal," or "I see coal—me!"

The three Olders were taken for a ferry trip. When they returned Edward was asked about it. His account was an adequate and effective piece of description. "I saw water—I went in boat. Boat go in water, sh—sh—sh," bending his body and moving his hands as if he were stirring up the surface of the water, hands held flat, palms down, then saying, "Gong-gong, gong-gong," his own interpretation of the experience.

Edward was allowed to walk in from the street to David's home with him a while ago. Since then he never fails to ask, "Home—Da—me?" when we approach the house.

MAY.

Thoroughgoing use of language. Gets over ideas. Joins in general conversation. Uses voice in singing.

We discovered more than once this month that Edward was applying his German vocabulary at the Nursery. He found an ugly two-pronged fork in the yard. We asked him for it, as it was a menace. He called it what sounded like "Garb" and we did not think at first that he was speaking German. He sometimes speaks of his hat as "hut" but generally calls other hats or caps, "hats." He shows a peculiar sentence construction. His habit of tacking on "Me" at the end of a sentence suggests the French "Moi." "I want to jump—me." "Can—me." "I see balloon—me." "I have home balloon." "Where dog?" "The dog has gone away." "Where is gone dog?"

He and George are in the stage of reiterative inquiry which is more a sort of exercise in language than real interest in finding out. What they want is to inform not to be informed.

E.: "Wha do man?"

C. R.: "The man is fixing the house."

E.: "Man fix house? I can fix house—me." Then immediately, "Wha do man?"

C. R.: "What is the man doing, Edward?"

E.: "Man fix house."

This type of conversation is repeated ad infinitum.

One day we made dire threats because his mother had dressed him in a button back suit which had to be entirely removed whenever he was taken to the toilet. He looked up with a twinkle and a sweet smile and said, with much emphasis, "No—s'goot mamma!"

He made a construction with the blocks which pleased him very much and after he had called C. R.'s attention to it said, "Tell John." (H. J.) He talked a good deal while building on this occasion, muttering "See-saw" at intervals, reminded by seeing a long block lying across another. Finally he found a very long block and exclaimed, "A long board" and laid it up on end on a pile of blocks. After that he piled up his blocks indiscriminately, singing a charming little phrase in a very sweet voice.

He is not to be taken in by childish jokes. The big packing box stood against the fence. He dropped his hammer behind it. We said, "Now the hammer is gone." "No, no," said Edward, "hammer not gone," and he set about moving the box so that he could get it.

One day he suddenly burst out, "Where Jane?" His question was turned back to him and he answered, "Jane sick." He was reassured. "Oh no, Jane is well now. She is in the country." In heartfelt tones he said, "Come Jane." We suggested that a letter should go to Jane. Half an hour later he came up and said, "Letter Jane." We inquired what he wished to say to Jane. He repeated, "Come Jane." We asked what he wanted Jane to do and he answered at once, "Come Jane play in the yard."

Arnold and Edward spied a cat walking on the fence.

A.: "O kitty, kitty!"

E. (begging): "See cat—me."

A.: "She's walking on the fence."

E.: "Walking on fence?"

C. R.: "Yes."

E.: "Fall cat?"

C. R.: "No, I think not."

A.: "Kitty won't fall. She can walk."

C. R.: "See how she jumps from one fence to another?"

E.: "Jump fence cat?"

Cat began walking away and shortly disappeared.

E.: "Come cat, come cat."

A.: "Goodbye, little kitty."

E.: (with feeling): "Come cat, come cat."

Edward found the rope and seat of a swing in a corner of the yard.

E.: "What's this, Carmen?"

C.: "It's part of a swing."

E.: "This—swing?"

C.: "Yes.

E.: "Want swing over there—me." (pointing to pebbled space).

C.: "I'm sorry Edward, but the swing is broken."

E.: "Broken?"

C.: "Yes."

E.: "Fix it—man." (pointing to workmen in adjoining yard).

Edward's progress from the first to the last entry seems to us to indicate his release from a cramping handicap and it has been encouraging to us to find that an analysis of our current records shows the steps in his development.

SUMMARY

As has been stated in the introduction, our Nursery School was not organized for the purpose of giving small children adequate physical care outside their homes, nor to relieve the needs of working mothers. We are trying to set up a laboratory in which growth can be studied. An environment favorable to growth must assure children physical care, but it must moreover provide them with opportunities for experience, experience in the use of their bodies and in dealing with things and with persons.

Our environment is not the product of one person's thinking. Long before the Bureau of Educational Experiments established our Nursery School, the City and Country School was conducting classes for children of three and four, and Miss Caroline Pratt's conclusions on equipment for small children have been the basis of our choice of play material. We have scaled down in some instances and made additions and changes as we felt the need on account of our lower age range. We are indebted to her, moreover, not only for her contribution to the subject of equipment but for the educational philosophy which underlies our method of approach to children. The establishment of a routine procedure, the development of a program for children of nursery age, and a policy on such questions as social and emotional control, discipline, etc., have been worked out by our staff, but there has always been opportunity for very free interchange of ideas between members of staff and Bureau. Our relations with the physician and psychologist have been very close. The problems of individuals, those of general environment and of method have been freely discussed with them. For two years we had Miss Harriette G. Hubbell, teacher of music in the City and Country School, on our staff in an advisory capacity. She conferred with us and very generously turned over for our use songs she had adapted for the children of the school. She also arranged and helped us to arrange many of the songs and phrases that we use as accompaniments to the activities of our children. The records have been the subject of frequent conferences with members of the Bureau and its staff, especially while Miss Mary Marot was working with us as Recorder.* Mrs. Mitchell has worked with us on language and we have based much of our approach on her conception of the function of language as play material.† Her contribution will be recognized in our statement of our procedure. On the whole I believe that the Nursery School may be said to represent a piece of "co-operative thinking."

It is too soon to draw conclusions. We believe that we have set up an

---

* See "School Records—An Experiment" by Mary S. Marot, Bulletin No. XII, Bureau of Educational Experiments, 1922.

† Op. cit. p. 37.

environment which is favorable to growth. We are attempting, as our experience widens, still further to modify and improve it. We believe that it will be possible within our laboratory to gather data of scientific value which will add to our knowledge of children's development. These data are still in the making. We must develop standards for making observations on children's activities, for taking records and for analyzing and assessing them. Further than that our aim and hope is that the knowledge gained may be converted into educational procedure for nursery children which is more fully adapted to their needs.

HARRIET M. JOHNSON.

TIPPETY-TOP!

MUSIC IN THE NURSERY SCHOOL

When the Nursery School bulletin was first issued we had had for two years a musician as a member of our staff, working day after day with the children and carrying on the musical program as an incident in the day's routine. We thought and still agree that such an arrangement where possible is advantageous. It reduces the number of adults in the environment and therefore the possibilities of confusion, and the music can be made a more intimate and coordinated part of the program when it can be on tap, so to speak, and can be given at odd times if the demand comes from the children. It can serve specific purposes too of meeting a mood or accompanying a play activity. It can be deferred if an especially profitable play experience is in full swing at the time when it is usually given.

We recognized from the first however that we could not in the nature of things have always on the staff a person whose special interest and training lay along musical lines and such a training is necessary if one is to work out a program for music with babies and to understand or even know how to attempt to interpret the responses one sees. For the past two years we have been fortunate in securing Miss Maude Stewart, Miss Hubbell's assistant in the City and Country School, who has taken regular periods in the Nursery School.

There has been a rather marked difference in the programs presented in 1921-22 and during the last two years. This was in part inherent in the changed situation but it was also decided to give a more limited and integrated program in the hope that the children's responses could be more definitely evaluated, or that at least certain factors present in the more complicated vocal music might be eliminated. We planned then, a tentative program with certain definite questions in mind and we agreed upon certain other details which in general followed our practice of the preceding years: Such details were that there should be no formality about the presentation of music; the children should be summoned to it from the roof or from other rooms if they were out of the large play room when Miss Stewart entered, but they should be allowed to continue their play activities unless they actually interfered with the music. Loud screaming if continued, and jumping and stamping were interrupted and the children were reminded that we could not hear the piano unless they were quieter. We also decided that we should make no attempt to get reproduction of songs from the children, nor suggest any specific sort of rhythmic response. This had always been our policy.

It is interesting to note that in going back to the procedure with which we began our experiment in music, that is in having the period taken by a person not regularly concerned with the daily routine, there was manifested none of the confusion or nervous strain noted before. It would seem therefore as if other factors entered in which may well have been the conventional presentation of the program which exacted or attempted to exact too sustained attention from the children, the use of instruments and also the fact that we were inexperienced in dealing with the problem.

The program for the past two years, together with notes taken of the children's responses are presented by Miss Maude Stewart.

HARRIET M. JOHNSON.

I.   MATERIAL USED IN NURSERY MUSIC PERIODS, 1922-24.

Whatever secondary aims music for children of nursery age may serve, its most significant use is the heightening of the babies' pleasure in their activities. These activities may involve materials, other persons, or they may be a quite independent and direct response of an individual. In any case music for these early years should be chosen that will best heighten child pleasures of rhythm (evidenced largely through big-muscle responses), melody (from cooings and gurglings, through spontaneous tunes with nonsense syllables, to short "songs" that make "sense"), or mere accompaniment that is evidently enjoyed but evokes no more tangible response at the moment.

The selections that we used were therefore short, regular in form, of distinct and simple rhythmic pattern, and possessed melodies characteristic of their type: skips, lullabies, walks, etc. This last requirement will be recognized as important by those who have collected music material for children. Of several skips, apparently equally good rhythmically, perhaps only one will have that inherent quality that invariably impels children to appropriate responses. Straight diatonic tunes in an unchanging tonality were favored, as chromatics and modulations introduce an element of complexity as foreign to the child's hearing capacity in music as long involved sentences would be in his language development, or as tasks requiring very fine muscle adjustments would be in his bodily growth.

A.   *Folk.*

These were largely played on the piano, a simple bass accentuating the rhythm. When sung, la or some other appropriate syllable was often used instead of the words, especially in the refrain portions. In this most simple way the child hears music, absolutely, as an expression. He will have ample opportunity to hear music with a program or definite word content.

Skippy.   French
En roulant me boule

Skipping
Morning Song (Tremp ton pain, Marie)
Bon Voyage
Polichinelle

English
Cock a doodle doo
Early one morning
Oats and Beans and Barley

German
Birdies
In Holland Stands a House
Flemish Song
Broader.
Tramp, tramp (English)
Dutch Hymn (arr. Josef Hofmann)
Hero March (Hungarian)
Turkey Buzzard
Lyric.
Lavendar's Blue (English)
Sun Song (Polish)
Sleepy.
Fais dodo (French)
Bergerette (French)
Sleep Baby Sleep (German)
Lullaby (Macedonian)

B. *Composed.*

Beethoven—Andante, C major
Beethoven—Menuet, E flat
Mozart—Trio from Menuet, Symphony E flat
Schuman—Soldier's March
Wachs—Menuet Pompadour
Mendelssohn—Fairies' March (first 8 measures)
Statkowski—Oberek

C. *Songs.**

Jog Along
Old Dan

---

* For most of these songs and adaptations, and continued practical help, we are indebted to Miss Harriette G. Hubbell, teacher of music in the City and Country School.

New York Horses
Galloping
Tucky Tuck
Peep Gray Mousie
Roll the ball along
Down Hill
Pound, Pound
Swing, Swing (8-5)
Climb up the Slide (1-3-5-8)
Music for Dona (8-1-1-1-1)
Good-bye Tony (8-5-5-5)
Sleepy Time
Dressing Song
Coats, Buttons
Singing, Singing, Barbara can Sing.

> These songs are extremely simple, utilize wide intervals for the most part, and are directly related to the activities or interests of the children. Some are mere phrases (major notation noted).

D. *Extra Music.*

For a period of five months (December, 1922—April, 1923) Mr. Morris Veder came once a week and played his violin for the children. At first the introduction of a new music medium fascinated the children, but when they became accustomed to it their responses were no different from those secured by the piano alone. Mr. Veder played the same group of French folk songs each time, supplementing them with general violin favorites, notably Wieniawski's "Kuiawiak" (main theme only), Beethoven's "Minuet in G" and Gossec's "Gavotte."

Fais Dodo
Polichinelle
Au clair de la lune
Il court.

An examination of the material used will show significant omissions. Of the conventional kindergarten music type, with its formless tunes of poor workmanship, its content relating to aspects of nature with which the city baby is not familiar, its adult conceptions of morality and even death — there is none. Nor is any "adult" music included which does not share childlike qualities.

Much of the above music is used with success by Miss Hubbell with older children (three, four, and five years). It might seem this was a loose, unstudied grading, but the same material is used with this vastly important difference in objective: with the older children a definite rhythmic response is expected (swinging with sticks, "on the floor," reproduction of songs, etc.) while with the babies all response is spontaneous and entirely unpersuaded, being observed in whatever activity they are engaged in at the moment.

II. MUSICAL PHRASES SPONTANEOUSLY.

The music we get from the children is very interesting and while we hesitate to call it "original," not knowing from what hang-overs it springs, it is their spontaneous expression, if only an unconscious and far-fetched adaptation.

Many of the phrases are on the arpeggiated tonic:

December, 1922.

Joan (2 years)

Good   night   Dol - ly.

Mollie Anne (2 years, 2 months)

6th

Up   slide,   down   slide,   up   slide, etc.

6th

Play   moo - sic,   Play   moo - sic, etc.

18th

Shoe,   lace   up   Shoe,   lace   up,   (5 times)

Moya (3 years)

Roll   it   down,   Mol - lie   Anne.

January, 1923.

Moya (3 years, 1 month)

Slide,   slide   down   Joan.   (Encouraging Joan to use slide.)

David (2 years, 11 months)

Ling - a - lang - a - long - a.

October, 1923.

Dona (2 years, 9 months)

I'm   all   read - y,   Mil - ly.

Much of the children's conversation is sung back and forth, and they continually chant. (This is especially true of Peter.) They often sing, accompanying their activities:

December, 1922.

Mollie Anne (2 years, 2 months)

I   want   din - neh !

January, 1923.

David (2 years, 11 months)

Need   a   screw   driv - er !

October, 1923.

Dona (2 years, 9 months)

Good   night,   good   night,   good   night.   (Bedding doll.)

Sometimes the children get started on endless sequences. Moya doubtless heard vocalises being practised at home.

When we get a phrase that is startlingly like some familiar theme we immediately link the two. It is quite possible that while the similarity suggests itself to us, the child's tune may not be derivative. Mollie Ann's is the same as the opening notes of Grieg's "Morning," but on questioning we found she had not heard it at home, on the victrola, etc. Marianna's has a hint of "Parsifal." Jane's has the rhythmic pattern of "Peep Gray Mousie."

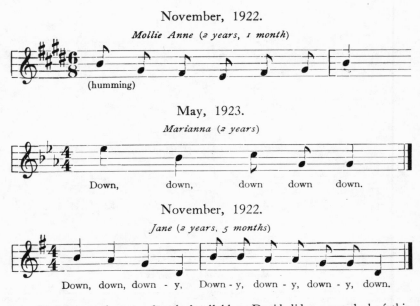

November, 1922.

Mollie Anne (2 years, 1 month)

(humming)

May, 1923.

Marianna (2 years)

Down,   down,   down   down   down.

November, 1922.

Jane (2 years, 5 months)

Down, down, down - y,   Down - y, down - y, down - y, down.

Tony sings along on detached syllables. David did a great deal of this, his syllables falling into more rhythmic patterns.

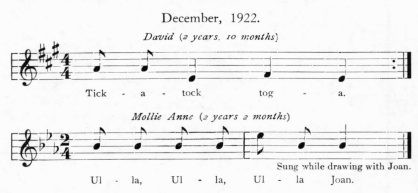

December, 1922.

David (2 years, 10 months)

Tick - a - tock   tog - a.

Mollie Anne (2 years 2 months)

Sung while drawing with Joan.

Ul - la,   Ul - la,   Ul - la   Joan.

The best full music sentence we got was Moya's:

December, 1922.

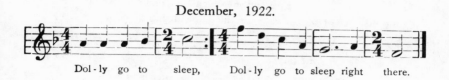

Dol-ly   go   to   sleep,   Dol-ly   go   to sleep right   there.

This is the type of thing we can get down in our music notation, but often the children's music eludes us. There is sometimes something about their tone quality that is difficult to parallel with our voice, and quite impossible to duplicate on the piano. This difference in timbre may explain why they sometimes seem to approximate quarter-tones.

III. OBSERVATION OF RESPONSES DURING MUSIC.

It would be more than rash to announce any dicta on the children's reactions, since the individuals differ so greatly and since so many considerations (physical, temperamental, muscular, etc.) affect their responses. Therefore in remarking the responses of most of the children, so extraordinarily in the spirit of the music presented, it is well to keep in mind certain general questions which shall guide our observation and make it more discriminating. For instance, it is hard to discern whether things noted are music responses, definitely, or part of the regular activity that would go on independently of the music. When thumping feet on chairs, patting, walking, etc. is *almost* in rhythm the question is not whether the response is actuated by the music, but if the music is even heard. Joan did a great deal of quick running and jumping, up and down, in circles, etc., but such activities seemed to result from her own excitement and were probably not occasioned by the music. She did that sort of thing when the music was soft or slow or both.

The regular Nursery staff took notes during the music periods, as did I, and in general our records are similar. The only difference is that they were more skillful in describing the motor details of responses, while my interpretations were often in musical terms. To illustrate, where I have "Dona tapping her foot" Miss Johnson has "Dona sitting on block—feet wide—moves them from out, in, out, in, several times—then taps with toe—heel on ground—toe turned in." Again, my "Perfectly beautiful dances from Peter. Unlearned, they are reminiscent of the large muscle movements Miss Doing has her older children do. P. had extraordinary balance and poise. Then he led out into a well-defined skip" becomes "Peter strides around room holding dumbell shoulder high—shakes it—then runs with a slide-step—shaking dumbell twice as fast as before. Later he drops dumbell and runs swiftly from one side of room to other. Seems a little more conscious of music than usual."

Our notes are very full, and in presenting representative ones some little pulling together of similar responses may "point up" this discussion.

Vocal (or at least lingual) responses and things I do to encourage them:

February 27, 1923.—When I began *Jog Along* after quiet music, J. C. (2 years, 2 months) raced through room singing "jog along" in key.

October 9, 1923.—Came down with children from roof. Sang *Down, Down* on 8-5, over and over. Same thing from P. W. (2 years, 8 months), same intervals, different key.

October 10, 1923.—*Galloping.* M. A.'s (2 years, 4 months) tongue went very fast, in a good imitative effect of the rush of the music, without producing any actual sound.

October 24, 1923.—M. A. talked with a mumble that was a good approximation of the rapid *Galloping* I sung. Delighted squeals from S. Y. (13 months).

October 25, 1923.—*Birdies.* M. A., chair at piano, singing *la.*
Old Dan (which features 8-5). M. A. sang "down, down" (8-5) during it.

October 26, 1923.—*Jog Along.* D. D. P. (2 years, 8 months), moved lips in time with each tone. No sound.

November 13, 1923.—*Bon Voyage.* M. A. and D. D. P. kicking on table. T. A. (14 months) bumping against box. I stopped several times to see if singing that went on during playing would continue without the music background. It seldom did.

November 14, 1923.—Found S. Y. singing "doo" on A flat, only child in room. I imitated her. She listened for several minutes, evidently delighted.

November 16, 1923.—I sang *Jog Along.* M. A. and D. D. P. at piano. When appropriate place in the music came I said "Shall I take M. A.?" "Yes." I stopped for next name. D. D. P. ventured, "Take me."

December 12, 1923.—When I entered the nursery and went to the piano, S. Y. was standing there. She gave a deep grunt when she saw me, something of a chuckle. I imitated what she did several times and she seemed delighted. I believe the sound pleased her, not my attention; and if we could be versatile enough to present simple, stark tones of various timbre, intensity and pitch—without their becoming outworn— I think we should do more of that sort of thing. I sang "Music for S. Y." (8-1-1-1-1). P. W. came up. "Music for me." When I had sung his he enumerated all the other children, now standing about the piano, for me to sing to.

December 14, 1923.—I sang "Music for—" to each child. B. L. (2 years) surprised Miss J. and me by repeating the octave progression after me perfectly, with words distinct, "Music for D. D. P." She sang in a ravishingly natural voice. Her interest I believe was in the brute sound of the words, not their meaning, as she still has her own peculiar speech, and this phrase she gave in flawless adult fashion. This would seem to indicate that our concern about suitable content for songs for this age is overdone, since combinations of smooth, jerky, soothing, impelling, etc., syllables engage the attention of the babies as well as, if not better than, those sequences that have a definite thought content. With the exception of the end rhyme, there is very often little in song words to commend them as successions of related, contrasted, or rhythmic sounds. Specifically, here, aside from the melody-swoop of the octave, the two long vowels, u and o, coming on the accented first and third beats of the measure, are reinforced. These are easy to hang on to, and the remaining short syllables slip into place. Repetitions of the same long vowel, or combinations of long vowels seem easier of reproduction by the children than sequences of short ones.

January 16, 1924.—Miss J. asked C. T. on roof "When does music come?" B. L. rose, flung away hammer and said "Wanna go down for music." Miss J. took her hand and they started down stairs. She chanted "Down for mu keek." Stood on stair, then jumped to next, hand on wall—chanted at each step "Jump-pp" blowing out the *p*- and over emphasizing it. I sang "Music for B. L., music for B. L." She gave back the intervals correctly. After period I called "Good bye" on E flat (high). All the children stood about. M. A. shouted on low note "Good bye." B. L. gave almost inaudible high tone.

This simple phrase is effective with all the children. One morning T. A. was alone in the room when I entered. I sang "Music for T. A.," touching him on head and tum as pitch was 8 or 1. Did this several times. Some seconds after he sang "Music," distinctly, on the octave (15 months). Once I stopped just before the last note of *Bon Voyage* to find T. A. singing the tonic. This very probably was not direct. I did it again, with no such result. The same day when all but S. Y. had been taken off to be washed for lunch I played *Lavendar's Blue* (allegretto, piano, and very lyric), singing it on "la." S. Y. just looked and looked. When she was taken out and T. A. brought in I did the same thing with him. He wagged his head in all directions and sang softly throughout.

Once when I sang *Galloping*, S. Y., D. D. P., T. A. and B. L. came to the piano. I intoned *WHOA* at the end. After the third time through B. L. sang "whoa" at end. T. A. full of rhythm. He has a special waddle from left to right. Using the same sort of device I held the last "la" of the Polish *Sun Song* for a long while. B. L., busy with doll, looked up. When I stopped again M. A. sang with very good voice about a three measure length.

January 18, 1924.—B. L. echoed exactly the phrase "Down, down, down, down" B.-F sharp-D sharp-B (1-5-3-1).

January 22, 1924.—*Bon Voyage*. B. L. came to piano, stood on chair. I sang "Barbra, Barbra, Barbra Bee" over and over through the song, fitting the music. Each time I finished she said "Barbra Bee" and laughed. I did the same thing with M. A. Sounds in her name not as successful. At any rate she paid little attention to my efforts.

January 23, 1924.—S. Y. sang what was meant to be "Hello" when I came in, and ran to me. As I went to piano she followed smiling, singing "Wuh d u h" on octave (G). D. D. P. and D. W. the only others in room. I began a very dramatic Slav mazurka. S. Y. at piano watching, hands at first thrust out at sides, fingers extended. Rose to toes, turned self about and started slowly up slide. Stopped to smooth the back of my blouse. Stalled on fourth stair murmuring "Too too" under her breath, pursing her lips in time with the pattern of the song (17 months). Went on up, then stuck foot out at stairs. "Dah dah," sharp and loud, as Miss J. asked her to go away from stairs. Then I began *Lavendar's Blue*, which never starts much activity, singing it on "la." S. Y. came over to the piano and watched. She loves to hear syllables sung.

January 25, 1924.—I sang *Bon Voyage* to B. L. as before. In chair at side of piano she said her name as if to correct my "Barbra Bee."

January 28, 1924.—T. A. at base of slide, watching. I sang "T. A." throughout *Tremp ton pain, Marie*. He seemed to enjoy it while slapping the block box in time. Did the same thing with D. D. P.'s name. Both long o-s.

January 30, 1924.—*Turkey Buzzard* (broad, fortissimo, full chords). D. D. P. and M. A. looked up for a minute. S. Y. sitting on window sill, feet in double time against the floor. No others responded. Then I sang "Tum-tum-tummy, tum-tum-tum" to fit the quarter-quarter-eighth-dotted quarter, quarter-quarter-half pattern, first with full chords, then playing tune only. M. A. brought her chair and watched throughout. "Can you sing M. A.?" "I sing home." "Can you sing here?" She said "Tum" at end. S. Y. on stomach on table, sang the song in key and continued after I stopped, getting the eighth-dotted quarter figure. I fitted the names of T. A., N. G., and M. A. to the tune. All listened with much interest around piano, but did not reproduce anything.

February 1, 1924.—*Sun Song.* P. W. asked me to play it "loud," then began a delightful walk around the room, head bobbing, holding index finger of right hand up throughout. I changed to soft. When I again played "ff", he began running, with same position of finger. Finally, walking, he sang for several minutes. When I sang *Oats and Beans and Barley* and left the end unfinished he sang in the last three notes, P. W. often supplies tonics. A. M. sings often, in her own language, with very musicial tone. Going up the slide seems to provide the best stimulus for her efforts.

May 6, 1924.—*Bon voyage.* T. A. and P. W. hidden in bottom of settle, waving to beat of the music. I sang each name on E flat-B flat. T. A. much interested and approximated the name, spoken, but no pitch response. P. W. echoed almost everything I sang.

May 9, 1924.—S. Y. in, crying. M. A., "I have a baby home." P. W. began singing "Baby sleep," several intervals. I played *Sleepy Time* softly, and sang it. He did too improvising his own words, always about two measures behind me.

The business of sleeping, or of bedding dolls, often starts the children on a vocal streak. This comes from a full-day record of D. W. (2 years, 2 months), March 12, 1924: ". . . I returned with new book. I had been singing with the music as I went out. As I came back she said 'Sing John Sing about a baby.' I sung. D. W., 'Here my baby.' I said 'D. W. sing about a baby.' D. W. began at once: 'Go to sleep Baby go to sleep.' I did and urged her to. She sang again high, then hummed: 'Go way Go way I tell baby go way Boy bee bey'."

Accommodation to various rhythms, timbre, dynamics, etc., and the notice they take of changes in the music are very interesting. "Atmosphere" in the grown-up sense does not get over to the children. They respond to rhythm and sharp contrasts more than melody and smooth flow. One day I played Purcell's *Passing By* (a seventeenth century song) merely as a tune. Afterwards I sang softly on "la," but with no words. It did not bring any response.

November 27, 1922.—I began with Mozart Trio. J. P. (2 years, 5 months) walked in perfect rhythm to two phrases, 3-4 time, as soon as it started. When I changed to 2-4 Schumann March, slightly different tempo, she walked in that time, keeping rhythm even when trains, cart, etc., were in her way on the floor.

January 23, 1923.—Children had scuffers when I entered. C. R. (2 years, 4 months) swished his in time first to a fast 2-4, then to slow *Jog Jog.*

March 6, 1923.—During *Jog Along,* 2-4, J. C. at table ironing, moved her iron in perfectly rhythmic strokes. When I began *Skipping* she left the table to go running about the room (2 years, 3 months). J. C. back to table when I began *Bergerette* 6-8 and ironed in that rhythm.

October 11, 1923.—*Skipping.* P. W. jumping up and down with a series of gyrations and a one-sided skip. Also tumbling antics on the mat. I changed to *Sleep, Baby, Sleep.* P. W. stopped. M. A. on mat imitating his antics. I played *Skipping* again and P. W. came back to the mat.

October 12, 1923.—*Fairies* (light, swift, no stark rhythmic pattern). P. W. turning somersaults on mat. Before, in *Jog Along* he had walked about with a slight effect of the "slow movie," very controlled.

October 16, 1923.—*Skipping.* P. W. began to strike the metal bell arpeggio, hanging near the piano. D. D. P. and M. A. joined in. Great racket. *Sleep Baby Sleep.* All to other quiet occupations, train blocks, etc. M. A. back to the bells. "That's a *big* one," hitting low C. She may have been impressed by the size of the bell, the volume of the sound, or the effort she expended in hitting the bell.

October 23, 1923.—*Polichinelle.* B. L., extraordinary poise in walking about during music. While her gait sometimes coincides with the spirit of the music, her determined walk seems independent of it.

October 24, 1923.—*Birdies.* P. W. standing at side end of piano, ear pressed against case, listening. I changed to pianissimo. He asked to "Play hard."

October 31, 1923.—*Polichinelle,* very softly. N. G. (1 year, 10 months) singing at cart. Extraordinary walking from T. A. M. A., rhythmic walk across room. P. W., tongue out, wagging it in time. S. Y. waving with left hand. N. G., lower jaw moving in time, no sound. All this quiet play, no balcony stamping, etc. This device, starting forte and continuing until the rhythm becomes established, then playing in the same tempo but pianissimo and with a marked lilt, seems to give a background that produces quiet singing and many rhythmic responses. D. D. P. patted her doll in time with each quarter note in *Birdies* (allegretto), played softly.

November 9, 1923.—*Fais dodo,* slow, soft, first time this year. D. W. started her patented walk but couldn't keep it up. M. A. got out doll. Began to bed it. S. Y. waved, but slower than usual. D. W. walked, slower.

November 14, 1923.—*Dutch Hymn,* broad and forte. All looked up when new music began. This is not true in changing from one light skip to another.

November 28, 1923.—*Bon Voyage.* P. W. on balcony, tapping one foot with perfect regularity, yet always slower than the 1-2 of the music. Did not seem to be disturbed by this.

December 11, 1923.—Began with *Fais dodo.* Usually I begin with a bright skip, simple melody and well-defined rhythm. This morning may not have been a fair time to notice any different response to the opening lullaby, as the children had been given musical dumbbells before I came in. These they shook with as much vigor at their activities as if I had been playing most exciting music. It may be too that the mere fact of having music, its announcement, my familiar entrance and what ordinarily follows, may loosen the babies up, no matter what the initial approach. *Morning Song.* Miss J. waved one of the dumbbells in rhythm. D. D. P. and P. W. tried it: they played quickly and regularly, but did not fit the music. *Dutch Hymn.* P. W. ran across the floor twice, shaking dumbbell in same time as he used in previous skip, but he couldn't keep it up. Went back to quiet play with Montessori material.

December 21, 1923.—*Morning Song.* S. Y. waved her arms quickly and sang slow, sustained notes. This is comparable to the sort of thing Miss Hubbell has the older children do when they swing the broad metre and clap the quicker, rhythmic pattern, both at the same time.

January 11, 1924.—I began playing soft chords and a kind of "endless melody." Not much notice was taken of the music. D. D. P. looked up expectantly and stood as if ready to begin one of her performances. Playing in 3-4, I kept up a half-quarter note pattern. B. L. ironed forward on half note, back on quarter note, for several minutes. I went into *Lavendar's Blue,* 3-4. T. A. walked in, swaying from side to side, legs wide apart. Has done it before, but to 2-4 or 6-8. N. G. doing much the same thing. Neither saw the other.

January 23, 1924.—*Bon Voyage.* M. A., D. D. P. and B. L. up the slide. I played the piece twice as slowly. No notice taken except by D. W., who looked up and stared from mirror.

February 8, 1924.—*In Holland Stands a House.* D. W. began jumping. Almost always she came down on the hard beat. Gave double jumps—short, long—and paused, as if to emphasize her action. During *Dutch Hymn* she continued but accommodated her jumping somewhat to the new accent.

Sometimes a "saturation" point is noted, when the rhythm established by a first selection hangs over in the responses that go on during a second and different activity:

March 20, 1923.—M. A. (1 year, 10 months) came into room while *Hero March* was being played. First slow music she has heard here. It so got into her system that she didn't seem to hear the following skip.

November 23, 1923.—*Bon Voyage*. At least seven kinds of responses from T. A., in chair. *Cock a doodle doo*. Just as much activity from T. A. *Fais dodo* (andante). T. A. seemed to be freed. Got up. Quick walking, nothing lullabyish about it.

February 15, 1924.—*In Holland Stands a House*, many playings. A stream of running and skipping activity between kitchen and window by D. W., N. G., S. Y. and P. W. I then played *Sleep Baby Sleep* for three minutes before there was any let-up in the procession of the four.

It often happens that there is a preoccupation with materials or an activity. Yet even within this, incidental individual responses are noticed:

November 28, 1922.—*Schumann March. Mozart Trio. Polichinelle.* Four children began train activity, with chairs in row, toot of whistles, engines, good-byes, etc. They continued right through the three compositions. Individuals banged time, etc., but the group activity remained undisturbed.

December 6, 1922.—All during the period D. D. (2 years, 9 months) played with small cubes, flat on stomach, paid no attention to music. L. F. (2 years, 11 months) with train of cars, also absorbed in his own play.

February 20, 1923.—Played *Skipping* over and over, but D. D. busy with a real hammer and nails, never noticed it.

April 9, 1923.—M. A. (1 year, 11 months) trying various chairs, swung feet vigorously no matter whether music was a skip, lullaby, slow, or heavy.

Jan. 15, 1924.—*Bon Voyage*. Little response. Selection usually stimulating. Perhaps due to previous rather quieting music and its attendant quiet activities during more than ten minutes. (Periods should never last more than fifteen minutes.)

The music may stimulate social activities and again a social feeling established previous to the music may preclude any attention to the music. Of course imitation is an element in both:

March 2, 1923.—M. M. (3 years, 3 months) so busy directing D. D.'s activities that she didn't seem to know music was being played.

May 1, 1923.—D. D. and M. M. on settle. When I played *Tucky Tuck*, D. D. said "It's going fast" several times. He probably referred to their "Train," but the tempo of the music set the mood.

May 21, 1923.—D. D. not touched by the music he heard distinctly yesterday. He and M. M. had begun a new absorbing play in the pen set up on the floor.

January 4, 1924.—*Bon Voyage*. D. D. P., a pirouette. M. A. imitated her but soon gave it up. P. W. began to run. Soon all but T. A. were racing about. Playing this again when B. L., D. D. P., M. A., P. W. and S. Y. were at table for apples and milk, all were quiet. Then all but S. Y. slapping both hands on table quickly. Kept it up after music stopped.

January 25, 1924.—D. D. P. and M. A. lying on floor with doll in dark corner. D. P. P., "I'll sing to you, M. A. Isn't this a pretty song?" Began "Dee dee dee" in tremolo voice on long involved tune, formless.

March 4, 1924.—*Lavendar's Blue*. P. W. up to M. A. asking for more covers. M. A. refused. P. W. dragged bed about. Into kitchen then out again. Left bed to dance lightly across floor. Back hurriedly to keep possession. . . . Music evidently calling him, for he stepped off from time to time in a lovely swing, arms and legs keeping time. Fear of losing bed and doll restrained him.

The play sometimes becomes quite dramatic, although this incipient sort may be deserted in its early stages for a second engaging activity. The stage is set only to be torn down in a few minutes.

November 27, 1923.—*Birdies.* Quiet. Almost all individual play. *Boy Voyage.* Much activity. M. A. busy with boat play. Whistle, etc., harsh, not singing. I changed to *Sleep Baby Sleep.* In forty-five seconds all were quieted but M. A. Miss J.: "Can you hear the music?" M. A.: "But this is a *boat.*"

January 9, 1924.—*Skipping.* P. W., "My doll's asleep. Will the music wake her? I don't want her to. Play soft." I continued *Skipping,* but pianissimo. D. D. P., to me, "Shh!" *Sleep, Baby, Sleep.* P. W., M. A., D. D. P., and D. W. engrossed in doll-bed play. I began *Bon Voyage,* suddenly and very loud. P. W., with approval, "Play loud now, she's awake."

May 25, 1923.—*Skipping.* D. D. and M. M. climbing up slide steps said they were "going in the boat." M. A. joined them on the balcony and all three made so much noise with feet jumping that Miss J. had to tell them they couldn't hear the music. When I played *Bergerette,* D. D. and M. M. began a beautiful play of finding little fish in the water and scooping them out with a wide arm motion in the rhythm of the music. Their steps from one "pool" to another were distinctly rhythmic, knees bent when the "dip" came in the music.

I was often requested to play or sing general favorites:

These requests came notably from D. D. and P. W., probably from some supervisory urge or simply to make conversation, for when I did not comply they were not insistent.

December 4, 1922.—When I had finished and all were dressed for taxi, M. M. asked for "More music." I played the melody of *Polichinelle.* M. M., delighted, said, "Yes, that one," and beamed when I played it with the accompaniment.

February 2, 1923.—D. D. asked for "the big pony music" but seemed contented when I played something else.

December 11, 1923.—P. W., whether going up slide or engaged in any other way, comes to me if I am not playing and asks for "Mustard," "horses," or "ponies."

January 8, 1924.—I sang *Oats and Beans and Barley Grow,* unaccompanied, then I played it. No comment from P. W., D. D. P., M. A. and B. L. at the piano. P. W. left to run about and clap. B. L. off, imitating him. When I played and sang it, D. D. P. said, "I have that on my record, too." Afterwards when I played it and did not sing, P. W. asked for "Barley again." This while I was playing it, evidently not connecting it without the words.

One afternoon the group, bound for the taxi, met me in the hall. I was carrying an armful of flageolets and they asked me to bring them to the Nursery. When I played *Hot Cross Buns* on one the next day all watched me intently as I played it through twice, but there were no comments.

With the very young children obvious responses are halted because of lack of co-ordination. This was especially true of S. Y., who at first seemed to have only one outlet for her rhythmic feeling. These notes are from Miss J.'s full day reports on T. A.:

"November 7, 1923 (15 months). *Polichinelle.* T. A. stared at Miss S. then walked slowly about backing up against big table where he stood. Off in a sidewise walk. Fell and slid. Rolled over and crept to me. Pulled self up by my foot and stood leaning against me and swaying. Revolved and leaned against me rubbing head. Waved arms and walked off—up on mat and down again without stumbling."

"February 6, 1924.—*In Holland Stands a House.* T. A. out, waving a blanket, then bounced. Beat with hand on table. T. A. does not go far from side of table."

"April 9, 1924.—T. A. rose and in steps approximating *Lavendar's Blue* went lurching about from one store of blankets to another, seizing them, making off with them, and hurling them at another child."

First observable responses and those characteristic of individuals were interesting:

January 24, 1923.—Played rather slowly, *Beethoven Minuet in G* (with violin). D. D. gave a really individual little steppy-toe movement to each staccato eighth note throughout the whole trio.

January 30, 1923.—M. A., new child (20 months) paid more attention when I began *Polichinelle* than others did who have heard it for a month.

February 6, 1923.—*Polichinelle.* M. A. nodded head in time to music for four measures. First response as definite as this.

February 19, 1923.—Played *Skipping* many times. When I stopped and went into Brahms' *Lullaby,* D. D. looked up and said, twice, "I just love that song" (evidently meaning *Skipping*). After the lullaby, I went back to *Skipping.* D. D. looked up and repeated his remark. *Galloping.* D. D. told J. P. it was "about horses." *Jog.* All responded to irresistible rhythm of *Skipping,* especially M. A.—hands, feet, body, head. D. D. with crayons at table gave remarkable finger reaction, the most specialized so far. A hurried skipping motion over the surtace of the table.

March 2, 1923.—A. C. (1 year, 11 months) on stomach at bottom of slide. Kicked legs in air in rhythm with *Skipping.* First response noted.

April 9, 1923.—New child, N. G. (16 months). I played two simple skips. N. G. the only child in room. He stood perfectly still at first then began to sway slightly from one side to the other, watching me all the time.

November 2, 1923.—*Skipping.* D. W. steps forward and back, with a curious bending of the body, yet upper part of body held rigid, especially the neck. A regular fox-trot walk. Seems taught or imitative. She kept it up after the music stopped. Very little spontaneous response noted from her before. When I changed the music, D. W. performed again for a few seconds, then walked to the window. (She continued this bouncy walk for several days.)

November 28, 1923.—T. A.'s activity almost continuous, but not all the same kind. Beethoven, *Minuet, E flat.* Waving hands, regular 1-2-3 for a few measures, then running in time; then, being against slide, bumping against the steps. Sang quietly on one tone long after music had stopped. Off, nodding head at the window. *Birdies.* His whole pace of living quickens when bright quick things are played.

December 18, 1923.—*Skipping.* D. D. P., a distinct pirouette and balancing on toes, arms out. She must sometime have had a model. Looked for an audience. *Birdies.* D. D. P. and S. Y. in chairs, feet tapping. This a new response for S. Y. She now seems much freer—has several different kinds of reactions now—while at first she waved her arms in just one way whenever she heard music.

January 9, 1924.—*Skipping.* N. G. has a bouncy walk, hands in pockets. Has many rhythmic manifestations of short span but excellent spirit. Similarly, S. Y. did a kind of Russian squat dance to *Morning Song,* lasting several minutes. Lovely. A continuity, but little repetition of definite movements.

January 22, 1924.—Lately in going about activities that engage their interest, D. D. P. is full of incidental responses, while M. A. is evidently untouched in any way by the music.

January 29, 1924.—*Skipping.* D. D. P. sitting in chair-train. Feet back and forth from ankle, and moving lips to time of music. M. A. in train, too, but no notice of music. *In Holland.* M. A. and D. D. P. standing over chair, playing with doll. M. A. walking about chair but not influenced by the music. D. D. P. taking steps, sometimes holding one knee bent, or jumping.

April 15, 1924.—J. K. (2 years, 4 months, new) unmoved throughout period until *Minuet in G,* when he began to sway. He caught me watching him and stopped with a shame-faced look.

In this month M. A. began to show again her many and varied expressions that we noted last year. She suffered a lapse that we could not trace. This day when music was announced she went with the others with alacrity and pushed up to the piano as soon as I sat down, but did almost nothing during period.

March 11, 1924.—*Lavendar's Blue*. P. W. got up on D. W.'s chair. She cried out but bore it for some time, then shook back of chair quickly and regularly in rhythm of song. This was not due entirely to music—partly to irritation from P. W.

I felt that some responses that related themselves to phrase lengths were more than coincidental:

April 11, 1923.—During *Minuet in G* (with violin) both D. D. and M. M., drawing carts, would take a few steps and hesitate, then repeat, roughly following the general length of the phrases.

May, 1923.—Activity during a selection of skippy nature with short, choppy phrases, brings a direct response, often exactly on the beat, and distinctly motor. During a selection having longer, more sustained phrases a kind of circle or long-rhythm activity comes,—running or walking in large circles around room, carrying iron or doll to one point and bringing it back, etc.

October 31, 1923.—*Polichinelle*. S. Y. crouched. Remained with knees bent until end of section, two phrases. Did this twice, as I played it over and over without pausing. Seemed almost to wait for end for her release, straightening then.

November 28, 1923.—*Bon Voyage*. D. D. P. running, stopped at end of phrases.

January 25, 1924.—*Skipping*. B. L. waving blanket. Preparation for flinging always came before down beat, and the thrust on the down beat. In phrases.

February 1, 1924.—*Birdies*. S. Y. bending by degrees till squatting position—took her a full phrase to get down.

Occasionally I played a familiar major tune in the minor mode:

March 13, 1923.—When I changed *Skipping* to minor, M. M. looked up and asked, "What's that song?"

April 29, 1924.—P. W.: "Sing *Cock a doodle doo*." I did, several times, then I played it in minor, without singing. P. W. came over to piano, "I don't like it that way."

We met puzzling, uneven responses to the same music.

It may be that we read too much into an experience. We think of a dashing mazurka and become emotionally excited even when we speak of it, talking in more rapid tempo and with animation. The first time the children heard Wieniawski's *Kuiawiak* there was a perfect tumult. The next time everything was decidedly dead.

January 3, 1923.—With violin. Tremendous response from group—body, hands, and feet—all during the French folk songs. J. C. (2 years, 1 month) sitting on table, singing lustily, independently, enjoying herself to the utmost. D. D. P. (23 months) doing a little dance step. All activities stopped, no use of slide. M. F. (2 years, 2 months) started up but stopped on stairway to listen. D. D. (2 years, 11 months) went to all corners of room and looked at violinist as if to get him from every angle. Suddenly, *Kuiawiak*. Almost immediately, deafening bedlam, rising in intensity as music continued (one phrase repeated over and over). D. D. P. (2 years) danced and twirled till dizzy. We played *Au clair de la lune* but there was no abatement until the end of the second playing. Then violin alone, soft, slow, minor—gradually group came back from slide they had been using during the mazurka.

The next time Mr. Veder came, playing the mazurka with vigor, absolutely no attention was paid to it. It might as well have been a lullaby.

May 22, 1923.—*Skipping*. Played many times. D. D. curled up to sleep on the settle. Certainly no impetus to this from the music.

Responses of different children to the same musical stimulus were varied:

February 5, 1923.—*Polichinelle*. M. F. and C. R. came running in from the other room, very brightly, almost skipping. D. D. P. began her pirouetting, without any reference to the rhythm of the music. M. F. imitated, but soon decided to "swim," moving about on stomach and waving arms and legs in the air.

February 16, 1923.—New *Skipping* played. M. A. very rhythmic, especially her feet. J. C. with her regular hippity hop skip across floor. New girl, A. C., did not move during entire period. M. M. eating apple at table, no response. No one else in room.

May 28, 1923.—I felt the necessity of a system of notation for different sorts of spontaneous "dance" steps. Just recording "D. D. stepped to *Galloping* or M. A. stepped to *Skipping*" does not give the distinction there actually was between the two responses. There was no obvious response from M. M. during the four things I played. In *Il court,* which has one phrase repeated many times, she looked up at me, but absolutely unmoved. She maintains a kind of intellectual aloofness or dissociation from the music.

October 26, 1923.—*Birdies.* S. Y., waving arms. Indiscriminate but lovely dancing. Curious response from N. G. Knees flexed, crouch, a stepping forward, lasting about length of phrase, then round, same thing in other direction. S. Y. walking in time in spite of stagger. N. G. crawling on all fours, very rhythmic.

November 8, 1923.—*Bon Voyage.* M. A. on stomach on slide step, legs kicking. N. G., many big muscle responses, but all of short span, not sustained. D. D. P., pushing cart on knees. One knee forward on each 1-2 beat.

January 4, 1924.—*Morning Song.* P. W. on mat at foot of slide. Lying on side, right arm flung back, quiet, left arm down and up on 1-2. Entirely relaxed. N. G., trunk swaying, then knee flexing in time. D. D. P., a nonchalant walk, shrugging shoulders, across room. P. W. running and clapping.

January 11, 1924.—*Morning Song.* N. G. off immediately, combination run, jump, and skip, vaudeville fashion. D. D. P. jumping on one spot, waving arms regularly. B. L. imitating her, but progressing with leaps. Beaming. D. W. walking, swinging arms, relaxed, front and back from shoulders. After I stopped D. D. P. chanted on C above middle C. (Song in Key F.) Nasal tone.

It is evident these children could be taught any set response en masse, but their spontaneous expressions were fully adequate.

Specimen days:

March 14, 1923.—Impossible to take down all the reactions noted while playing. Even A. C. responsive. *Skipping, Bon Voyage, Polichinelle, Birdie, Il court,* and *Dutch Hymn* used. C. R. and M. A. extremely quick in changes. During *Polichinelle* four children had marked reactions, all different but all appropriate.

November 21, 1923.—Sang "Music for —" to each one, then "Ready for music" to same tune. *Cock a doodle doo.* D. D. P., hands on side of piano, jumping up and down to every quarter note. I played twice as slowly, D. D. P. kept exactly the same time, now jumping to every eighth note. D. W. jumping and running with short steps. N. G. singing. M. A., D. D. P. and B. L. evidently interested in the tumbly sound of the words as I sang *Bon Voyage.* In stopping just before the last note, no child has yet sung in that last note. D. D. P. and M. A. in chairs at piano. I said "Can you make your tongue sing too?" M. A. began in strong voice which continued throughout, but at end she said, smiling, "I don't *have* to do it." *Fairies* (light, breathless). P. W. looked up from crying spell. M. A. with wheel in hand, running about in aimless circles. D. W., a curious step, with right foot in air most of the time. D. W. in chair, heels kicking.

May 13, 1924.—New French song. *En roulant ma boule, roulant.* I sang the French words, which have no variation. M. A. and P. W., the only ones who would listen for sense in the words, came to piano. They listened intently. Finally M. A.: "Don't sing that any more" S. Y., over to piano, listened a long time, smiling, watching my lips. Rhythmic response from everyone. M. A. a light skip. P. W. on balcony stamping a perfect 1-2. Even J. K. picked up his chair and moved to a different spot at end of each playing (no stops). *Flemish Song* (allegro, minor). P. W. began racing around table. I played faster, he ran faster. M. A. joined him, tearing at full speed. I stopped. It took them 30 seconds to stop. I began again. T. A. joined the two. Some slackening by them when I played slower. I stopped again. P. W. stopped in 15 seconds. M. A. and T. A. kept it up for a full minute and a half.

SCHOOL RECORDS—AN EXPERIMENT

by

MARY S. MAROT

This report is the result of three
years' research as Recorder of the
Bureau of Educational Experiments

BUREAU OF EDUCATIONAL EXPERIMENTS
144 West 13th Street, New York
1922

DOWN,

DOWN,

DOWN,

DOWN!

SCHOOL RECORDS—AN EXPERIMENT

PURPOSE AND HISTORY

In March, 1918, the Bureau of Educational Experiments began an experiment in school records. The undertaking arose from a practical need felt by all experimental schools,—the need to know what subject matter, equipment, and methods bring promising results. Another desire, held in common with most school experiments, was to accumulate material which should in time contribute towards a better knowledge of children's growth in school. To these ends the Bureau felt it necessary to work directly on the technique of school recording.

At the outset of the experiment the old forms of school reports in common use were discarded as inadequate to convey real information concerning school procedure. The question of form and method of keeping new records was left open, the only requirement being that each record should supply educational data in a sufficiently organized form to be readily used by the Bureau and by the school or teacher co-operating in the experiment.

The active participants in the experiment were the City and Country School (formerly the Play School), the Nursery School, several experimental classes in public elementary schools, and a Recorder. The City and Country School children were from three to nine years old, in groups of eight to fifteen children. The Nursery School children were between one and a half and three years old, in a group of eight children. The public school children were of the First, Fifth, and Sixth Grades. The illustrations in this report are nearly all from notes of these schools, and most of the children were under ten years of age.

For the last two years, to June, 1921, the experiment was confined to the City and Country School and the Nursery School. In both of these schools the recording was attempted by the teachers and by myself. In the public school classes I undertook the classroom recording alone.

The teachers of the City and Country School had been working upon notes of their work for several years before the Bureau began its experiment. They had kept notes of individual children and of the teachers' methods, but they were not well satisfied with their material. They had followed the plan of making daily notes. Most of the teachers in the school followed this plan until the last year of our experiment.

But it was a burdensome method for the teacher, and it was not practical for general use because it set before the reader too unorganized or too detailed a picture.

As recorder I made many notes in these schools and classes, but they also were unsatisfactory, though for another reason. My notes of specific subject matter, for example, always missed significant connecting links which only the teacher could supply. When I tried to record the interesting first reactions of a group of children to some new experience, I had to go to the teacher to find out what other experiences had led up to this one. Moreover, I did not always know which remarks of the children were important enough to record. My usefulness was temporary and experimental. I helped to do part of the work of recording while we were all learning how, and I sifted out and generalized into conclusions the many differences of opinion and the many ways of taking notes.

For a limited time we tried continuous literal note-taking every day, to record certain subject matter. A stenographer had to be specially trained for this type of recording. It was expensive and the notes contained much irrelevant matter. Even an expert stenographer loses much of the significance of the byplay because nobody but the teacher understands its implications. Not even the teacher can catch everything that goes on in a class of children, but she can catch more than anyone else even while she is teaching. The verbatim notes did not prove to be of special help to the teachers and we discarded them except where we desired to quote the children exactly, and we decided that these quoted remarks must be chosen by the teacher in order to assure their significance.

These experiences in recording and the conclusions we drew from them threw the responsibility for making records squarely upon the teachers. The teachers and directors of the City and Country School and the Nursery School accepted this responsibility with my help until June 1921. They were ready then to assume all of the work themselves. The plan finally adopted by the teachers, after much experimenting, was that of taking rough notes daily or less often as expedient, and of making an organized summary of these rough notes at the end of a week. The summary was to be the record. Later sections of this report will give illustrations of the teachers' notes.

The organization of the teachers' summaries was, in each school, the organization which was finally adopted by the school as its guide for procedure as well as for its system of recording. We had experimented with several outlines for organizing the teachers' notes, but no outline proved satisfactory in practice until each school had organized its procedure, and had made this organization a basis for reporting the children's responses.

The teachers in these two schools recorded primarily for their own use and for their school. When their material developed into organized form a demand for the records began to come from other experimental schools. The City and Country School and the Nursery School then decided to mimeograph or to print from time to time records which were more or less satisfactory. Some of these records are now ready.* They are not sent out as finished products, but are tentative both in form and as statements of educational procedure. They are experimental records of experimental procedures. They are limited to those school activities which the teachers themselves are responsible for; they do not include the physician's and psychologist's records. This report also is limited to a discussion of teachers' records.

At the beginning of the experiment I formulated several tentative principles of recording which had grown out of past experience in making school records. The teachers of the City and Country School, and later the Nursery School, cooperated in trying out these principles of recording and in adding to them as working hypotheses. This cooperation was necessary to the success of the experiment. One teacher in particular made the experiment as a whole possible by her untiring willingness to test out hypotheses, and to experiment with various methods of recording. Our experience showed that it must be the class teacher who makes the record of her own class, although other people may make contributions to it. This decision caused us to drop the public school classes as contributors to our study of recording. We could not ask public school teachers to record in our way in addition to making the records required of them by the public school system.

A discussion of recording finds its logical place in a discussion of teaching. Recording is only one of the necessary factors in an efficient teaching procedure. A treatment of recording by itself is presenting the cart without the horse which makes it function. But this experiment was only concerned with recording. We are thus obliged to confine our present discussion to recording, with references to educational procedures only in their application to recording.

---

* See "A Nursery School Experiment," by Harriet M. Johnson, Bulletin XI, Bureau of Educational Experiments, 1922, and "Record of Group VI," by Leila V. Stott, Bulletin of The City and Country School, 1922. Record of several other groups can be obtained in mimeograph from The City and Country School, and a second bulletin, "Record of Group V," is in preparation.

STANDARDS OF OBSERVATION AND GUIDING PRINCIPLES

Our experiment required a definition of terms in order that we, the Bureau and the teachers, should understand each other. When we talked about growth, curriculum, environment and experience, what did we mean? We defined these terms and they became our standards for observing children in school. We tried out several principles as guides to our recording and we adopted those which assisted us in gathering the material we desired.

STANDARDS OF OBSERVATION

The teachers in our experiment made records as an aid to their teaching and as a report of the children's progress in school. They were not responsible for the work of the doctor and the psychologist, nor for the parents at home; and, although they cooperated with all of these people, their own records were records of what came under their own observation. When they talked about growth, for example, they did not mean weight and height, they meant progress in school.

Growth (for teaching purposes) we defined as a child's progress in ability to use his environment. This progress can be indicated only by a continued recording of a child's reactions to an environment. Progress is not continuous in the sense of a constant rate, but it does take place, and how it takes place is what we must observe. For example, a teacher's note in October stated that B.'s attention was held only for a moment by any kind of work. She gave an illustration. In November she reported some progress, "B. steadies now a little better; she is making a more direct connection with the class work; her interest is always awake, but she guesses rather than thinks." Specific reactions to different types of work were given, and it was shown how B. compared with the other children and how she reacted socially. In the following months these points were all followed up until any reader could see how, and in what respects, B. was progressing in her use of the school environment.

Environment (for teaching purposes) consists of those parts of a child's surroundings which may provide experience for him. Environment for us includes the material setup, the children, the teacher, the school, the city streets, and the interrelationships of all of these. A child's environment is not static, it is relative and changing. His environment stimulates him, he responds, and an experience gets started. We must observe these experiences and what part of the environment produces them.

Experience (for teaching purposes) is a child's use of his environment, his participation in it. A school is responsible for supplying to its children opportunities for first hand contacts and for making their own discoveries. The children's progress in ability to get this kind of experience is the measure of their school growth, and the measure of the success of the school environment. The teacher must observe the environment to see that it offers opportunities for this kind of experience.

Curriculum for us is the school's plan in so far as it is successful in providing children with a succession of experiences. Curriculum in this sense therefore is concerned only with those parts of the school surroundings which the children make definite use of. Subject matter, materials, the city streets, what the other children and the teacher bring to the group, are the raw material of the curriculum: when they are utilized by the school and actually give experiences to the children, they become curriculum.

The curriculum is not found in the books the children read, nor in what the teacher tells them, until the children begin to get experience from this presented environment. The course in science is not curriculum until the children begin to get from it, or through it, a stimulus to scientific inquiry; until they begin to ask spontaneous questions, not directly suggested by the teacher but by their own desire to learn. "What is this button?", "What is that jar for?" may or may not be a beginning of scientific inquiry. "This button is not in the same place as that one, what does *it* do?" "There's a wire from that jar. Does it go to a bell? I don't see any bell. Where does it go then? What is it for?" Records of such questions as these indicate that children are making use of the school environment, that they are ready for more experience, are using past experience to draw their own inferences in a new situation and to ask for new explanations.

GUIDING PRINCIPLES

We decided, then, that records would provide reliable data for school purposes only if we made our observations of children's responses with our school definitions of growth, environment, experience, and curriculum clearly in mind. We decided furthermore that our records must contain certain information and must be gathered according to a certain method. This method was supplied by the guiding principles which we adopted.

Records must provide information for making changes in school procedure. Our school records were planned to help the schools to know what they were accomplishing and where to make changes. A school cannot stop satisfied, it must continue to change. A record should help a school to build up standards which it expects to put to use as measures of its efficiency in meeting the needs of its children. For this purpose school records must be under the constant scrutiny of the school staff, who will use them to see that the school environment is successfully providing experience for the children. The various parts of the school curriculum must be subject to change when they no longer effect progress. But the old school methods of recording do not provide specific information which will assist a school in making changes in procedure, either for the benefit of individuals or for the whole class.

The old methods of recording attempt to record individual progress, but they do not succeed in this. "Percents," or "poor," "excellent," carry different meanings to different people. "He has greatly improved in behavior" is an opinion which may or may not be colored by the teacher's personal attitude toward children's behavior; it carries with it no evidence. "Very independent," "good cooperation," "highly original," convey no real information. They are subjective terms which merely give the teacher's own feeling in the case; they supply no basis for comparison, for watching progress. Nobody is independent or original under all circumstances; people cooperate sometimes but not always. A school report, to be of real use, must answer questions like these: "What were the conditions when the child showed independence and who were with him? What part did he play in the group when he cooperated and who were the other children? What kind of activity was going on when he showed originality? Did he differ from the other children in this? Did he generally show originality when working with certain material?"

Whether a child is progressing satisfactorily or not a teacher must be sure that she has real information about his school growth, that she is not depending upon vague impressions, that she is depending upon concrete evidence. When a child is not growing in originality, independence, skill, the power to get knowledge for himself, etc., his teacher must know how he shows this, how he is different from the other children, or like them, and what the environmental conditions are. This information is essential if the teacher's purpose is to find out how to change his environment to fit his needs.

The old school methods of recording lend themselves no better to the purpose of changing the curriculum. A high percentage of a class average in history, or the words "All showed much interest," may mean merely that the children memorized what was presented, or that the teacher made the lessons interesting. What sort of progress these lessons brought to the children is not shown at all. A supervisor could not tell from reports of this kind whether these history lessons were educating the children or not. The only kind of records which show this are records which show the spontaneous reactions of the children to the material presented. Few schools supply such records, and they base most of their changes upon wholly inadequate data, or upon no data at all.

In fact the majority of school records report the child's success or failure; they do not report the success or failure of the environment to fit the children. They ask the children to change; they forget to watch for faults in the curriculum.

The careful observing and recording, the willingness to modify the environment which this new recording implies, take time. But the alertness, initiative and originality which this procedure encourages in teachers when they follow the method should give pause for thought to a superintendent who finds a lack of these virtues among his staff.

Concrete illustrations are necessary to a school record in order that the picture may be clear enough to base changes upon. These illustrations must show the actual activities of the children, what they do in response to what the environment presents to them. A picture of what really happens will contain concrete notes of typical or significant occurrences. For example, a teacher noted what a five-year-old said while playing with his block building. "There is oil in this building. Have to take it up this way." If to this illustration the teacher added, "This dramatic content is characteristic of most of the children's play," or "This play with their building is common to only a few," we should have information to work upon and something to watch for. We should expect future reports to show what changes in building took place, and in what new ways the children played with their structures when built.

A teacher of a certain class was called upon to report what her children were actively engaged in, and what they were getting out of their school time. She chose, as her method of reporting, a detailed word picture of the children's experience during one school day. This day, she stated, was a characteristic one with these children at this particular stage. She then noted that such and such changes in the children had been going on since school began, and that she was watching for other changes. This kind of a report is practical. The supervisor, or the teacher herself, can go back to this report and look forward from it when she wishes to know what her children are achieving.

What the children are achieving is shown only in the responses of the children themselves. What they do is what we wish to know when we ask for a school report. What the teacher gives them makes no difference unless we know what the children do with it. It is only by watching and recording the children's responses that a teacher can give us this information. Only a picture of the children's responses will show whether the school has set up surroundings which bring the desired results and whether the teacher's methods work to the same ends. A report of what subjects and what equipment the school sets up does not show what educational values the children actually get out of these subjects and materials,—that is, how they use them.

Both parents and supervisors wish to know whether the school is a success, a success from the point of view of the children's development. A school may surround the children with everything it can devise as an educational expedient. The children will appropriate and make their own only a part of it. The world as well surrounds children with a varied and complex environment, but much of it makes no impression at all upon them so far as we can see. What we wish to know about a school is what does make an impression and what impressions assist in the children's school growth. The only reports which can give us this information are reports which show the children's developing and changing reactions to the school environment.

Records which are to show school progress must show processes of growth in the school. It is *how* a child attacks his work or play which determines his growth. It makes little difference whether he learns the capitals of all the states, but much difference whether he is forming the habit of going after what he wants to know when he wants to know it. He may want to know the chief salt manufacturing city to-day; he may not need to know the capital of his state until he is a man. It is the habit, the process, which is important. This process of growth is what we must watch and cultivate and record. It is not measured by the quantity of geography or spelling he is accumulating.

A record of growth processes (for a teacher's purpose) must be a report of what takes place *while the children are learning*. An examination shows only how much information they have acquired, and a recitation seldom shows more. A school that undertakes to watch processes, and to base its procedure and what it supplies of subject matter upon what it knows about the children's habits of thinking and habits of working, will find little need to worry about how much the children know. A teacher in such a school will be kept busy satisfying the children's demands for knowledge. A record of processes of growth in school will show that a child's environment acts continuously. He reacts to it continuously and spontaneously, but not with the systematic regularity of the formal school programs and reports. Both the child and the environment change. We did not make use of the formal school reports, and we also did not use the modern objective tests of the psychologists for our school records nor the standardized measurements of progress in school subjects because they do not show this continuous interaction and change between the children and their environment. We needed to know as much as possible about the children's processes of growth in school in order to teach them, and we could get this information only from records which would show (so far as it practically could be recorded) the children's continuous interaction with their environment.

The activity of the group must be observed and recorded. Our purpose in recording was to study children's habits of learning in school. A child's habits in the school environment are formed while he is among other children. Other children are an influence in his growth. Consequently we based our records upon notes of the group activities which surrounded him and of which he was a part. Children acquire most of their knowledge in company; we teach them together. We must know the group's reaction to the environment if we wish to find out what brings about the growth of habits in school, and what changes in curriculum we must make in order that better habits may be formed or that progress may continue.

Detached reports of individuals, whether percentage ratings or descriptive words, do not show what is actually going on. They do not show an individual's progress in experience, and still less do they show the success of subject matter, materials, or the teacher's method. An average percentage of the individual successes or failures in a class gives no real information about a subject that has been studied by the children. It gives no indication of the complete situation, of the influences which, acting together, produce the effect. The only record which will show the curriculum in the sense of our definition, with its effects in growth, is an account of children and teacher working together,—a record of group activity.

The teacher herself must be the recorder. The only person who can approach a telling of the whole story of the children working together in their daily school activities is the teacher. A teacher who accustoms herself to watching the group as a whole, to seeing interrelationships that take place, will appreciate the value of group records. The very necessity of observing group reactions in order to report them, will make a teacher more keenly alive to the influences of social contact. She is the only person who is in a position to see the majority of these interrelationships and who is able to estimate their value. It is she also who brings about a continuity of experience, who suggests and supplies new subject matter or materials as they are needed. It is the teacher, then, who must be the recorder of the activities of her own group of children, in order that there may be continuity and accuracy in the recording.

A teacher should also be a recorder for her own benefit. Recording in some systematic fashion is the only way for a teacher to check up her own procedure, to make sure that she knows what is continuous, what brings interruptions, what is important, what is merely trivial occurrence. A teacher cannot trust her memory, her unsupported opinion. Even a highly skilled teacher needs something to guide her in making changes, and in deciding when these changes should be made.

The impulse to record by the teachers of the City and Country School and the Nursery School is that of the experimenting scientist. One of these teachers said of recording: "In any scientific experiment notes are necessary. A teacher in an experimental school should keep track of individual children, and also of the steps taken in the class work. She should do this in order to follow up and compare results with different procedures. She should include enough of the children's responses to compare one procedure with another," as well as for the purpose of keeping track of individuals.

The organization of a school's record material will correspond to its organization of procedure if its records are to be of use to the scool. In our experiment no outline or organization proved satisfactory until each school concerned decided in the first place why it was keeping records; that is, how the school wished to use them, who wished to use them, and what information they should contain. Secondly and obviously this information must be so arranged that it could be readily used. Finally, the headings under which the teachers' notes were organized must be as objective as possible in order to be intelligible and to be unmistakable in their meaning. We experimented with the terms "creative activity" and "cooperation," among others, but they were not concrete enough. They did not mean the same thing to all who used them.

The teachers of the two schools which were experimenting adopted different outlines for organizing their notes. These outlines may quite fail to meet the needs of other schools who have children of the same age. But whether they do or not is beside the point; the point is that an organization of any kind within a school is more likely to be lived up to in practice when it is made by the people who have the responsibility of carrying it out.

A record of recording, which this report undertakes to be, must fulfill its own demand that a record shall provide concrete illustrations. I have divided these illustrations into two heads for practical reasons of reference,—Records of Curriculum Functioning, and Records of Individual Children. This division is made in answer to two common questions from experimental school people: "How can I let a new teacher know what our course of study means and how we use it?" and "How can we make the children's reports give real information to the next teacher?" Our own queries were, what kind of records will best serve our schools, and what information must these records give as a basis for changes in curriculum?

The discussion of these two topics, Records of Curriculum Functioning, and Records of Individual Children, will contain many repetitions because they are based upon the same guiding principles and the same standards of observation. But the illustrations have been chosen from school occurrences which in the one case were weighted with curriculum information, and in the other with information about individuals. Often an illustration telling about an individual would also indicate the curriculum just as well. But this only serves to confirm what the discussion of our guiding principles implies, and what our experience proved for us, that one and the same record must be used for recording both curriculum and individual progress, and that neither record will be clear if these interrelated topics are kept separate.

RECORDS OF FUNCTIONING OF CURRICULUM

FORMAL CURRICULUM DETERMINED BY TRADITION OR AUTHORITY

The traditional school curriculum only recently has become open to suggestions of fundamental changes. It is difficult for any of us to see clearly enough to break away from the old leading strings. Most of us still keep the old course of study, the subject matter required for culture, even when we add other more practical subjects. We still ask "When?" We ask at what age shall this cultural subject be placed in the course of study. We do not ask, "What is the evidence that this subject is cultural?" It may be, but we only have hearsay to prove it. No school can be sure that such and such a subject is good or otherwise unless it has concrete evidence at hand.

Schools have based their choice of subjects and materials and methods, not upon concrete information showing their own use or need, but upon what has been done before by other schools. When school directors do contemplate making changes, they adopt those a school somewhat like their own has found successful; or they plunge into a haphazard method, first this and then that device or material. When these prove misfits, they look up another authority whose plan they try.

Superintendents who wish information usually inquire whether the children have learned all that the teacher has been directed to set before them, and what they have been unable to learn in the time allowed. They seldom ask whether the children have acquired the habit of making use of whatever may be about them which contributes to their experience of the subject under discussion; whether the children themselves have been making spontaneous contributions to the group's progress in learning. If a superintendent should ask such questions his teachers would have no adequate data by which to answer them. Few schools have these data; they do not have evidence to base their changes upon. Many teachers, when asked for information, advise materials or methods because the children like them, or because the teacher herself is used to them and does not wish to change. This unwillingness to change is not always due to inertia or indifference. Both superintendents and teachers are a hard-working class. They do not wish to change because no convincing reasons are given for the changes proposed, and because no way is suggested of finding out whether the new will be any more successful than the old. The usual trial and error method of making changes is discouraging to a teacher. She has no standards of observation, no organized and continuous method of recording to guide her.

The difference between a school having a flexible curriculum determined by its own conditions and one that is run on traditional lines is simple. The former starts out with the knowledge that we still know very little about what makes children learn and grow. It bases its choice of an environment upon what it knows about the children who will come to the school. It chooses an equipment which can be changed at least in part as changes are needed. The school then watches and records how this environment (including the children themselves) reacts upon the group as a whole, whether it promotes school progress, and how it may be changed in order to bring better results.

The usual formal school on the contrary provides a course of study which is based upon what the school has decided beforehand that the children should know and how the children should act. This traditional curriculum can be changed at best only at the end of the year. It is widely recognized as inadequate and cumbersome, and in the end expensive of time and energy. Schools unlike in procedure or in enrollment adopt the same course of study,—tradition or authority decide upon it for them. Schools which make changes as they are needed in their own classes are rare. Still more rare are schools which depend upon their own carefully kept records for suggestions of changes in subject matter, equipment and method.

TEACHERS' RECORDS A BASIS FOR DETERMINING CURRICULUM

Data showing what experiences the children get out of the environment provided by the school, give a practical basis for making changes in the course of study, in the material equipment, in the teacher's methods. The teacher can best supply these data. Only the teacher can show the steps, the processes of growth in school. The Nursery School says of note-taking, "We set up hypotheses" but without "our own notes" . . . "we cannot make accurate discriminations, . . . We must have evidence in order to prove or disprove and to change."

Systematic concrete notes are a check to the teachers who write them. They furnish a supervisor with material for judging what it is that is bringing progress or the reverse. A school principal sees "spots" when he sets forth on a tour of inspection. He does not see what preceded nor what will follow the lessons that he observes, he only sees what is going on at the moment. He can gain enlightenment only through continuous records, records which are concrete enough to take the place of his own sight, and which will supplement his isolated visits. The Director of the City and Country School has such notes to read. From one teacher she had notes upon number and drawing which covered a considerable period of time. After reading these notes she made calls during class time, and was able to make helpful practical comments because she had concrete information for a discussion with the teacher of changes in method.

RECORDS OF SPECIAL SUBJECTS

A teacher's systematic concrete notes are the only safe basis for determining the value to children of special subjects of study. A certain subject was adopted in one school because the teacher's plan of work and her materials seemed very attractive and suitable. After months of trial the class teachers expressed varying degrees of satisfaction, and equally varied opinions about the effect upon the children of this subject matter and its presentation. Nobody had notes to back up their opinions; the teachers supplied only isolated, remembered incidents. The school wished to reach a just and reliable conclusion and began careful notes of the children's responses to these lessons. Notes were made of all the lessons in all the classes for some months because the information that had gone before had been confusing. It was contradictory; it was opinion, not concrete evidence. Summaries were made of this new body of continuous, concrete information, summaries of the responses of the children at different ages.

These summaries gave rise to general conclusions about each class and together they formed an intelligent basis for decisions upon the subject matter as a whole. In a class of three-year olds the children merely looked on. They were either quite passive or were excited; they showed no initiative towards the material and soon wandered off to some more active occupation. In this class the subject was dropped; there was no growth for the children, they gained no habit of learning for themselves. In an older class the children were so pleased, so attentive and responsive, that only a continuous record over several months served to show that these children also only looked on. They made exclamations of pleasure; but they took little action on their own account; they acted upon what the teacher suggested, "Do you want to . . . ?" The subject as presented did not arouse the spontaneous inquiries of these children; it did not of itself stimulate action. The lessons were an entertainment only; the children's activities had to be directed by the teacher. Notes of the other classes were equally illuminating, and the school finally gave up the special lessons but kept the subject in an altered form. The teachers kept notes of the changes in procedure which they had made that they might have data for future judgments.

A mere list of subject matter topics is of use neither to a new teacher nor to parents. Catalogues of private schools are obliged to add photographs to show the children's active use of the subject presented. The actual response of the children is needed to tell the tale. Traditional subject matter terms do not describe these reactions. "History: the Revolutionary War" gives no real information. The following notes show what the children did: "The class paid three visits to the ruins of an old fort. They read up local history between visits, and reconstructed the positions of the two armies on the spot, comparing their respective advantages and disadvantages. These comparisons unexpectedly led to the discovery that the course of the stream close by had changed since revolutionary days, and the discussions that followed formed a new topic which required a good deal of research by the children in geography books."

The teacher of a new class cannot afford to neglect the information about the class contained in the preceding teacher's notes. A teacher of eight-year-old children did not look up what their teacher of the year before had written about them. Her own notes criticised their slowness in arithmetic. She said she had "tried having a match, . . . which the children were not familiar with." In this case it was the teacher who was not familiar with her children. The notes of their previous teacher showed that they had delighted in all sorts of arithmetic games and matches the year before. When, in January, the second teacher read the previous year's notes of these children she frankly admitted that she herself had confused and retarded them by not finding out what they had done before. She had asked for quantitative reports,—how many, how much of each kind of subject matter, and for some time she was not interested in concrete reports of the children's responses, or how children use material, but only in what she or a preceding teacher had presented.

Important facts to get into a record are those which tell whether the subject noted has developed spontaneous activity on the part of the children, and what conditions, or what treatment of the subject by the teacher helped to bring spontaneous response from the children. The notes of a teacher of seven-year-old children show their active use of number and the spontaneous drill they gave each other in order to achieve a group response.

NOVEMBER SUMMARY: The feeling of a need for number has centered largely around the store. The class office of treasurer is a highly esteemed one, and it was decided by the group that only children passing certain tests could aspire to it. The tests are reading and writing numbers to 100 by ones, fives and tens. As soon as anyone passed these tests he began helping the others. . . . A certain facility in making change is also demanded of anyone wishing to sell food (which the children had made) at the sales. Two or three times in a free period the children have played store. On the 8th C. with some help counted to 40, the seven others listening intently. (A free period is undirected by the teacher.) . . . The children feel responsible for slow children on account of the store.

A class teacher of six-year-olds also reported a spontaneous use of the school environment. Her notes included the children's use of information brought from home,—their contribution to others' use as well as their own use,—and her method of organizing their activities and the information made use of during class discussions. Class discussion time was the teacher's opportunity to encourage a habit of inquiry, and to make use of the children's spontaneous inquiries to organize their information and to connect it with common occurrences in their daily lives.

> Week of February 7.—The block scheme this week was entirely spontaneous and well launched before I saw it. It involved an iron mine drawn in chalk on the floor by Cl. "An iron factory" . . . "where the iron is melted up and made into things," was built near by. Close to the factory docks were built, and barges pulled by tugs were loaded with iron products, and taken to "N. Y."
> As this play scheme carried over several days and included nearly all the class, I made it the subject of Thursday's discussion. The interest was chiefly in pursuing the mining end of iron industry and the children introduced the subject of the use of dynamite for breaking up rocks containing iron. They were very much interested in the details of dynamite explosion, wanted to know what made the rocks break, how dynamite could be set off without blowing up the man who lighted it. Comparisons were made (by the children) to the push of hot air as seen in their science experiments, and to the familiar push of steam.

Other notes of the same class show the children's experience in language and some of the teacher's ways of getting practice and originality.

> Week of February 7.—L. for the first time told an original story. I had to suggest the topic, home experiences, and keep out extraneous matter by criticisms, . . . but he enjoyed the effort and produced a pretty good narrative. E. also told several stories which she wanted written into a book she had made, to correspond to the illustrations. M. on Friday dictated a story meant to be dramatized. All were enthusiastic about the idea and went up to the sun room to prepare for playing it. . . . (They arranged a stage setting of blocks.) . . . The story included a two nights' journey on a ship, which was tossing badly in a storm. . . . M. made a real attempt to picture in words the rolling of the boat on the waves. He began by using gestures to help out, and C. gave him the word "tossing," but the rest was all his own, and he used a sort of refrain to emphasize the roughness of his trip. Proof of his success in this seemed to me to be found in the fact that the other children featured the stormy trip in their dramatization later and did so not in his words, but in motor expressions of their own.

In L.'s and E.'s stories I put all my effort into centering their attention on unity of thought, as both were much inclined to wander off into
irrelevant concerns.

Another record of language teaching in a class of six-year-old children is a record by a special teacher of English who was making an
experiment along new lines. Her report is a statement of her purposes,
of how she planned to work them out, and of her success as shown in
several of the children's stories. This was not a planned-beforehand-
and-put-through so-called experiment. It was an experiment carried
out by the special teacher assisted by the class teacher, both of whom
watched and recorded the children's responses, and changed the approach,
the teacher's suggestions, to fit these responses of the children. It was a
scientific experiment. The purpose was the development of an art, but
this in no way altered the necessity for a scientific recording of results.
The report, part of which follows, was written after a careful study of
the concrete notes taken by both teachers. It was accompanied by several
of the group stories, only one of which is given here.

The work in language with the Sixes in the Spring of 1920 was
started distinctly as a pre-reading experience. I had two primary aims.
The first was to get the children interested in listening to sounds in general,—street sounds, water splashing in the tub, the fire, etc.,—and so
gradually to the sound quality of language, both of individual words and
their rhythm when combined into sentences. The second aim was to
get the children to give verbal expression to their sense and motor experiences. The school felt that listening and verbal expression might be
regarded as preliminary techniques to the technique of actual reading.
The method used for this pre-reading training was experimental. It included the reading of much verse and a few stories which had marked
rhythmic and sound quality, and the telling by the class of group stories.
I tried to have each period include some listening and some expression
by the children.

All the group stories aimed to make vivid some experience common
to all. When possible, we chose an experience—such as rain on a rainy
day—in which we could make immediate sense observations instead of
relying upon memory. This definitely interested the children and gave
them an idea of a story in which plot did not predominate. Sometimes
in order to get the whole group to think about the same thing in their
group stories I introduced pictures. I chose pictures which had little
narrative suggestion. The children discussed how the picture made them
feel, as "sleepy" or "cool and quiet" or "happy and dancing." Then
they told the story, various children volunteering and I writing down
their remarks, frequently reading back the story as far as it was written. We agreed to put into the stories only the things which made us
feel "sleepy" or "cool and quiet" or "happy and dancing." The children
quickly became their own critics. Some of the group stories had real
literary merit.

Second group story, told on a rainy day: The rain is falling. It's
damp and cold. It's coming down in flocks. It's part cloudy and part

sunny. And it's half and half. It's raining in New York, but maybe not in California. The rain goes pitter-patter on the windows. It falls on the umbrellas. The rain drips off the roofs on the houses. The little wet drops they fall on your face. We all get wet. The rain falls on the ground and our shoes get all wet. The rain falls on people's hats in the street. And the men run when they haven't any umbrellas. The rain falls on your rain hats and falls on your face. Your foot hits a puddle and the water splashes up on your knee.

RECORDS OF GROUP METHODS OF LEARNING

A teacher's record of curriculum functioning is not complete unless she supplies information which will show how the children are learning together. The children work and play together, and they influence each other as grown people influence other grown people's ideas and actions. Realizing this, schools make provision for social play time. Some schools also make provision for studying and learning together,—a social organization not simply allowed because a class is too large to be taught as isolated individuals, but deliberately planned because learning together is part of the experience of living together, which experience we wish all children to be ready to share.

When the Director of the City and Country School, after visiting class-rooms and reading the teachers' notes, sees a common need for some specific suggestions she sends them out to the teachers in the form of bulletins which help the teachers both in their teaching procedure and in their recording. The bulletin which follows points up this school's emphasis upon group discussions in each class as a method of organizing the children's information and of encouraging the habit of making their own inquiries.

> Bulletin. . . . Perhaps this is a good place to emphasize the fact that what makes for social organization in our school groups is: (1) the common experiences the children have in their past and are still working on; (2) the organized body of information which they have and which is common to the majority of the group. These two things are inseparable and can be separated only for convenience in discussion. What we wish to catch and record is not so much what the children are exposed to as what they get. This may be obtained only by specific recording of discussons, activities, and inquiries.

The use of a group discussion period for teaching language was illustrated in the preceding topic. A discussion period is always a language period. The following record also illustrates the teacher's use of this opportunity to help the children to organize their information and to plan their activities.

A MONTH'S SUMMARY: OCTOBER —Six-year-old children. "Discussions have included the school program, practical needs such as . . . the election and duties of a class committee, . . . marking the attendance. . . . Other discussions have dealt with different types of farms. . . . All of this has centered very clearly around the children's play schemes. . . . The children's lead has been followed rather than a definite program of information and has led off occasionally from the general subject of farms to specific interests. . . . The general purpose of the discussions has been to encourage language expression in the group, and to find out what information the children have available for use in their play and to help this to function.

Week of February 21—(Same class.) The last two days of the week the discussions returned to the general subject of geography. On Thursday we reviewed the origin of rivers and in particular the source of the Hudson and the way water is brought from the Catskills to supply New York City in connection with—(their science teacher's) illustration of this. I read the story of the Singing Water, recapitulating the informational material, and it held their attention well. . . . On Friday morning the picture map of the city and harbor proved very absorbing, and all took turns in very orderly fashion. . . .

Week of February 28.—Children from five to six years old. Enthusiasm was high on Monday over the new blocks which had been stacked in the room over the week-end. Almost as soon as he was seated (for discussion of the morning's work) . . . B. M. said, "Oh, let's build a town." This fired the group, and one said, "Let's put in a church," another . . . Since there was now such deviation from the first suggestion of a town, I remarked, "If we are going to put in all of these things, we'd better build New York City." This was taken up at once, and I sent a child for a map. . . . The buildings had all been on or near Broadway or Fifth Avenue. I pointed out these streets to the children on the map. We found the north and south, then discussed the best arrangement in the room to show uptown and downtown. This came readily, for we have had games of direction in the room. . . . The next day I showed the children pictures of the buildings they had chosen. . . . T. Z. had built Old Trinity the day before. He had put it downtown, but not on Broadway, and the construction was not a creditable one. After seeing the picture he said, "It is going to be different when I take it down and build it on Broadway."

The scheme was a general one, each child co-operated by making his own contribution of one or more buildings. . . . Occasionally two or more worked on the same building.

Week of March 7.— . . . This (week's) scheme as that of the previous week was initiated very evenly in the group. The suggestions were given rapidly and with excitement. One child did not wait for another to get an idea, but was ready with his own.

Discussion time may bring opportunity for a group's control of their own behavior as well as of their work during a free (undirected) hour. An observing teacher's notes of such an occasion are given below. The class of nine-year-old children was taught by Miss B.

Before beginning, Miss B. remarked, "There is a serious thing for just one hour, do you remember it?" Several children replied, "Yes,

H. and T." Miss B. cautioned, "Don't mention names. . . . You all understand?" . . . The two boys then went into the most secluded corner of each room. Their punishment had been chosen by themselves, at H.'s suggestion. . . . Both were very conscientious. . . . When Miss B. called "Time's up!" both boys went quietly to look at . . . (something which had been going on during their hour of punishment, but which they had not watched).

A few minutes after the announcement that the hour was up, Miss B. said to the class president, "They are not putting away." Said J. (the president), "They won't put them away." Miss B. laughed at a president's tolerating this, and made suggestions how to manage. Then they sat down to report "whether you did, during your free period, what you said you were going to do; . . . whether it was something harder and better than before." There was close attention to this brief suggestion of Miss B.'s and to the reports from each child about his satisfaction with the work he had done; close attention from all but P. All the children made reports that the teacher and children were satisfied with except P. and M. P. said she was satisfied with the work she had done, and when no one commented, Miss B. merely said she did not agree with her. M. said he had nothing to say, and he had to be prodded before he would give any account of his wasted time.

Records of trips taken by a group in search of information or on errands to buy something are very fruitful sources of information to the teacher and the school about how and what the children are learning together; how they are developing, through their own spontaneous inquiries, the habit of going after the information they want when they want it,—going after it themselves, not waiting until it is handed out to them.

Week of May 9.—Four-year-old children. On Monday the children went with me to the butcher's on 8th Street to get meat for the turtles. On the way back they noticed men apparently mending the roadway, and asked to look at it. We crossed the street and found three men making a square hole in the ground. M. said, "Why are you doing that?" A man replied that they were trying to mend electric light wires. One man was holding an iron bar with a sort of tongs while two others hammered on this to break up the stone under the roadway. A. explained to me that the man wasn't holding the bar with his hands for fear he might get hammered. Some stones loosened, the workman leaned over and picked out pieces with his hands. "Why doesn't he use a shovel?" asked M., just before the man did reach out for his shovel. The men were so impressed by this time with the children's intelligence that they told me we could see the wires in a hole farther up the street. . . . T. remarked that some trolley wires are above ground, so we looked at the cable between the tracks on 8th Street.

Another group of four-year-olds made several trips to see a concrete mixer. The teacher did not point things out, she answered questions. On their second trip, they asked among other questions, "Who makes it turn around,—that man over there?" "How does he open it?" The same children on another trip stopped to look at a sewer being cleaned.

"Where is the other pail?" some of them asked when only one came up.
"How did they make the fire?" in the small iron stove.

While the extension of Seventh Avenue was being built the five-year-olds were especially interested in watching its construction. The following are my summaries of their teacher's more detailed notes of their many visits.

> NOVEMBER.—During the first trip the children noticed the piles of stones, dirt, sand, etc. During their second visit they were too absorbed to raise inquiries about the wonderful mixing machine, the men carting stones, sand and cement to put into it, and others dumping out the mixture. Miss M. let them watch the whole show in silence for fully twenty minutes. On the third visit they were again absorbed and asked no questions. They were not asked any until their return to school, when it was found that every child but one had taken in all the processes of the machine and could describe them accurately.
>
> DECEMBER.—On the fourth visit the children remarked, "Stones and sand and cement all go into the big wheel" . . . "they get mixed up inside the wheel" . . . "The water gets into the wheel through the rubber pipe." They were told the name "concrete mixer." On their return to school they gave separate accurate accounts (except one child). While passing by some days later bound for another destination the children called out "There's our friend!" When asked what part of the road the mixer had been on and where concrete had not yet been deposited, they jumped up and down and pointed to show that they could tell by feel as well as by their eyes.
>
> JANUARY.—The children pointed out to Miss G. where the mixer had filled in, that they could walk on it, and that where "it was only dirt" the mixer had not been at work. They told her how the concrete was made. On another day they watched the stones laid, the tar and then the sand put on top, and described it all. Miss M. asked what would be the next thing they would see on another trip and some of them shouted "Horses and automobiles."

RECORDS OF EMOTION, OF FATIGUE

Records of emotional states, of fatigue, are not available in most schools. Sometimes a single incident of a spectacular type is recorded, but no isolated occurrence is valuable as evidence of cause. "I think so and so is very bad for the children," or "A. and B. were very much tired out after . . . " are the usual contributions to questions about what brings fatigue or irritability, etc., in school. The concrete data, systematically recorded over a sufficient period of time are lacking. Keeping notes of many instances of the emotion in question, with the surrounding circumstances, is the only method which will produce evidence upon which we can base our judgements.

The matter of fatigue is given a good deal of attention in private schools where doctors and psychologists assist the teachers. But specific data of experiences in school are not often at hand. A teacher, B., said, "Whenever I go into A.'s room I am impressed by the quiet and good order everywhere. My children are so often noisy; I am sure I let them get too excited." She was asked what she had recorded; had she notes that showed which activities aroused excitement; whether they always did so; which children were most excited, how they showed it; etc. She had some notes in answer to the last question, but nothing adequate upon any. She had very full notes of individual cases of excitement but the complete conditions were not noted. There was not an accurate following up to show whether there was repetition under similar conditions, nor how the children in the other teacher's room reacted under similar conditions.

This question of excitement and fatigue was often brought up by A, B, and other teachers during several years. They questioned their own procedures or criticized the environment; and they made some changes, by guess not by concrete evidence. They asked and accepted advice from the doctor and the psychologist. But no decisions were reached,—there were not sufficient data to make sure of anything, there was only vague opinion. The only suggestive contribution was made at a meeting when A. and B. each read her record of the content of her group's activities,—the information they used and how they used it. The contrast in richness of content and in productive activity was strong and in favor of B.'s class. The query then narrowed to, "Which is better for children of this age, the rich experience going on in B.'s room, or the much less active but serene and quiet experience in A.'s room?" There was no evidence to answer this question in regard to fatigue.

An interesting beginning has been made in recording emotional states by the Nursery School. Notes are taken to determine just what produces strain in individuals and in the group, so that changes may be made in the environment as indicated. The following illustrations of their recording are especially admirable in the way points made in a preceding summary are followed up:

> Week of January 24.—The children play together with almost no friction or crying, a very different atmosphere without J. (one of the oldest children.)
> Summary at end of January.—Integration of group seems still further advanced, that is, the integration of the two groups each within itself. There is a very distinct line dividing the babies from the older children (two or three years). The friendliest relations prevail between groups, and the "Bigs" show great forbearance with the little ones who naturally interfere considerably. . . .
> Summary at end of March.—As a whole the group atmosphere is serene most of the time since J. left. . . .

RECORDS OF EQUIPMENT

A school's equipment is a significant part of the environment which provides experience for the children. It is used by the children; and a record of how they use it, what experience they get out of it, is necessary if we wish to know whether the equipment we have supplied to the children has contributed to their growth, and whether we shall continue to use it.

A school cannot afford to guess at the usefulness of its material set-up. Teachers must record what use has been made of the materials provided when they ask for more or when they ask for changes. A teacher of six-year-old children was asked whether she needed more blocks. "Yes," she replied, but when further inquiries were made as to how many more. she did not know. She did not know whether they were used for social play or quite individually. Another teacher said she needed no more blocks, yet a frequent visitor had noticed repeatedly that the same two or three boys used up all the blocks before anyone else had a chance to get at them. A teacher of the same grade in the City and Country School reported specifically that she needed twice as many blocks and gave the sizes she wanted. She had recorded and followed up for weeks to find out which children used the blocks, how many used them at the same time, at what stage in the building the blocks were apt to give out, and how worth while was the activity that the blocks commonly stimulated.

A teacher of six-year-olds in another school asked for more balls. She had no record of use and was disconcerted when she was asked whether the balls were used individually or in group play. She was further confused by the question whether the same children used them each time. She had never been asked such questions before. "I guess so," was all she could reply. Requests for more equipment are based upon guesswork in many schools. Another teacher noted, "two long chains were added to the yard equipment to-day, and greatly delighted the children. Their first use was . . . Later the chain was attached . . . Still later . . ., etc." This was a promising beginning to work from, to report changes in use. But these chains were not mentioned again in this teacher's notes. If they were never used again, a statement of just this fact would have been adequate for further inquiry at least.

A systematic recording of the concrete facts, followed up to report changes or nonchanges of use, is the only method of getting reliable data about school materials. The following illustrations are from the notes of teachers in the City and Country School. These notes were not written to report the use of materials only; they were part of each teacher's regular weekly summary. Each summary was a record of how the children had been learning during that week and how the curriculum had functioned to stimulate their learning processes.

> Week of March 7.—Four-year-olds. Block building. The squares, half squares, prisms and cylinders introduced last week were the only blocks used this week and they brought about entirely new types of construction. Towers were made several days of the week. . . . M. was able to place her blocks so accurately that her tower, which was about five inches above my head, remained standing all morning. The upper half was made entirely of the small cylinders. M. A. and A. tried to imitate the towers, but . . . , etc.
>
> Week of Feb. 7.—Six-year-olds. Yard play. Outdoors the play in the morning has been principally with the big slide and knotted rope, and "jumping" on the swing. D. is now completely a part of the social group. . . . He and C. have played together in a box house every afternoon, using the big blocks for furniture and stairs, and building a roof of boards. M. and S. have found a congenial interest in . . . E. and Cl. played together on the slide a good deal, inventing games like last week . . . , etc.
>
> Week of March 7.—Six-year-olds. Shop. In the shop most of the children are working on articles wanted for specific purposes, like a box to plant flowers in at home, toy furniture for doll houses . . . , a bird house . . ., and a bread board.
>
> Week of January 31.—Three-year-olds. The slide. A new game developed. J. B. and D started it, P. and J. F. joined: another step in J. F.'s better, physical activity. (The game was described in detail here.) They all tumbled off together in gales of laughter. J. F.: "Oh, isn't it fine!" More abandon by him than I have ever seen before. Great abandon by J. B. going down slide backwards. No other child has done this, though a few have announced that they wanted to and have climbed the steps to the top of the slide for that purpose but have changed their minds when actual time came for letting go their hands.

Records of the curriculum,—of subject matter, materials, etc., kept by one school will be invaluable to other schools having children of the same age. Mistakes and discoveries by one are enlightening to another school. There should be a free interchange of such records between schools.

RECORDS OF INDIVIDUAL CHILDREN

TRADITIONAL OPINION OR CONCRETE DATA AS BASIS FOR CHANGES IN ENVIRONMENT

Our experiment in recording held to the same guiding principles and the same standards for observing individual children that we used in records of the curriculum. The discussion of records of individuals will repeat many of the same arguments, and the illustrations used will often be records of curriculum as well as of individuals. As I have said before, this repetition is necessary for the purpose of answering the question which is so frequently being asked by school people, "How can we make children's reports give real information?"

Our experience proved for us that the same data are needed for information concerning individual children as for the curriculum, and that neither record will give full and clear information if these two points of view are kept separate. When we wish to take intelligent action, in the case of individuals or to change the environment, we must have concrete data of the children's own activities; we must observe and record processes of growth in school; we must report group responses in order to tell the whole story; and the teacher is the only recorder who can approach a recording of the whole environment and can estimate its importance in terms of continuous experience.

Grown people's judgments are seldom based upon closely observed activities of children. The most well informed of us still judge the behavior or the scholastic achievements of children in school more or less by traditional standards. We are dependent upon what we, in common with most other people, believe a child "should" learn, and how he "should" behave. As in the case of the curriculum, we have only recently begun to doubt, to suspect that our traditional ideas about children may be mistaken. We have only recently begun to watch the responses of the children themselves in order to discover what these responses really mean. We are beginning to find out that they frequently mean something quite different from what we have supposed, and that our action in regard to these responses must be quite different from the action we have been in the habit of taking.

When we wish to understand a child we must observe not only his responses, but what it is in the environment (so far as we can see) which stimulates these responses,—these behaviors and interests and accomplishments. Perhaps something other than what tradition has taught is the real source of stimulus. Some non-scholastic people go so far as to say that the most valuable training, the most important experiences for living the lives we all have to live, come not from school but from outside of school. Schools have not looked upon themselves in this light; but if it be true, it is a challenge which the schools must answer. They must find out what share the schools should take in supplying opportunities for these experiences. Psychologists have recently made large contributions to our knowledge of how we learn, of what teaches us. Teachers have contributed little; in fact engineers and other business men have contributed more by showing their dissatisfaction with the uneducated products which the schools turn out.

Psychologists are more and more commonly basing their judgments upon concrete data, less and less upon subjective inferences of what is probably the matter. A teacher must follow the same method. She must follow it for herself. She cannot, even in schools where a psychologist is part of the school staff, wait for the psychologist's examinations. She needs to know too often, she needs to know what to do. Moreover it is the teacher alone who has opportunity to see the children's day-after-day behavior, and their influence upon each other. She is responsible for changes in the school environment which shall bring continued progress for each of her children. She must depend upon her concrete data for information that will indicate what changes she should make in the school environment.

The measure of a child's growth (for a teacher's purposes) is his progress in ability to use his environment to satisfy his own purposes. This was our standard of what we must observe to know whether growth is taking place. It is his own experiences which teach him, it is the satisfaction of his own purposes which brings experiences to him; it is these experiences which a teacher must watch and record if she wishes to understand him. The environment that a child uses, through which he gets his experiences, consists of people as well as things, and his desires are both social and material. It is the school's business to provide the material and social setting which shall supply each child with an environment which he can use and which the school can change to fit his growing needs. It is the school's business to know whether these needs are being satisfied. It can only know by the help of concrete records of the children's activities.

The recording of children's activities, of their processes of learning and growing, for the sake of having a reliable basis for making changes in the school environment, is chiefly for the school's own information. These records relieve the home of no responsibility for changes which the home makes. But they form a basis for bringing home and school into cooperation instead of into conflict, which percentage reports, for example, so often do just because they convey no real information and in consequence are confusing and misleading. The City and Country School and the Nursery School have been working upon reports to parents and reports from parents. These reports are based upon the teachers' and the parents' concrete notes of the children's responses to the school and the home environments. These schools have worked upon home reports independently of the experiment now being discussed and further discussion of that topic will not be undertaken here.

A teacher's record of her children takes into account those home conditions which may be responsible for each child's methods of attack upon his school environment, for his attitude in general; but her judgment should be formed and her procedure determined chiefly by what she herself sees and by what she can control. Her record must be critical of the school environment, including herself, before it is critical of the child; and it should be critical of the child only for the purpose of finding out what she can do in the situation.

"Elizabeth is lazy and stops before she gets her work finished," is a kind of report that is often sent on to the next teacher or even to a parent. If this is to rise above the level of mere fault finding it must tell a good deal more. What kind of work is it that she avoids doing, is there none she does well? Does she work better when alone or when with other children? How do the other children behave towards her? Does she show her idleness ("lazy" is an inaccurate term to apply to children) by dreaming? Or by doing something else than the work in hand, or by talking? How were the other children behaving in the same situation? What has the teacher done to alter the behavior? Unless a new teacher has answers to these questions, she will have to work them out for herself; the mere statement as quoted above will convey no real information and would better be left unsaid. If the first teacher has taken notes showing the conditions and how the other children reacted, and if for each child she passes on to another teacher she gives page and paragraph of these notes, she will be giving invaluable information. The new teacher will also be finding out about the other children at the same time, she will be seeing them in contrast with Elizabeth; and if the first teacher is a good reporter she will see what methods have failed with Elizabeth, and will have some basis for choosing a different procedure.

A teacher's account of Elizabeth or of John must contain a description of how the child works, what he is curious about, in what ways he is like or unlike his companions. The account must be continuous; that is, it must follow up a significant action and state whether it develops and how. This account of John must show how he grows, how he learns among the other children who are also learning, learning in a different way from John perhaps, and at a different pace, with interruptions to their learning which are not the same as John's. Is this too difficult a task to set a teacher? The ordinary markings by percentages, or the newer character studies, take a great deal of time if conscientiously undertaken, and they tell very little to the next teacher when they reach her. The new teacher is obliged to go to the other teacher to obtain more information, when she wishes information which will be full enough to act upon.

The first essential difference between our records and those in common use is the difference in responsibility. Most reports of children throw the emphasis upon what is the matter with the child; our reason for making records is to show what is the matter with the environment and to change it. Even if we are satisfied with an environment for the time being, we know it must change, it cannot stay as it is because the children change; they change enough to call for some different approach or material every week at least. A teacher must be on the lookout for changes in the children and be ready to provide some variation for each child.

Re-reading her notes will convince any teacher that she cannot trust her memory for each child's learning processes. She must take notes, and keep referring to them; she must know what his changes of activity or attitude have been and what influences have brought about his changes. A teachers' meeting was called in the middle of a school year to discuss several children. One was reported as very unruly at home but not at all troublesome in school. The home wished advice about managing him. Specific misbehavior at home was mentioned and the class teacher was asked whether he had shown none of this when he entered school in the fall. "None at all," she replied, yet her first notes of the child were of just such conduct. She had not looked up her notes. She had forgotten the child's early behavior because her action at the time had so readily brought about a changed attitude. She did not remember that he had ever been a problem. Nevertheless this very fact was a valuable one to report to the meeting and to his mother as showing what the teacher's management and the school environment had done for the child.

Individual Records Must be Records of Group Reactions

The second essential difference between our records and others is the fact that we do not separate individual records from records of the group. We claim that they cannot be separated. Individual records must be records of the group if they are to give a clear picture of the individual working and playing, learning and growing with the other children who are associated with him. The other children are part of his environment; their activities have a share in his growth.

We experimented for a short time with separate individual notes until we realized that separate notes of each child are confusing to the teacher. Notes of the activity of the group as a whole are necessary for an understanding of an individual's reactions to the school environment. It is necessary for the teacher to observe group situations and to record them in concrete form for comparison and reference, if she wishes to have a true picture of the child in school. When she wishes to pass on to the next teacher a report which will suggest how the new teacher shall manage him, she must show how the other children were reacting at the same time under the same circumstances.

SUMMARY FOR OCTOBER.—Four-year-old children. There is a good deal of difference in the children's ability in handling their clothing, which ties up with their general facility in using their hands. All can take off their own hats and coats, but some are much slower than others. Marie still retains her pride in the speed with which she accomplishes the operations, and her triumphant "I beat you" has hurried up the slow ones and added interest to the whole proceeding. There has been a special problem with one little boy who really seemed to suffer from a complex in regard to clothes. This was manifested by extreme sulkiness and negativism. His usual behavior was to get into a corner and pretend to be a turtle or lion, instead of going to work as the other children did. A new method of treatment was decided on, i. e., not to mention clothes at all until he had become interested in an occupation . . . (other details and child's responses.) Since then there has been no difficulty at all. I am careful not to ask him directly to take off his things, but usually he does so when the other children do.

The reports of Marie and the little boy would not be complete without the comparison with the other children. A new teacher has the information that this group of four-year-olds has a certain facility with their hands, but that they varied very much in their willingness to take care of their own clothes. She also has a clear idea of a method of managing the boy which will be useful if he reverts to old habits while in her class. She sees, as well, the influence of Marie's skill (or perhaps it was her energy) upon the slower children; they learned something from her.

The social environment determines individual progress,—for adults and for children. The race has lived in groups because of the stimulus of social experience; the give and take which follows from social contact, from relating experiences as they are alike or different, and as they are repeated by the group. If this be true of adult life it must be true of children. We wish them to live a socially active life, consequently we send them to school with other children. A record of an individual's progress must then include environment, must show enough of the general activity going on in the group to report what sort of stimuli arouses the individual to inquiry and effort and what does not, what contributions he makes to the group activity, how he makes them, and how he is learning to make more inquiries and more contributions. When a teacher studies one child at a time or writes up each child separately, she focuses her attention upon the one child, not upon the child plus the social and material environment within which his behavior took place.

The Nursery School, with children three years old and younger, makes very careful records of the children's experiences, their learning processes. The contrast between the following children is informing of both. In this case the "group" happened to consist of only the two children.

> Weekly summary, May 23.—George made a very complicated three-story construction about two feet long. The big blocks were laid lengthwise, short ones were placed across them and triangles. Edward still tends to the helterskelter piling. This week, in his first attempt, he seemed to continue intentional much longer than usual. He announced he would make a train. He laid about 12 blocks in a long track and then George, whose specialty is that type of construction, joined him and they worked together for ten minutes or more laying a wonderful track. In some places it was seven or eight tiers high. . . . It was amusing to see George straighten a block put in crooked by the temperamental Edward. Their method of work is very different. George works with absorption and is meticulous over details . . . but his schemes are not likely to be bold. Edward enjoys doing a stunt. His towers were well executed and he showed some skill in devising ways of placing blocks after he could no longer reach the top. On the other hand it took him longer than it did George to discriminate in the size. Experience teaches Edward without his taking much responsibility about it.

We do not become informed about a child when we study him alone. We may record what he is doing when alone and how he does it, but we do not know him. We may catch some of his characteristics, but we can know his possibilities only when we see him working with his kind with whom he must live. A teacher of a five-year-old class reported many weeks of active block building. The children's play was rich and varied in its informational content and its constructions. Almost every child took part in this building. The exceptions noted were significant; but without the notes of the responses of the group as a whole they would have been of no value except to report that there were exceptions. The first and second paragraphs noted below illustrate this teacher's notes of the building during two weeks. The next paragraphs show the same class at dramatic play in the yard. Different children are emphasized in the two settings, in these particular weeks because they stood out as reacting differently.

Week of March 21.—Building. When boats were suggested as the objective in block building for the week . . . one child suggested that the boats go to the West Indies. (The children had seen a West Indian boat during a trip to the docks.) This was agreed upon. . . . All kinds of craft were built. . . . Grace modified her boat, however, putting on many passengers and dressing them up. Though she was co-operating in the floor scheme, the dressing of the dolls was, I believe, more her interest than the boat and its destination.

Week of April 4.—Building. Contributions (to the discussion of trains and boats) came from all the children with rapidity and enthusiasm. . . . My suggestion met with approval and going around the circle each chose what his contribution would be, except Grace who chose to build a house. She seemed utterly outside the spirit of the class. It is difficult to think of any child being able to withstand the enthusiasm of this group.

Week of April 4.—Yard Play. The yard play has been very intent and interesting all week. The constructions of blocks, or boxes and blocks, were made in order that dramatic play could be carried on. Very often the dramatic activity is taking place or being planned during the course of the building. . . . Jervis plays well alone, building with blocks, making boats or houses. He has a great desire to be included in more social play and appeals to me. I am endeavoring to have him accomplish the social contact himself in so far as it is feasible. However, when he invites other children to play with him he does not make his requests attractive and hence meets with no response. If he wishes to join the play of a group he goes right in it without making any request to be allowed to play. This annoys the others at once. . . . He makes no contributions when he gets in, but I believe this will come since he shows good content in his own play.

Week of May 9.—Jervis built well alone and occasionally has made a satisfactory contact with other children. He is apt to play with the others expecting them to carry out his directions or to allow him to be in the play without contributing ideas or help,—consequently he is not included long and finds it hard to be included at all.

A teacher of a country school discovered by experience that records of group activities gave her far more information about her children than records of individuals. The teacher was new to the school and began by keeping notes of the character study type (a rather new method in those days,—some years ago). She also kept notes of their academic work along the usual lines. All of these notes were separate individual records. She studied these records separately and drew subjective inferences concerning each child's behavior, in his school work, on the playground, and what she knew of his home. But she did not find these records helpful. She was confused, she could not keep connections in mind, and she did not get help in making changes which she was sure were needed both indoors and out. This was especially true of the two oldest boys, Leonard and Randall; she knew something was ineffective but she did not know what it was.

For a different purpose, that of making a special study of play, the teacher took concrete notes of the whole group while they were on the playground. The fact that small groups remained constant over a period of many days became evident, and the teacher discovered that the individual composition of these groups, and the relationships of the groups to each other, were of great value in judging the character of each child.

The two big boys, thirteen and fourteen, when studied as isolated individuals, had not shown the teacher what was the matter with them, nor what she could do to bring about changes in attitude. She had also kept trying to see them in the light of outside public opinion, and the reports preceding teachers had left. These opinions were that Leonard was a trustworthy leader and a good student, while Randall was the village bad boy who came to school only because his father forced him. The teacher's individual studies had thrown doubt upon these opinions, but they gave little information except that the bad boy had done nothing bad so far, and that the good boy took no interest in his studies. The teacher got no clue to understanding and handling the situation adequately until she studied her continuous notes of a group activity. Here there were noted enough interrelationships between varying situations and personalities to show up both boys in considerable relief. Leonard was mean; he got the younger children to run after his balls and he usurped all the desired positions. Randall was generous towards the younger children, taught them the games, comforted them when their feelings were hurt and encouraged them to be good sports. Randall and Leonard were not particularly good friends on the playground.

The teacher began to observe these two boys, and the other children, as groups, at work together. She did not allow herself to form judgments about individual occurrences nor individual children until she had observed them working together repeatedly under similar conditions. That is, she observed and recorded continuous group activities. She was able therefore to draw positive instead of negative conclusions, conclusions which were based upon a series of concrete related facts,—evidence, not opinion. She found Leonard, for example, expert in devices for deceiving her about the work he had done. Randall would cover up nothing from a teacher he liked. The teacher had sensed this before, but she had not taken the right way to get the evidence. Her action, following these positive leads, was direct and in time brought results she had not been able to get before.

A teacher of nine-year-old children, after overcoming several difficulties in her children's play in the yard, read over her rough notes and summarized the situation at that date in regard to each child. This summary forms an excellent basis for a continued following up and reporting upon the progress of each one.

NOVEMBER-DECEMBER.—Tom was then the best athlete, Martha and Ellen entered into the games with most abandon. James, Violet and Frank were good sportsmen. Edmund played at this time with great zest but had not much muscular control. . . . Jack, who at first was often accidentally hurt, and who liked to play alone, had become quite one of the group. . . . Edwin still had a tendency to take it easy, giving up a chase if he saw near the start he hadn't much of a show. Henry enjoyed play but wanted to be "it" most of the time. . . . Mary and John fitted in nicely with no outstanding characteristics.

A final summary at the end of the year by the same teacher contains the following partial report of the children's drawing and painting. This report would be complete only when accompanied by the actual paintings made by the children, and when preceded by an account of their beginnings, their progress and what teaching or help they had had.

Judging from the hundreds of drawings, I think we have succeeded in getting free expression, and in the case of A., B., C., D., and E. I think I can say that the majority of their drawings and paintings have been real art expressions. F., G., H., I., and J. have also produced some pictures worthy of mention.

One interesting characteristic of the drawings produced this year has been the type of subject chosen. With the exception of Violet, whose paintings have been of an imaginative order, all the drawings and paintings have been the outcome of observations and feelings with respect to the real world surrounding the child. . . . Certain of the children have developed a decided style, in particular . . . (seven children including Violet).

Whether or no it be argued that our method of recording can be used in the standard, the usual public school, it can be shown that even a large class may be given opportunities to study socially, to work out their problems together. It can be shown that, while giving her class these opportunities and while observing the individual responses within the group activity, a teacher will understand her individuals more thoroughly and may thereby record achievement and behavior with more accuracy and justice, even though she may be obliged to report each child's performance in formal terms. A visiting-teacher, who had been trying to persuade the teachers of a public school to adjust the school procedure more nearly to the needs of several girls in an eighth grade, offered one day to take the class in geography, in order to show the class teacher how these girls would act when thrown upon their own initiative, with opportunity to discuss and compare notes with other girls, and with opportunity also to use the knowledge of the subject which they had acquired outside of school.

The teacher had complained of the lack of interest in their study of Central Europe. All these girls were of Central European descent, and the war had recently begun. The teacher of geography knew of their descent, but she did not take it into account. The visiting-teacher took it into account, and when she assumed charge of the class (as a demonstration to the teacher) she talked this fact over with the girls and suggested that many would have a good deal of information from home to contribute. She then divided the girls into groups as they sat, from four to six in a group, and gave them a common problem to work out. Each group was directed to discuss, confer and pool their information, whether gained from the text-book or from home.

There was no confusion in the classroom; the geography teacher moved about and watched individuals who had given her trouble with especial interest. She had time to do this because she was not conducting a recitation; she was not engaged as usual in discipling idly listening girls while only one was reciting. Very few out of the forty-five girls were idle, and these few disturbed nobody because the others were too busy. When the groups were called upon to report, the formerly troublesome girls showed up remarkably well. "I thought of them as so troublesome that I never found out what they really knew," said their teacher.

This teacher realized that she had learned more about her girls when she had given them an opportunity to work together. She herself had had a new experience in observing. She had seen what an entirely practicable change in the classroom environment would do, to produce in certain girls a greatly accelerated process of learning what she wished them to learn. She would probably have no time to make concrete records of such lessons, but if she could keep up this method of observing the girls while they were working in groups she would have a much more accurate basis for estimating which of the required A, B, C, or D marks for scholarship she should enter in their monthly reports. And she would also have a more accurate basis for answering that common and very puzzling question, "Should Anna's greater willingness to do her work make her conduct mark higher this month, or should it add to the scholarship mark?"

TECHNIQUE OF RECORDING

Our method of recording calls for a new habit of observing children. New methods of teaching will follow these new ways of considering children; but this report is a record of an experiment in recording and must not discuss methods of teaching, except in relation to the observation and recording of children's activities. The last illustration in the preceding section showed a class studying with more than their usual interest. This energy did not arise merely because the girls were set "free" of their habitual classroom restraint of passive listening. Their interest and energy were aroused by the stimulus of sharing in a group activity. A teacher who gives her children opportunities to be "free" in their reactions to the environment, has far more to do and far more to observe than the teacher who carries out a predetermined recitation. She must be ready to act at any moment, to divert, to direct, to suggest, in order that the environment shall function adequately; she must be ready to change or to add to the environment when need is shown.

A teacher who wishes to record by our method must develop the habit of observing children working together. She must learn to recognize what sort of contribution each child makes to the group and how he makes it. She cannot record everything, nor can she always tell what is of most significance, but she can make tentative notes for her own use, leaving the sifting of evidence to a summary later. A teacher will find that the making of summaries will help to point up her observing. One teacher wrote, "A new feature in block building this week has been the fine cooperation displayed. * * * Marion was the only child to build alone." This teacher had been observing group activities; Marion had not changed with the group, and the teacher's note emphasized this fact in her weekly summary. There it will stand as a point needing attention, further observation and perhaps action.

The director of the City and Country School visited a class of five-year-olds and handed the teacher the following notes about their yard-play with the big blocks:

> The best contributions during their construction (of a "fire engine") were from O., A., B. and Tim. Tim had most information but he could not get it over to the others . . . seemed more interested in what he knew than in ways of carrying it out. . . .

These notes are valuable to a teacher only as points of departure. If she includes them in her summary (at the end of the week or other length of time) she does so in order to follow up with further observing and action until she has progress or the lack of it to record.

Skill in our method of recording depends upon how well a teacher follows our standards of observing children's activities. She must observe the children's progress in ability to use their environment; she must observe this environment to see whether each child uses it, whether it actually functions in experience for him. She observes the children's growth, and their school experiences, in order to criticize the school environment,—to test the curriculum. She records these observations so that she may have concrete evidence of each child's processes of growth in order that her criticisms may have a reliable basis for making changes in the environment to fit the children as they grow and change.

Many teachers have to teach themselves to give up the habit of criticizing the children and asking them to change, before they can develop the habit of criticizing and changing the environment. A teacher made long detailed notes of a little girl's dominating personality and her influence in the group. She affected the environment, but the notes did not indicate that the environment, including the teacher, had made much change in her. Was this due to the teacher's method of observing or was her recording at fault? The next teacher's record was clear. It showed that changes in the environment were followed by changes in the child. This record noted that specific action by the teacher diverted and controlled Nancy through the daily group activities. The child was much less frequently mentioned in the notes of the group, and though still a problem, the notes clearly indicated her wider efficiency, her narrowed and more natural dominance, and how this had been accomplished. This was a record which will be of great value to her next teacher. It was also reported that the child recognized her need of discipline and enjoyed her own greater productiveness under it.

> March 7.—Shop. . . . Nancy was sent out for misbehavior on Tuesday and has not been allowed to go back to shop since, but has worked at the classroom bench. For one whole hour she stuck to the self-chosen task of cutting out a round table top with a circular saw and finished the table next day to her great satisfaction. "If I had been in the shop I wouldn't have got it done so quick. I would have been thowing shavings instead of working." Nevertheless she is eager to go back and is trying to prove to me that she can be trusted. . . .

Reports of this kind need take no more time when teachers become skillful than the ordinary percentages do in the hands of conscientious teachers who vainly struggle to calculate justly. Our recording takes less time than the elaborate character studies which some schools are substituting for percentages. "Percents" do not indicate what should be done and personal character studies omit much of the environmental situations or are too elaborate for practical use. Records which are not used are a serious waste of a teacher's energy.

Teachers who expect to share in making changes in the school environment will have to keep systematic concrete notes if their share is to be effective, if it is to carry weight and avoid the confusion of conferences where discussion is based upon uncoordinated, vaguely remembered or inaccurate facts. Beginnings of new activities must be clearly stated, enough notes kept to show continuity and progress, and these must be looked over and organized into summaries upon which the teacher will base her judgments and make her recommendations. We cannot declare that a teacher who takes poor notes or no notes is a poor teacher; but we do say that a teacher who is aware of what she is doing and of the significance of what the children are doing, makes a good recorder of material which will be useful to herself, to her school and to other schools; and we also say that a good recorder makes a better teacher than if she took no notes.

A teacher does not need to note all the detailed variations of each child's progress each day. This is not only an impossible task but it obscures the teacher's vision; she is not seeing the tree, she is only counting the leaves. She would better take no notes at all, but take time to watch for significant relationships, for processes of learning. When a teacher gets into the habit of watching how the children gain from day to day, what brings about this progress,—not the quantity they memorize but the way of their growth,—she will not be willing to work without taking notes, because she will know that only so will she catch what takes place, will she see how irregularly continuous the process of growth is, and with the help of her notes be able to make use of what she sees to control the children's environment.

Teachers should have some experience in recording children's activities before they are given the entire responsibility of a class of children. Experience in recording is experience in seeing; it is experience in recognizing originality and initiative; in distinguishing between what is directly suggested by the teacher and what spontaneous responses and inquiries the environment has called forth. Whether a student expects to teach in a formal or an informal school, systematic note-taking of a practical kind (which she or a teacher expects to use) is training which she is unlikely to acquire in any other way,—it is laboratory work in pedagogy.

Skill, and consequently practice, is called for in the making of records which undertake to give the school, and the next teacher of a class, a clear idea of what and how the children have been learning. Notes must be brief and to the point or they will be too much of a burden to the writer and not useful to the reader. Until teachers acquire skill in recording, they need supervision and following up to see that each teacher pulls her notes together, that each record of the year's work shows continuity within itself and also shows relationship and progress from the year before. The organization of notes adopted by a school must be determined, as has been said before, by the organization of that school's procedure,—and by what use the school expects to make of its record. An outline proposed for one school might quite fail to be useful to another school.

There are however two essentials without which no school report is worth making. First, a teacher who makes an observation which she believes is important enough to enter in her record must follow up this statement by further observations and notes. An isolated observation is of no account until it is continued by further observations. It may be crossed out of her rough notes and left out of her permanent summary entirely, but if put in it must be followed up. Second, a teacher must be able to distinguish between what is, and what is not, evidence in regard to her conclusions concerning her children, and the environment she provides for them. Opinions are not evidence, nor are phrases characterizing the children, unless they are supported by concrete illustrations. These illustrations, in order to be good evidence, must illustrate the point at issue. This has the sound of truism, but teachers and parents, in fact everybody concerned with children, have a traditional habit of judging children not by the concrete evidence but by what they think children ought to do and be.

Follow-Up

Following up is a habit it is necessary for a teacher to learn if her notes are kept for practical use. Following up a subject that has been mentioned, or a statement that has been made tentatively, requires a re-reading of old notes. But no teacher can afford for the sake of her teaching to do anything else. She cannot trust to her memory, and she is teaching thoughtlessly if she lets each day's procedure depend upon what comes up or upon what she remembers of the past. If she wishes to share in making changes, if she wishes to be responsible for her own procedure, she must take some sort of continuous notes. Two teachers using the same yard and equipment made a full report of the children's use of some new heavy blocks. A third teacher did not mention these blocks at all in her notes,—yet it was of just as much importance to the school to know how her children used this new material as to know how the other classes did.

When a teacher takes notes of what she wishes to remember and use, she is likely to give information which another teacher will find useful. When note-taking is perfunctory, it is of no use to others. A teacher wrote, "The children evolved a self-directing system * * * for going downstairs at lunch time." She did not mention what this system was, nor how the children carried it out; she did not mention it again at all. Why did she note it in the first place? If it was worth mentioning at all it was worth explanation; if it did not function, this was worth mentioning. On the other hand, specific questions concerning an absence of functioning, even if the teacher never discovers a satisfactory answer, are of great value. "My children use the sandbox so little. Is it worth while to have it at all?" was a question of practical value to the school and to the next teacher.

A teacher's failures, and the children's, are often more illuminating than successes and call for as full reporting. They are even more important to follow up with statements of outcome and of changes which brought success. But it is neither success nor failure which are of themselves important,—they are parts of the process of learning, incidents. It is the flow of progress, with its ups and downs, its variations, which tell the story.

> Week of May 2.—Four-year-old group. Block building. Marion was the only child to build alone, but when Henry began a track on Thursday, he said, "I want somebody to build with me," and Marion, putting away her own blocks, joined him. . . .

This summary would have been worth nothing by itself. Preceding notes indicated a different social activity, and the weeks that followed showed variations. This teacher reported progress in building together, week by week, and how she herself helped.

> Week of May 9.—Interest in building together strong this week. Henry and Marion began a track on Monday, and were soon joined by Thomas. . . . The two boys were better able to cooperate than Marion. . . . I did not want her to be discouraged, so I suggested that . . .

It is during the re-reading of her rough notes to make a summary, such as the above, that a teacher organizes, readjusts her previous evaluations and makes plans anew. It is this summarizing which is of educational value to her, which helps to make clear to her how the environment has functioned, and what experiences she should encourage.

Evidence

The mental notes which a teacher makes will be endless in quantity; her written notes may be few or many according to need and skill. These

notes will be valuable just in so far as she has taught herself to discrimi-
nate between an opinion she wishes to hold and the actual evidence. She
takes notes because she wishes to use them; she wishes to have something
other than remembered facts as a basis for making her more important
changes in curriculum or in her procedure. Her decisions to make
changes or to take specific action must be based upon an accumulated
body of occurrences of the same kind. She makes decisions because, "B.
has acted thus every time so and so has occurred," or, "It is only when
I arrange such and such a situation that the children respond as I want
them to." The writer of these notes may be mistaken in what she wishes
to bring about, but at any rate she will be learning to know what she is
doing, because she is collecting real evidence concerning the effect of the
environment. "The children ought to . . .," or "Anne should feel
sorry but . . ." are not evidence. "R. seems listless part of the
time and at others is inclined to be mischievous. He still has a bad cold
and this may be partly the cause." As rough notes to be followed up
by more specific evidence these may be good enough. But "seems" and
"may be" are terms a teacher should avoid. Listlessness is a visible
manifestation, and she could use "is listless" with accuracy. The second
sentence would be much stronger if asked as a question, "Is his bad cold
the cause?" and would imply an intention of following up. "Evidently"
is another word that is worthless unless the teacher is in possession of the
facts. The following is good evidence because it was a summary of many
observed incidents of the same kind:

> January 14 was cold and windy. This kind of weather evidently
> affects the type of yard play; either it is of the monkey-shine type, tossing
> each other's hats and chasing each other, or else the activity slows down
> and complaints of being cold are made, and I have to enter in with sug-
> gestions, a thing I have not had to do for many weeks.

Another teacher's notes upon two children are in strong contrast
with each other as evidence. Her first note is valueless because it gives
no evidence for her conjectures. The second is a statement of the facts
in the case, and no inference is drawn unless one is implied by the last
sentence.

> Albert was willing to try this today, although the other day he re-
> fused to; but either his circulation is not so easily started, or else his
> spirits are too easily depressed.
> The children were very quiet and interest was sustained in their
> own plans for activity without suggestions from me up to 11:45, with the
> possible exception of Max, who was inclined to be pugnacious and fretful.
> He has a cold.

A mother who was also a teacher, a specialist in a science, told another teacher, "Baby sees a long distance. She really recognizes that church on the hill. Whenever I ask 'Where is the church?' she points to it." A few days later at the dinner table, the mother asked, "Baby, where is . . .?" The mother mentioned this person and that and the baby pointed until one was named whom she refused to point to. "Ah, little baby, that is too far away, isn't it?" This mother had no real evidence that the baby recognized or was pointing to the distant church, nor had she any ground for making the contradictory statement that the baby could not see far enough to recognize some one across the table. Although an accredited specialist in a science, this teacher had no sense of what constitutes evidence. Her statements about her pupils in school were as inaccurate as about her baby at home,—they were colored by the requirements of the moment, they could never be relied upon as evidence.

A teacher who was a keen observer of children's activities, made so few notes of her own share in promoting these activities that her weekly summaries were very incomplete as histories. After giving weeks of discriminating assistance and encouragement to the one child of her three-year-old group who was still afraid of the slide, she succeeded in overcoming his fear, and he let himself go down. She had noted his reactions, but her own way of meeting them, without which the child would have done nothing, was not mentioned. Her note of his victory, in which she played an active though unmentioned part, was:

> On Friday John for the first time went down the slide alone. He was beside himself with ecstacy, jumped around like a clown on the pebbles, telling everyone to watch him, and he proudly repeated his performance many times for his mother when she came for him at noon.

The December summary of a teacher of eight-year-old children, on the contrary, stated her own purpose and efforts, but not what the children got out of the environment which she set up. She set up standards, but she did not tell whether they were effective; she did not follow up her statement of purpose with any responses of the children. This is a type of report which many superintendents feel obliged to be satisfied with, yet it tells nothing at all.

> The general work so far has been standardizing, that is giving the children something to measure themselves by. In behavior the ideals have been set of moving quietly . . ., leaving other children alone except when help is possible and deserved. . . .

A teacher's record of school functioning must report the essential related facts of functioning,—the interaction of environment and children. Teachers who are content to follow a dictated course of study are not the teachers who are in question here. This discussion of our experiment in recording is meant for those teachers who wish to share in the changes in curriculum which any progressive school finds necessary to make from time to time. It is meant for teachers who are willing to take the time to record those concrete facts which are necessary as evidence of the changes that should be made, in order that their curriculum shall continue to function adequately for their pupils' growth. When a school manages its record-making with skill, when it uses an organization of material appropriate to its purposes, when it gives its teachers time to re-read and summarize, the records so made will be invaluable to the school itself. They will be valuable to other schools also.

A year's record of a group of six-year-old children has recently been published by the City and Country School.* This record was made by the class teacher, Miss Leila Stott, to show "the school as it functioned through the children." Many such records of actual experiences in many schools may some day provide us with a body of reliable evidence concerning the functioning of different kinds of school environment. At present we are uninformed concerning school functioning; we are still guessing when we sit down to plan a school curriculum.

MARY S. MAROT.

---

* Op. cit. p. 5.

STUDY OF
ANIMAL FAMILIES
IN SCHOOLS

By

LAURA B. GARRETT

BUREAU *of* EDUCATIONAL EXPERIMENTS

70 FIFTH AVENUE, NEW YORK

THE BUNNY FAMILY

"The babies huddle under the father. He's a good one."

Introduction

CHILDREN and animals have always seemed a natural and wholesome combination. One hates to think of a childhood without pets. Yet that is the sort of barren childhood which the vast majority of our city children nowadays are spending. There is no place for these little dumb friends in the crowded homes, the crowded streets and the crowded days of our modern city life.

As in so many other ways, if old privileges are to be kept for children under new conditions, the school must be the means of bringing this about. If modern city children are to know the joy, the beauty, the significance of animals, it is necessary that they be included in the children's school home. The description in a book is but a tame, a pathetic substitute for the live creature. A chipmunk was taken as a visitor to a New York East Side class. Those twelve-year-old children thought the little striped creature was a tiger! They had studied a tiger in a book.

To use animals in a school room along with other lessons is quite in keeping with the general loosening up of school practices. It is one more way of letting a child learn through his natural curiosity and pleasure. But, like other expansions within a class room, it involves adaptations. It raises practical problems which need practical answers. Perhaps the answers contained in the following paper may show teachers how to open the doors of their class rooms to admit the historic friends of children—the animals.

Committee on Toys and School Equipment

"THE HOME WE BUILT AND THE FAMILY WE RAISED"

STUDY OF ANIMAL FAMILIES
IN SCHOOLS

No CHILD should be allowed to grow up without having the training which the care of pets gives him. The values of animal friends to children are so many that it is difficult to think of them all. The most important is the joy of the child as he plays with his friends. He learns at the same time respect for life, and incidentally gains an understanding of reproduction, as he sees his pets bearing young, and is automatically instilled with the appreciation of parenthood and the cleanness of the sex instinct. Kindliness develops with even the roughest little "tacker" as he is trained to handle and to be responsible for the care of these friends. The children also learn self-control and become more quiet, not from discipline superimposed by teacher or parent, but because they want to get closer to the pets, and because they must be quiet to see what the animals do. The whole subject of sanitation—which greatly needs to be taught in a vital way to the children in the public schools—can be taught in connection with animal study: proper housing, ventilation, clean food, and the protection of the animals from their own excreta.

Criticisms of Work With Animals

MANY people feel that there are so many objections to work with animals that it is not wise to take it up in the city schools. Thus it seems that the only children who may realize the joy of knowing animals are those who live in the country. As a matter of fact, country children acquire knowledge of animals and their habits, without that correct scientific study and ethical training which should always accompany work with animals, if it is to be of educational value. The chief objections to work with live animals in city schools are these:

1. That the animals lose their freedom and that this reacts upon the children;
2. That it is difficult to keep them clean;
3. That they distract children from their work;
4. That the children are naturally cruel, and constant care is needed to protect the animals from them;

5. That the untrained teacher does not know how to handle animals, nor how to give the children the freedom which is essential for the development of this work;

6. That there is no one to care for animals over week ends and holidays.

The most difficult one of these criticisms to meet is, that we have to confine animals and keep them under unnatural conditions. Any one who loves animals feels this intensely; but the value of this study to the children is so vastly more important than the life and comfort of the animal that, after all, these objections are overbalanced.

The difficulty in keeping the animals clean and sanitary is not in the least an objection to the work, but rather a point greatly in its favor, as many lessons can be given in sanitation and hygiene, to which the children eagerly listen because they want to give their pets the best care.

The fact that the animals distract the children from their other studies may be of real good, for little school-work is equal in value to the training in keen observation, kindliness and composure which the children thus learn.

The statement that children are naturally cruel is very true; but the training they get to counteract this and the class ostracism which is developed toward the boy or girl who is cruel is most valuable.

The difficulty of caring for animals over week ends and holidays is easily disposed of. The real difficulty is to choose from the big group of applicants who clamor for "One, just one, to take home! Mother is waiting for one to visit us!" One teacher made trips from Brooklyn to our school in Manhattan to care for a mother rabbit and her young. Janitors, too, help to watch over the families.

During the summer we have found a settlement house glad to welcome our pets—rabbits, pigeons, and guinea pigs. In the future, as more schools undertake the work, these animal families will be found valuable assets to the equipment of summer playgrounds and school gardens, and thus their care in the long vacation will be hardly a problem.

Values of the Work

One of the most important values of the work is the training it gives to the teacher. Many of the teachers know nothing about the animals or how to handle them. They are not accustomed to think-

THE COMMITTEE, "HAVING OUR PETS PHOTOGRAPHED"

ing or talking frankly where sex is involved and therefore are easily
embarrassed by the naturalness of animals. Many of them are
unable to teach the children with regard to the animals which are
mentioned in their history, geography or other lessons. Teachers
know little of their children except in the regular work of school
routine, and as the children become keen in their interest, unselfish
toward other members of the class, forgetful of the ordinary school
discipline and quiet in behavior because of their new interests, the
teacher sees a different group develop from her old class.

Another value is that of the mutual interest and friendliness
which soon grow up between those classes having families of animals
in their charge. They soon learn to lend and borrow pets and
exchange information about them.

A surprising number of superstitions have been unearthed during
the study of animals. The one we all think of, of course, is that
hop toads make warts. This is a common superstition with every
nationality. (See Riley's "Mr. Hop-toad"). Interesting, though
perhaps more local, are these: "Guinea pigs take away the 'sticks'
(rheumatism). My father, he had a guinea pig that took away
his sticks. He let it run up his back. Then he got well and could
go to work, and he sold the guinea pig to a sick man for five dollars."
"If you blind a rat and let it run away, it will carry all the disease
out of the house and if you keep the rat's eyes and dry them and

hang them around your neck, you will never get sick any more. My brother, he knows just how to take the eyes out of a rat. He can squeeze the rat, and when the eyes bulge out he takes them out, and then he lets the rat run away and saves the eyes. He knows how to do it."

These are not isolated stories. The same or similar stories have been repeated by class after class in New York schools, where all the children have been ready to contradict the teacher and protest that these were real ways to get well and keep well. These superstitions should be recognized as a groping toward health. They should be met with respect, not scorn, and the discussion which follows—perhaps weeks after—will lead to a better, saner understanding of the laws of health.

The elimination of fear is another great value of animal study. It is very interesting to study in our kindergarten classes the supposedly inherited fear of snakes. A few children are somewhat nervous with anything that moves, but they show no more dread of snakes than they do of any other animal. In fact, they are not so afraid of them as they are of animals that move more quickly. Very soon all of the children learn to admire the beauty of color and scale markings and the graceful form and movements of the snake, and they are full of astonishment to learn that the snake "can walk and it has no legs." At the same time, a careful study is made of the economic value of the snake as the enemy of rodents and insects. In the older classes the same work is done, but there are many more children here who have been taught fear. By suggesting to the ones who show signs of fear that they stay away while the rest of us play with the animals—snakes in particular—the nervous ones quickly learn to touch them and handle them without fear. This elimination of fear is one of the most valuable results of the work with animals.

The only animals the city children know are the alley cat and the stray dog who suffer intensely from cruelty, and the horse who is abused by his driver until every one who loves animals suffers with him. When I say "animals children know," I mean the ones they can fondle and love and care for or get near to. The reaction against cruelty as shown by our children in their attitude toward the above-named animals has been very strong. In connection with this part of the work, classes are taken to the street to study the whole problem of the street cat with regard to its misery, its food—the garbage—and the harm it may do by spreading disease. In the same way dogs are studied, and a more careful study is made of the

OUR FAMILIES—RABBITS AND PIGEONS
"We helped them raise their little folks."

horses we see in the streets. We study their loads, their harness, and the treatment given them by their drivers. Surely those of us who see horses in the streets of New York must feel that many of their drivers have never had pets of their own when they were children. We have made a careful study of the "Prayer of the Horse," by F. H. Burgher, ex-Deputy of the Police Department. As a part of this study of street animals we visit the blacksmith shop and stables. Many a horse has received better food or his harness has been readjusted at the suggestion of a class of little folks who watch the same animals from day to day. The almost immediate response from the children if the animals suffer, shows one of the valuable lessons in connection with the work.

It is very interesting to notice the different reactions of the animals to the children as they are fondled. With some children the animals snuggle down and go to sleep, or sing, or purr, or talk to their friends. Certain types of children cannot handle animals at all. The animals run away or squeal. The children notice this immediately. A sturdy little fellow in the kindergarten once protested as a guinea pig was to be given to a classmate. He waved his hand vigorously and said, "Oh, don't, don't give it to him! He has a 'fraid!" There sat a weak, nervous, little fellow who had poor co-ordination and who would probably have injured the animal by nervously throwing it aside. A long and persistent training is given these little folks who are afraid of the animals or who do not know how to handle them. Gradually all the children can be taught, and their pride is developed till they are able to announce that the whole class can be trusted.

Method of Introducing Work Into Schools

This work should be introduced in the school in the following way: First the animals should be taken to the children as visitors. After they have learned to handle the pets and to care for them, the children should be encouraged to build homes and to bring pennies for food and to get ready for families they want to raise. If they have the means, they should buy their own animals. This develops in the children a sense of ownership which brings with it a feeling of responsibility for the proper care and protection of their animal friends.

The work should be varied according to the needs of each school group, for the interests, superstitions and fears differ greatly with the different nationalities and with the varying opportunities of different children for knowing animal life.

The same animal can be used throughout all the grades. The little folks show joy and interest in observing and hugging the pets. As children grow older they ask questions about the habits, habitat, enemies and economic uses of the animals. Gradually, beside all these other interests in the animals, their place in the animal world and their values to man become of absorbing interest. Throughout the entire work sketches are made, stories told, poems learned and games, which have been developed by the children to represent scenes in the lives of the animals, are played.

The children should have a chance to select the pets whenever possible, or should appoint a committee to buy them. It seems almost an inborn trait in the children that they select the parents which are mature and in a healthy condition. They reject with scorn any animal which does not look well. Parents which have different genetic traits should always be selected. For instance, a white (albino) doe mouse and black or lilac buck; in guinea pigs, a short-haired English male with an Abyssinian female. Where there is an opportunity for raising chickens, an interesting cross is that between a bantam rooster and a Plymouth Rock hen. The children notice the traits of the parents cropping out in the second and third generation and soon announce with intense interest that it makes a difference what kind of parents the babies have.

Inasmuch as the time to begin to teach children is while they are very young, this careful selection of the parents of their pets is of vital importance and leads to many interesting discussions with regard to eugenics, reproduction and sex hygiene.

The knowledge that the child gets about animal life should be accurate and scientific. If the "life history" of an animal is presented to a child—as it ordinarily is—with reproduction entirely omitted, it is not only a lost opportunity to give the child in a natural way the information which he may otherwise acquire in a twisted way, but it is an actual distortion of fact. It is essentially an unscientific point of view to expurgate your material for ulterior purposes. This does not mean that reproduction should be stressed. It should not. It should merely be treated honestly as a part of the situation when it really is a part. It thereby becomes related to something understandable and ceases to have the glamor of mystery. The children's own questions and attitudes are the best guide in this matter. This teaching when young, prepares the children for a better understanding and respect for the great surge of the creative instinct which comes to them later.

These discussions arise as an inherent part of the study of animals. They create no undue interest and are very normal; they simply fall into their rightful place.

In connection with this animal work, Dr. Hornaday, the director of the Bronx Zoological Garden, loans animals to supplement our school study, and animals are chosen which are either related to our residents or which are a strong contrast. The immediate result is that the children want to go out of the school and to other parts of the city to study the animal life they find.

The Museum of Natural History loans mounted animals (cousins of pets) which are studied with great care and with much interest after the children have become familiar with the live animals. Whenever young children are given their freedom, though wonderfully mounted animals are at their disposal, they crowd around one little moving animal and desert the mounted specimen altogether.

LAURA B. GARRETT

New York, March 1917

WE STUDY THE ANIMALS OF THE STREET

A BETTER WAY OF CARING FOR THEM

ANIMALS USEFUL
IN THE SCHOOL

FISH must be kept in a rectangular aquarium. They are generally over-fed, and if kept in globes they smother for want of air. There is probably no pet in the city homes which is more generally kept and more abused than gold fish (dealers are interested only in selling globes and fishes). A book on the care of aquaria can be obtained from the Aquarium Society at Battery Park.

Two aquariums, one for fish, tadpoles and snails, and another for snails only—where both life breeding and egg laying varieties may be kept—are valuable in the school-room. If a well-balanced aquarium is kept in the school and the children are taught about the relation of plants and animals to each other, the lesson of mutual helpfulness is thus taught without any moralizing on the subject.

Various sized aquariums can be used in the school room, costing from $2.50 up. The bottom should be covered three inches deep with sand and pebbles which have been boiled to kill all germs before being placed in the aquarium. Then various water plants should be placed in the aquarium and allowed to root there about a week before any fish are put into the tank. The fish should be fed regularly every other day and given only the amount of food which they eat. All extra food should be taken out of the aquarium and not allowed to sour in the water. There are many beautiful details about the aquarium life which can be got from books on the care of aquaria. Fish respond to friendliness and learn to eat from the hand.

PIGEONS can be raised in the school room and have, in one class, had the freedom of the whole class room. They learned to drink from the cups on the window sills and the children scattered peas and grain in certain places on the floor for them. These pets built their nests and raised their squabs to maturity in the class room. Pigeons are valuable because of their variety of color, their gentleness, their incessant cooing and their home traits—both parents feed, protect and train the young. The parents partially digest the food and regurgitate it into the mouths of the young, a step toward the milk giving mammals.

Pigeons that are confined should have a cage which is a yard cube and the top of the "house" should be protected from the rain and sun. The nesting box should be at least 6″x6″x10″; a cigar box is very good as it is sufficiently large and it keeps away lice. They should be fed green food, peas, corn, buckwheat, barley, and some salt fish should be hung in the cage where the pigeons can get to it. Some kind of grit (oyster shell, for instance) should be kept in the cage.

CANARIES can be bred in the school room, but they are expensive, especially since the war, and they cannot stand the changes of temperature which occur over week ends. They are not very practicable except in places where much more care can be given them than in the public school. Therefore it is not wise to try to breed canaries, though they are very good parents and both male and female feed and care for the young. Get books on breeding canaries, or better, go to any German who breeds them. A German neighbor of mine who lives in a tenement can give more helpful hints in ten minutes than one could get from a book in a year.

WHITE MICE (or any variety) are most valuable in city schools, as they need but small boxes and they breed very rapidly, and both parents, if well fed, help to care for their young. They can be kept in very inexpensive boxes, which from time to time should be thrown away as new ones are to be had at any grocery store. For one pair of mice, a box about 12″x8″x6″ is desirable, covered on one end with ¼-inch wire and provided with a movable, or removable, side. All the rough edges of the wire must be covered to prevent the mice from injuring themselves. A smaller box 3″x2″x2″, without a bottom, should be kept inside for a bed and a small circular opening should lead into it. For bedding, sawdust or pieces of paper, which the mice chew up, can be used. They should be fed hard bread to keep their teeth sharp, and bits of green vegetables, small amounts of oats and wheat; and the nursing mothers should have milk after the little ones are born. In fact, the food should be varied. *Plenty of water should be accessible to all animals all the time.* Mice mature in three months, and may live to be two years of age. The period of gestation is 21 days, and from 4 to 8 young are born at a time. The little ones are born naked and blind, and are intensely interesting to the children; they sometimes think they are worms and then suddenly decide they are baby mice. The mother builds a wonderful nest with a little hole for entrance, and if the babies are removed, carries them back with great haste, grabbing them by the neck or any part of their bodies. Mice mothers differ in the way they care for the young. At one time an experiment was made with four mothers who had 18 young. We took all the young from their boxes and put them outside. One big, black mother ran around the box and played, paying no attention to the absent little ones; one immediately went to work and fixed up all the nests and the other two dragged the fat, naked babies and put them into the nests without any apparent thought as to where they belonged. Mice cannot be handled in this way until they are about two weeks old. If disturbed before this, the mother may become nervous and in her anxiety she may kill them.

WHITE RATS (or any variety) are very valuable and less objectionable than mice in some ways, as they have practically no odor and will run around the school-room and "make tricks" which the children enjoy. The children immediately learn the difference in intelligence between the rats and the guinea pigs and rabbits. A box 2′x1′x1′ is big enough for the rats' home. It should have a ½-inch wire mesh side and contain a small nesting box 6″x4″x4″. This should be an inexpensive little box such as can be obtained at any grocery store. It should be thrown away very frequently. Sawdust, cork, excelsior, or newspaper may be put on the floor as an absorbent. Both boxes for the mice and rats can be hung by the back on the wall and thus become a part of the school equipment in a very normal way. The class can select a color and the box can be painted, *on the outside only*, to make it more attractive. If the mice or rats are to be kept where either domestic or wild mice, or rats can disturb them, the wire on the front should be put on in two layers so that an inch or two of space lies between the two surfaces. This is to keep the wild varieties from disturbing the others, as they sometimes bite their toes and tails. Rats should be fed and watered the same as mice.

GUINEA PIGS—"cavies"—make the most satisfactory pets for the school-room. They are clean, have very little odor, are perfectly harmless (in fact, too much so, as they do not protect themselves from the children) and are very friendly. They reproduce rapidly and make very good parents. The only objection to guinea pigs is that they are so short legged that the slightest fall, even from the lap of a child, may paralyze them. However, though this is hard on the animals, the children soon learn to protect them,

and an occasional tragedy is a valuable lesson. A box 3'x2' x 1½'
will house one male and three females. The door should have a
half-inch wire. There should be a movable box inside for sleeping
quarters. The nesting box must be protected from wet and dampness with hay or sawdust for bedding. They should be given two
meals a day (oats, bran, vegetables or greens). Nursing mothers
should have bread and milk. Plenty of water should be provided.
The period of gestation is about 62 days. There are from 1 to 4
young at a time and they mature in 8 to 10 weeks, but should not be
bred until 5 or 6 months old. Hence the sexes must be separated
when about 4 weeks old. Food cups should be placed low on the
sides of the cage so that the pigs cannot soil the food, and preferably
should be made in such a way that only a small amount of food will
come down at a time. Water cups should be made of galvanized
tin and should be of the kind which cannot be upset. These can be
procured at Wanamaker's for 35 cents.

RABBITS have always been loved by children because of their
beauty, their friendliness and because they stand mauling. Rabbits are not affected by the cold and can be kept in cages in the
school yards. They breed very rapidly—that is, two or three
families a year—and the mother shows wonderful care of her young.
Just before the young are born, she vigorously arranges the nest,
using straws, hay, etc. Then she pulls great mouthfuls of fur from
her breast to line the nest, and she often attacks other rabbits and
grabs great mouthfuls of fur from them. After the young are born,
she cleans them and puts them into the nest. The little blind, naked
babies are a wonderful surprise to the children. In a week the
young can be handled and examined with care, and from then on
they are a source of constant joy and interest. (When handling the
little ones, rub the hand over the nest and then over the mother
so that she will not be disturbed by a strange odor. She may kill
her young if frightened). There are no animals that are more
abused than rabbits by pet fanciers. They not only lift rabbits by
the ears, but tell children that this is the way to handle them. Of
course the ears are surrounded by blood vessels and well developed
nerves; no part of the body is more sensitive, and it is very cruel to
lift a big, heavy rabbit by the ears. This is, however, a very hard
superstition to eliminate as stock dealers insist that it does not hurt
the animal. All animals need water and the succulent vegetables do
not take the place of water. If five or six babies are born, four are
all she can care for, and the weakest should be destroyed or should

be taken away from the mother and raised by hand, or all will suffer. The young are weaned in about four weeks, and in about two months the males and females should be separated to prevent their breeding before they mature. Rabbits should be fed hay (clover hay is best), oats, greens and dried bread. Again, nursing mothers should be given bread and milk. A desirable box is 2½'x2'x2' with half-inch wire mesh and removable sides. Clean sawdust or paper should be put on the floor and should be changed at least two or three times each week. A handful of Sanitas is good to keep down the odor in these cages. In cold weather rabbits should have hay or straw for bedding.

PLAYTHINGS

Third Edition
(Revised)

BUREAU *of* EDUCATIONAL EXPERIMENTS
144 WEST 13TH STREET, NEW YORK

COULD THERE BE A BETTER USE FOR A LABORATORY FLOOR?

PLAYTHINGS

Before attempting any sort of dissertation on playthings, it is necessary to say a few words about the needs which produced this bulletin,—the needs of play. These needs require discussion, not because children do not know how to play without adults; but because they have so often become sidetracked and meaningless in their play because of adults and the sidetracking and meaningless playthings adults have foisted upon them.

When an adult says he plays, he means he is wasting his time, he is not working, he is amusing himself. For some unknown reason, he has applied the same connotation to what a child does,—a child who is no more like him in his play than in his work. The adult thinks, "During all the hours of the day from his rising to his going to bed, a child is free,—free to amuse himself, free to 'play.' He has nothing else to do." And, unconsciously, in so thinking he is marking the playing child as negligible, an incompetent; he is estimating the play in terms of what products result, not in terms of what the child gets out of it; he is caught in the most fundamental but, alas! the commonest fallacy in the education of little children. And consistently, in order to make these "negligible" hours of amusement easier for the child—and often for the adult as well—toys, playthings—are meted out.

Now because, as is being more fully recognized each day, this fundamental conception of play as merely amusement is wrong, it makes us do wrong things to children. It makes us, in the first place, give them wrong things to play with. And in the second place it makes us take a wrong attitude of amused tolerance towards their accomplishments. We measure them by standards of our own, and we "talk down" about them. A child is only "playing" at the things that are real, are vital to us. As a matter of fact, experiences in the real world are just as vital to the child as to the adult. And the most significant measure of growth is in terms of these vital experiences.

A child's day is a busy one—far busier than that of many adults who "work," for there is all the world to learn about. All day long a child is busy educating himself. He learns, as does the adult, by doing, by experiencing, by making mistakes. In their mental attitude, the adults of yesterday drew a line, saying "To such and such an age you are a child, you have nothing to do with the world; later you will go to school and you will learn from books about life; and then later still you will begin to live, and you will discard all you have learned from books because you will find that only by experiencing for yourself can you learn." But the adults of today are adding, "And you will realize that if only you had been helped to learn by experiencing when you were a child you would not now have wasted so much time."

Suppose we take a different interpretation of the word play as applied to children and see to what it leads us.

A child is in the position of someone who has been plunged into the world of unfamiliar things. He is uncertain of everything. He does not know on what he can depend. Objects that appear neutral have suddenly strange reactions. His chief interest is to "find out"—find out just what things do what, and just how far that doing leads them. Haven't you, for instance (to appear absurd for a moment) felt distinctly reassured to know that an automobile was back-firing for a perfectly explainable reason and that it was going to be content with this and was not going on to explode?

When a child has come to some sense of certainty in his environment through what we more or less vaguely call an "experience," at once he utilizes this new certainty for play purposes. So we find the child constantly endeavoring to reproduce his environment, and to reproduce it in such a scale that he can manipulate it, that he can handle it as a superior; in other words, free from the handicap that goes with a sense of not knowing,—the sense of inferiority. He relives his experiences: he recreates a world he can control. That is his play, that is his method of learning. For play, instead of being a wasted interlude in the learning process *is* the process itself.

Of course, this constant endeavor of a child's to reproduce his environment has been seized upon by mothers and teachers alike to attain their own adult ends,—to get over to a child certain valuable facts. The baby piles up some blocks. Mother or nurse says at once, "How many have you? One, two, three, four, five!" He scrawls a figure on his paper—father gets the child's attention to say, "Yes, my son—that is a triangle,"—and both mother and father flatter themselves that real progress toward the goal of being educated has been made. It is obvious that play-schemes in the classroom may be made an excuse for making children swallow sugar-coated pellets of arithmetic and reading and writing. Devices of this sort to beguile the unsuspecting child have multiplied like weeds in recent classrooms. They are largely responsible for the common suspicion that freedom within a schoolroom must mean either coaxing or license. They are devices, nothing more. And they are a bit unworthy of the situation. It is not being argued that the play of children affords an opportunity to slip in unnoticed something which an adult values, but which the child would repudiate if he were not duped. It is that interpretive play, constructive play, depends in its very essence upon the same relations, whether expressed in human terms or in books, upon which our real world depends. Play, for the child, is not opposed to reality and to the relations which control the real world. On the contrary, it is a reliving of the real, in the way which best deepens the sense of reality and of the relationships upon which the real world rests. Little children who are having rich first hand experiences in the actual world and are let alone, play in this way. Of course, children whose lives have been largely filled with vicarious experiences drawn from books and pictures (and certainly this should not be the first phase of life) have only this second hand world to reproduce. Later, in order to carry on organized life, we find it necessary to use symbols. These symbols have grown up just because they are necessary to facilitate the processes of the world. The same necessity will be felt by the children in any play which reproduces these processes. And the use of symbols will grow up in the same natural way as it has with adults. Children cannot reproduce an environment which implies a number sense without using that number sense; children cannot do exact bench work without measuring; children cannot play store without arithmetic.

This is the point toward which educators in the last few years have been dimly groping their way. It is the point of departure from the old-fashioned view of children as little animals to be cared for physically and let alone mentally until such time as the school stepped in to pour knowledge, all ready made, through a funnel into their dormant understanding.

When these facts are appreciated, the problem of school and home assumes an entirely new aspect. How can they be made over into places where children can educate themselves, can learn through experimenting the meaning of the world they live in, and do it by the natural means of play? What must be done to furnish a genuine laboratory for children? What are the necessary appliances with which it should be equipped?

These are searching questions. They send a challenge to nearly everything which has been thought proper in a small child's home and school surroundings—the furniture and the equipment, the teacher's, the mother's attitude. Let us consider these things as necessary complements to the proper use of playthings, and hence to playthings themselves.

5

If possible, instead of a nursery where pictures of fairies and goblins, kings, queens and palaces crowd in to confuse the naturally clear thinking of a child, substitute a play-room, which, construed into the new sense of the term, is a laboratory,—a laboratory free from the hampering frills of what grown-ups think children ought to like, free for the child's own experiments in education; and where, it has been proved, he will "play" enthralled hour by hour, not wasting his time, but using every moment of it to acquire knowledge.

If a laboratory is to give each child full freedom for his own expression, it has to provide not only appliances which he can easily manipulate to his own ends, but physical space and guarantee from interruption as well. The ability of even well-to-do homes to command these last essentials is seriously threatened in these days of congested cities and small apartments. The school's task is no light one. It must, then, not only see to it that children have the playthings which are the nucleus of a significant life-process known to them through their own experiences;—that is, toys which are related and suggestive; that they have at hand materials with which they themselves can supplement these provided toys; but it must also see that they be given time and space in which to work out their own experiments in their own way. The easiest place for a little child to play is on the floor. Why not a school floor? Why not let him construct his scheme on the floor and then use this scheme to carry out in action whatever miniature dramatic situation he has created? Could there be a better use of a laboratory floor?

Up to the age of six, a child is an extreme individualist. He does not naturally do things co-operatively. There comes a time, however, when he steps from his individualistic into a social world. The school should meet the requirements of his individualistic period and bridge the gap when he begins to be a communistic soul. Here again, playthings, free materials, are the school's chief reliance. They adapt themselves to the needs of a project in which a whole group of children spontaneously develop joint floor schemes such as a section of a city with its streets full of autos and carriages, lined with trees, flanked by houses, restaurants with outdoor gardens, grocery shop, baker's shop, railroad station with incoming and outgoing traffic, river with wharves and shipping, factories and all the endless array of industrial activities which make up our modern world. This is not a theoretic description. It is the kind of thing that those who work with free materials and comparatively free children constantly see.

UP TO THE AGE OF SIX A CHILD IS AN INDIVIDUALIST

There are, to be sure, some practical difficulties in devising a school-room where little children may have both ample privacy and ample social life, particularly if they work with free material. In one school the mechanical difficulty has been met by two simple devices. Small, low, and easily handled screens are placed so as to give each child his own isolated space on the floor. Here he is free to develop a miniature dramatic scheme, as he may desire. And when the individual expression is completed and the floor space is needed for common purposes, the screens are removed. By the other device—a small balcony, easily built in any room—the additional space needed for co-operative "floor schemes" is secured. This balcony may be too low to let a grown-up pass underneath, but it doubles the space for the children.

Much of the furnishing of a schoolroom, such as screens, folding tables, chairs, rugs, etc., is good dramatic material. And so is whatever there may be in the way of outdoor apparatus. If children are encouraged to use materials freely, they fashion almost anything into their dramatic purposes.

In a little child's school or home laboratory, the teacher or mother through observing becomes a specialist in play. She does not impose her personality or her methods upon the child. The child's world is his own world. He wishes to interpret that and not another's. The work

CHILDREN FASHION ALMOST ANYTHING INTO THEIR
DRAMATIC PURPOSES

of the teacher is not to lead him to see *her* world through his eyes, but to put before his eyes a world which he may make his own. For the child, the stimulus to experiment should come from the observation of the life of the city streets, or the farm, or the home, or whatever his environment happens to be. The teacher should put her energies upon the ordering and simplifying of this larger environment, rather than upon suggestions as to what the child shall do within his laboratory in experimenting with or interpreting this environment. The child's interpretation of his environment *is* play. No child need be taught it.

But if the child himself is to get from this interpretation all that it has to yield, he must have more than space and furnishings and observant teacher or mother—for all these are but necessary complements to the proper use of playthings. He must be given the very best appliances to express this interpretation. And these appliances are technically "free materials"—colloquially, toys.

With this in mind, the whole meaning of the term plaything is altered. Playthings should be the tools which help the child to reconstruct the world about him. They should be scientifically thought out. It is the unthought out, the hit-or-miss, the plaything built only to amuse for a transient hour—that is the true waster of time. It is only in the presence of these that a child is bored and begins to whine and complain. His tools are not adequate to his purposes. He can do nothing with them. He has not the adult capacity to be merely "amused."

The climax of absurdity in playthings is the so-called "mechanical toy." It does all the work. The child does nothing. Watch a child in front of a mechanical toy—say a miller who runs up a ladder and dumps a sack of grain down a chute. It seems to hold much of promise for interpreting a child's surroundings to him. He is fascinated by the first few trips of the miller. He endows the man with human qualities. He names him. Then, after the novelty has gone by, he longs to have his miller do something besides race up and down the ladder at superhuman speed. But the miller has no other possibility. So the toy is finally discarded, or, more probably, dissected by a bored child who wishes to find out how the little man works. The net result is a disappointed donor, an "ungrateful child," and a little heap of un-usable rubbish. There exists, to be sure, another type of mechanical toy of which the electric engine is a good example. A toy of this type may be used as the basis of very wonderful constructive play for children old enough to "run it" themselves. But the usual type of mechanical toy should never be classed with toys at all. It is destructive of play.

"FREE MATERIALS" AID HIM TO ENTER THE SOCIAL WORLD

Again, toys, even good toys, which help a child to duplicate the processes going on around him have never been planned together. They remain separate objects, unrelated units, disjointed bits of the universe, which grown-ups, having forgotten their own play-thoughts, imagine children are interested in. It is difficult to reconstruct a sector of life with a two-foot rag baby, a four-inch wagon and a rocking-horse.

As has been said, toys,—real toys,—are the tools of play. And since play is serious business for children, these tools must be selected with serious intent. They should be selected in relation to each other, both in size and in kind. They should be consistent with the environment of the child who is to use them. They should be constructed simply, so that they may serve as models for other toys to be constructed by the children. They should suggest something besides domestic play, so that the child's interest may be led to activities outside the home life. They should be durable, because they are the realities in a child's world and deserve the dignity of good workmanship. Only toys that a child can "do with," fulfill these requirements.

Toys of this sort may obviously form an equipment for a child's laboratory, and anything which answers these requirements becomes in this sense a toy,—a tool for play. Some toys of this sort—for example, blocks—are as old as the proverbial hills; they are common even in the schoolroom. But to use them as a basis for constructing a miniature world, a world in which the related toys—the dolls and the horses—live, move, and have their being, an incomplete world which may be supplemented by all sorts of plasticene and bench-made things, a world, moreover, which may be decorated to any extent—to use blocks in this way beyond the kindergarten, is an innovation in education. Yet there is no appliance better suited to a laboratory for play than simple blocks.

Work benches, with real tools, are an essential for the laboratory. The possibility for purposive action which a work-bench holds is literally boundless. At the bench a child is a creator: and his crude creations, his boats and wagons and engines, his own reproductions of the moving world in which he lives, become, moreover, the tools for further dramatic play. So, too, with play materials such as crayons, colored papers, plasticene and clay. If children are let alone with paper and pencil, they will quickly learn to use these playthings quite as effectively as they do blocks and dolls. Left to dig out for himself the "soul" of an object and transfer this soul to paper, which is, after all, the true province of art, a child under six may produce something that at first sight seems to our hide-bound imaginations grotesque. But rest assured that this absurdity is based on some reality. He has drawn the essential

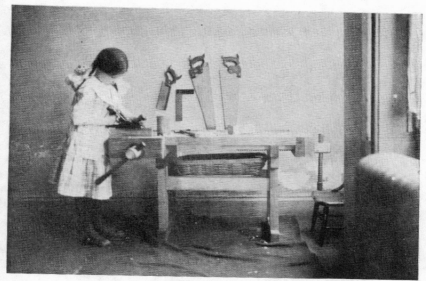

EVERY CLASS ROOM SHOULD HAVE A WORK-BENCH

rather than the object itself. Take the small boy of six who drew areo-planes, guns, ships, and then smudged the whole thing with red crayon. When asked what his drawing represented, he said, "Why, that's war. Isn't it a mess?" Or the child who drew a barely perceptible automobile in white crayon because, as he explained, "It's going so fast you can't see it." Or, again the seven-year-old who passed green crayon lightly over a sheet of paper and placed at the bottom a tiny figure who "thinks he is walking in the grass, but he really is in the bottom of the sea."

What about playthings called books?

The effort to amuse has produced a literature of fairy tales—steeped in the imaginary romance of an imaginary world—a world which often confuses a child's thinking and seldom has any significance in understanding the very real romance of the modern world; it has produced the "story of adventure" with its basic appeal to excitement, its familiarity with killing, impossible heroisms and violence of all sorts; it has produced the "animal story," in which the animal leaves both his nature and his habits and masquerades in human form, not uncommonly in human apparel. The effort to instruct children has produced a quite different but hardly more happy literature—if indeed it de-

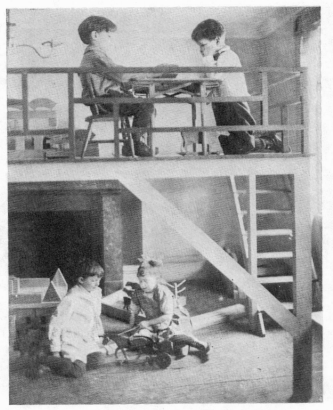

BY A SMALL BALCONY THE ADDITIONAL SPACE
NEEDED FOR CO-OPERATIVE SCHEMES
MAY BE SECURED

serves that name at all.   Facts chosen by an adult because of his own interest in them, presented to a child without being related to the child's experience, in a form which too often a child cannot perceive—such is the stuff of most of our informational books for little children.   Readers—which constitute most children's introduction to "literature"— are pieced together from these two types of stories—the amusing and the instructive—and cast in a language intended to facilitate the technique of reading and the technique of writing regardless of the effect upon the art of reading or the art of writing.

We all agree that the test of what we give to children is in what they give back to us. The following illustrations speak for themselves, telling us on one side of confused thinking, of mental indigestion over unrelated ideas and unexperienced facts; and on the other side of a sense of pattern and rhythm,—real play with language,—and of a feeling for the romance of the modern world. They were both dictated by six-year-old children. Can one uphold what adults must have introduced into the environment of the first child—tigers and theatres—when one sees how little the child could use this foreign material? The second story is a recall of an actual first-hand experience.

I

"Once upon a time there was a man and he had a moustache. Once upon a time he met a tiger and then the tiger came and ate him up. Then the tiger went away—Then another man came and the tiger didn't come—And he walked and he walked till he found a house where they all act and he went in that house and so he took his hat and coat off and went into the play."

II

"Who-o-o, who-o-o, the big Aquitania ship going and all the people hurrying down to see their friends off.

The sailors were all letting down the ropes from the big ship and hoisting up the anchor and the little tugs were pushing and pulling and pulling and pushing.

And the people were still waving their handkerchiefs to their friends, little white things, and all sorts of flags too.

Way, way up on the top, the Captain was up on his bridge guarding the wheel and the band was playing on the decks and the little tugs were pushing the boat around, and then the boat was off out into the open seas going for distant lands far away.

Whoo-oo, whoo-oo.

My fog horn!"

Care for a child's sensitiveness to sound, care for a child's natural play use of words, care for a child's interest in his own experiences and for his method of reaching the remote and the unfamiliar through the immediate and the personal, care for a child's creative power in language —these are not the things that have guided most of the adults who have written the books for little children.

We need a new literature for children. We need stories which recognize the art—the play spirit in words and which are cast in patterns which a child is equipped to see and enjoy. We need stories which start from a child's own experiences and environment and through following the line of his own inquiries, lead out from his immediate limited surroundings to richer, wider environments. We need parents and schools who will test the stories and verse which they give to their children not by what a child takes in but by what he gives out in stories and verse of his own creating. For create he will, if he is not diverted from his natural bent by some adult conception of what he should enjoy or should know. There is no telling how far the dramatic appeal of a story might carry a child into genuine scientific habits of thinking. There is no telling through what new forms of play expression, of "literature," he might express himself, if language were to him "free material" suitable for play purposes. Not till we have this new literature shall we have anything like a well-equipped laboratory for our little children.

Such then, are the needs of play; such are the requirements of playthings. And when it is remembered that everything a child touches —block, chair and table or language—becomes a plaything, for with it he plays, with it he interprets the world around him, with it he learns of this same world, does not that raise playthings to a dignity which entitles them to the same scientific consideration as other laboratory tools? Does not that put upon parents and schools the obligation of subjecting playthings to the most rigorous of our educational standards?

A CATALOGUE
OF PLAY EQUIPMENT

Compiled by

JEAN LEE HUNT

THIRD EDITION—REVISED

BUREAU *of* EDUCATIONAL EXPERIMENTS

144 WEST 13TH STREET, NEW YORK

1924

INTRODUCTION

WHAT are the requisites of a child's laboratory? What essentials must we provide if we would deliberately plan an environment to promote the developmental possibilities of play?

These questions are raised with ever-increasing insistence as the true nature of children's play and its educational significance come to be matters of more general knowledge, and the selection of play equipment assumes a corresponding importance in the school and at home.

To indicate some fundamental rules for the choice of furnishings and toys, and to show a variety of materials illustrating the basis of selection has been our aim in compiling the following brief catalogue. We do not assume the list to be complete, nor has it been the intention to recommend any make or pattern as being indispensable or as having an exclusive right to the field. On the contrary, it is our chief hope that the available number and variety of such materials may be increased to meet a corresponding increase of intelligent demand on the part of parents and teachers for equipment having real dignity and play value.

With one or two exceptions, the materials listed were originally assembled in the Exhibit of Toys and School Equipment shown by the Bureau of Educational Experiments in the Spring and Summer of 1917, and we wish to make acknowledgment, therefore, to the many who contributed to that exhibit and by so doing to the substance of the following pages. Chief among them are The City and Country School (formerly the Play School), The Ethical Culture School, Columbia University Teachers College, The School of Childhood at the University of Pittsburgh, and other experimental schools described in our Bulletins, Numbers 3, 4, 5, and 10.

For the philosophy underlying our basis of selection we have been chiefly indebted to our co-worker, Caroline Pratt, Director of The City and Country School, and a pioneer in the field of play materials.

The cuts shown were chosen, for the most part, from photographs taken in the City and Country School, and show the informal equipment devised by Miss Pratt. Schools and homes can maufacture equipment of this kind for themselves, and thus secure an environment rich in play opportunities, at a minimum of expense.

While the materials shown are especially applicable to the needs of children four, five and six years old, most of them will be found well adapted to the interest of children as old as eight years, and many of them to those of younger children as well.

BUREAU OF EDUCATIONAL EXPERIMENTS.

New York City, September, 1922.

OUT-OF-DOOR FURNISHINGS

OUT-OF-DOOR Furnishings should be of a kind to encourage creative play as well as to give exercise.

Playground apparatus, therefore, in addition to providing for big muscle development should combine the following requisites:

Intrinsic value as a toy or plaything. "The play of children on it and with it must be spontaneous."*

Adaptability to different kinds of play and exercise. "It must appeal to the imagination of the child so strongly that new forms of use must be constantly found by the child himself in using it."*

Adaptability to individual or group use. It should lend itself to solitary play or to use by several players at once.

Additional requisites are:

Safety. Its use should be attended by a minimum of danger. Suitable design, proper proportions, sound materials and careful construction are essentials.

Durability. It must be made to withstand hard use and all kinds of weather. To demand a minimum of repair means also to afford a maximum of security.

---

*Dr. E. H. Arnold, "Some Inexpensive Playground Apparatus." Bul. 27, Playground Association of America.

The City Yard Equipped to Give a Maximum of Exercise and Creative Play

THE OUTDOOR LABORATORY

In the country, ready-to-hand resources, trees for climbing, the five-barred fence, the pasture gate, the stone wall, the wood-pile, Mother Earth to dig in, furnish ideal equipment for the muscle development of little people and of their own nature afford the essential requisites for creative and dramatic play. To their surpassing fitness for "laboratory" purposes each new generation bears testimony. If the furnishings of a deliberately planned environment are to compare with them at all they must lend themselves to the same freedom of treatment.

The apparatus shown here was made by a local carpenter, and could easily be constructed by high school pupils with the assistance of the manual training teacher.

The ground has been covered with a layer of fine water gravel, a particularly satisfactory treatment for very little children, as it is relatively clean and dries quickly after rain. It does not lend itself to the requirements of organized games, however, and so will not answer for children who have reached that stage of play development.

A number of building bricks, wooden boxes of various sizes, pieces of board and such "odd lumber" with a few tools and out-of-door toys complete the yard's equipment.

OUTDOOR EQUIPMENT

All figures given in the following descriptions of out-door equipment are for *outside measurements*. Apparatus except see-saw board and sliding board should be painted, especially those parts which are to be put into the ground.

THE SEE-SAW

Board — Straight grain lumber, 1⅛″ x 9″ x 12′-0″.
  Two cleats 1¼″ x 9″ bolted to the under side of the board to act as a socket on the hip of the horse.

Horse — Height 25″. Length 22½″.
  Spread of feet at ground·20″.
  Legs built of 2″ x 3″ material.
  Hip of 2″ x 3″ material.
  Brace under hip of ⅞″ material.

THE STAND AND SLIDE

STAND OR PLATFORM — 26" wide, 30" long, 5'-4" high.

Top made of 1⅜" tongue and groove material.

Uprights or legs of 2" x 3" material.

Cleats nailed to front legs 5" apart to form ladder are of 1⅛" x 2" material.

Cross bracing of 1¾" x 2⅝" material.

Apron under top made of ⅞" x 5" material nailed about 1⅛" below to act as additional bracing and provide place of attachment for iron hooks secured to sliding board.

The stand is fastened to the ground by dogs or pieces of wood buried deep enough (about 3') to make it secure.

SLIDE — Straight grain piece of lumber, 1⅛" x 13⅝" x 12'-0".

Two hooks at upper end of sliding board are of iron, about ⅜" x 1½", set at a proper angle to prevent board from becoming loose. Hooks are about 1¼" long.

293

THE SWINGING ROPE

UPRIGHT—3″ x 3″ x 6′-9″.

TOP PIECE—3″ x 3″ x 2′-9″.

Upright and top piece are mortised or halved and bolted together.

Bracing at top (3″ x 3″ x 20½″ at long point of mitre cuts) is nailed to top piece and upright at an angle of about 45 degrees.

Upright rests on a base measuring 3′-0″. This is mortised together and braced with 2″ x 3″ material about 20″ long, set at an angle of about 60 degrees.

Unless there are facilities for bracing at the top, as shown in the cut, the upright should be made longer and buried about 3′ in the ground.

The swinging rope (¾″ dia.) passes through a hole bored in the top piece and is held in place by a knot. Successive knots tied 8″ to 9″ apart and a big knot at the bottom make swinging easier for little folks.

THE TRAPEZE

TWO UPRIGHTS—3″ x 3″ x 6′-10″.

TOP PIECE—3″ x 3″ x 2′-10″.

Ends of top piece secured to uprights by being mortised or halved and bolted together.

Uprights rest on bases of 2″ x 3″ material, 3′-7″ long, connected by a small platform in the form of an H.

Bases and uprights are bolted to dogs or pieces of wood 2″ x 4″ x 5′-8″ set in the ground about 3′-0″.

Adjustable bar (round) 1⅜″ dia.

3 holes bored in each upright provide for the adjustable bar. The first hole is 3′-0″ above ground, the second 3′-5″, the third 3′-10″.

Swing bar (round), 1⅜″ dia., is 20″ long. Should hang about 16″ below top piece.

2 holes ⅝″ dia. bored in the top piece receive a continuous rope attached to the swing bar by being knotted after passing through holes (⅝″ dia.) in each end of the bar.

THE LADDER AND SUPPORT

LADDER—14" x 9'.

Sides of 1½" x 2½" material.

Rungs 1¼" dia. set 11" apart.

At upper ends of the sides a U-shaped cut acts as a hook for attaching the ladder to the cross bar of the support. These ends are re-inforced with iron to prevent splitting.

SUPPORT—Height 4'-6". Spread of uprights at base 4'-2".

Uprights of 1½" x 2½" material are secured to a foot (1½" x 4" x 20½") with braces (11½" x 2½" x 12") set at an angle of about 60°.

Tops of the two uprights are halved and bolted to a cross-bar 1⅛" x 2½" x 10" long.

The uprights are secured with diagonal braces 1⅜" x 3½" x 3'-9" fastened together where they intersect.

A Practical Adaptation

The ladder detached from the support is an invaluable adjunct to building and other operations

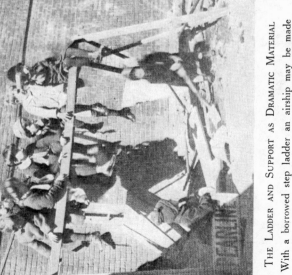

The Ladder and Support as Dramatic Material

With a borrowed step ladder an airship may be made

THE PARALLEL BARS

The two bars are 1½″ x 2½″ x 6′-3″, and are set 18½″ apart (inside meas.) The ends are beveled and the tops rounded.

Each bar is nailed to two uprights (2″ x 3″ x 5′-0″) set 5′ apart and extending 34″ above ground. An overhang of about 6″ is allowed at each end of the bar.

THE SAND BOX

The sloping cover to the sand box pictured here has been found to
have many uses besides its obvious purpose of protection against stray
animals and dirt. It is a fairly good substitute for the old-time cellar
door, that most important dramatic property of a play era past or rapidly
passing.

THE YARD BLOCKS

UNIT BLOCK—6″ x 12″ x 24″, average weight 11½ lbs.

HALF UNITS—6″ x 12″ x 12″, average weight 7½ lbs.

　　Made from ¾″ stock and painted (dark green) to protect from weather.

　　Two small holes are bored in each end and side to prevent dampness and warping.

NARROW BOARDS—⅝″ x 3¾″ in lengths of 48″ and 60″ are used as accessory material. They are painted like the blocks and made narrow to secure against warping.

　　Light in weight but of a size and shape calculated to bring the big muscles of trunk, arms and legs into vigorous play, the yard blocks used at the City and

Beginning Operations

Country School afford ideal material for a combination of outdoor exercise and constructive interest.

Where home manufacture is not practical they may be secured on order from the firm supplying the City and Country School, Pendleton and Townsend, Patterson, New York. Orders will be taken only for lots of one dozen or more of each size.

A Second Floor Apartment

BOX VILLAGE

The child is to be pitied who has not at some time revelled in a packing-box house big enough to get into and furnished by his own efforts. But a "village" of such houses offers a greatly enlarged field of play opportunity and has been the basis of Miss Mary Rankin's experiment on the Teachers College Playground.*

In addition to its more obvious possibilities for constructive and manual development, Miss Rankin's experiment offers social features

---

*See "Teachers College Playground," Bulletin No. 4, Bureau of Educational Experiments.

Of Interest to Carpenters

of unusual suggestiveness, for the village provides a civic experience fairly comprehensive and free from the artificiality that is apt to characterize attempts to introduce civic content into school and play procedure.

A Boom in Real Estate

INDOOR EQUIPMENT

THE requisites for indoor equipment are these:

A Suitable Floor—The natural place for a little child to play is the floor and it is therefore the sine qua non of the play laboratory.

Places to Keep Things—A maximum of convenience to facilitate habits of order.

Tables and Chairs—For use as occasion demands, to supplement the floor, not to take the place of it.

Blocks and Toys—For initial play material.

The Carpenter's Bench—With tools and lumber for the manufacture of supplementary toys.

A supply of Art and Craft materials—For the same purpose.

The Indoor Slide

THE INDOOR LABORATORY

The *floor* should receive first consideration in planning the indoor laboratory. It should be as spacious as circumstances will permit and safe, that is to say, clean and protected from draughts and dampness.

A well-kept hardwood floor is the best that can be provided. Individual light rugs or felt mats can be used for the younger children to sit on in cold weather if any doubt exists as to the adequacy of heating facilities (cut page 27).

Battleship linoleum makes a good substitute for a hardwood finish. It comes in solid colors and can be kept immaculate.

Deck canvas stretched over a layer of carpet felt and painted makes a warm covering, especially well adapted to the needs of very little children, as it has some of the softness of a carpet and yet can be scrubbed and mopped.

For the younger children the facilities for active play that an ample floor space affords may well be supplemented by more definite provision for vigorous big muscle exercise within doors. The slide pictured on the opposite page is used in the Nursery School of the Bureau of Educational Experiments and is a special resource in stormy weather. The platform to which the slide is attached is 5'-5" from the floor. One end of the balcony is raised 11" higher. The stairway measures 6'-7" and has a light pipe railing. The treads are 9½" apart. Climbing the steps and viewing the room from a height are in themselves play experiences greatly appreciated by very little folks. The slide board, 9'-9" long and 14" wide, is provided with side pieces (2¼") raised above the sliding surface to ensure safety. A gym mat is placed under the end of the slide board to make the landing easier.

Second only to the provision of floor space in importance is the supply of *lockers, shelves, boxes* and *drawers* for the disposal of the great number and variety of small articles that make up the "tools and appliances" of the laboratory. The cut on page 24 shows a particularly successful arrangement for facilities of this kind.

Seating equipment to be adequate for the needs of a play laboratory must combine the following requisites: it must conform to orthopedic standards; it must be plastic; it must be practical; that is to say, durable and not prohibitive in price. Models fully meeting these requirements are few, and in some cases difficulties of manufacture and costs of transportation further narrow opportunity for selection. The Mosher kindergarten chair (cut page 24) is easily available, however, and comes in three sizes, 10", 12" and 14".

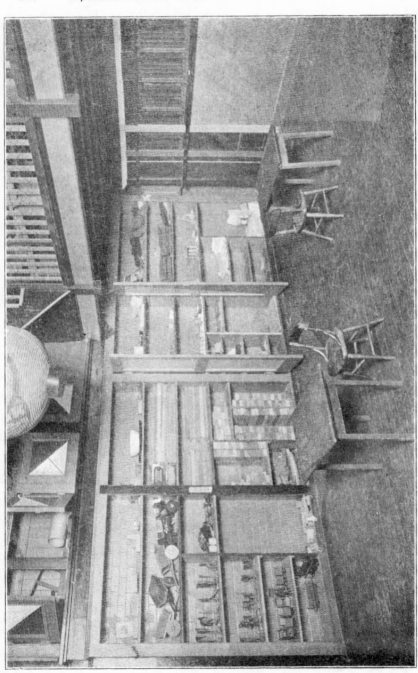

A Place for Everything

For older children the chair shown above is especially good. It is the "model industrial chair" approved by the American Posture League and reduced in size for children's use: The wide space between the center back brace and the seat, and the slight tilt of the seat downward from front to back are special features of the Posture League specifications that make for comfort and correct position. The chairs are made in seven sizes ranging from the usual kindergarten measurements, 10″, 11″, 12″ and 14″ in height to those of adult height, 16″, 17″ and 18″, but with seats of the smaller size.*

Individual *tables* with tops of generous proportions will be recognized as the next need. Several manufacturers offer good tables in kindergarten sizes, but for older children the selection is limited. The general tendency with tables as with chairs is to cater to public school standards and manufacture only heavy equipment. Thus plasticity is sacrificed for an appearance of durability that is often misleading. The folding tables shown in our cuts have been specially designed and carefully executed to ensure steadiness and resist hard wear. They are made of yellow pine with tops 22″ x 30″, in sizes ranging from 15½″ to 28″ high, and can be obtained on order from Pendleton and Townsend, Patterson, New York, in lots of not less than one dozen.

From a supply of chairs and tables of varying heights each child should be carefully outfitted with his own equipment, according to his individual proportions, and changes should be made as frequently as growth requirements may dictate.

Unfortunately these chairs are no longer obtainable.

The Balcony

The Unsocial Novice

To increase floor space, the City and Country School makes use of an indoor *balcony,* a device very popular with the children, as it contributes effectively to many play schemes. The tall block construction shown in the picture on the opposite page would never have reached its "Singer Tower proportions" without the balcony, first to suggest the project and then to aid in its execution.

Drop shelves like those along the wall of the "gallery" can be used for some purposes instead of tables when space is limited. It will be readily appreciated, however, that where a balcony is added special care must be exercised in regard to provisions for lighting both the "gallery" and the space below it.

Materials for store-keeping play fill the shelves next the fireplace (cut page 26) and the big crock on the hearth contains modelling clay, the raw material of such *objets d'art* as may be seen decorating the mantlepiece in the cut on page 34.

The low *blackboards* shown on page 34 are 5'-5" in height and 2'-0" from the floor.

All the furnishings of the laboratory should lend themselves for use as dramatic properties when occasion demands, and a few may be kept for such purposes alone. The light *screens* shown in the cut above and those in the right hand corner of the cut page 34 are properties of this kind and may be put to an endless number of uses.

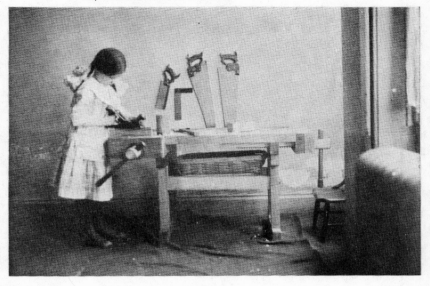

THE CARPENTER BENCH

The carpenter equipment must be a "sure-enough business affair," and the tools real tools—not toys.

The Sheldon bench shown here is a real bench in every particular except size. The tool list is as follows:

Manual training hammer.
18 point cross-cut saw.
9 point rip saw.
Large screw driver, wooden handle.
Small screw driver.
Nail puller.
Stanley smooth-plane, No. 3.
Bench hook.
Brace and set of twist bits.
Manual training rule.
Steel rule.
Tri square.
Utility box—with assorted nails, screws, etc.
Combination India oil stone.
Oil can.
Small hatchet.

Choice of lumber must be determined partly by the viewpoint of the adult concerned, largely by the laboratory budget, and finally by the supply locally available. Excellent results have sometimes been achieved where only boxes from the grocery and left-over pieces from the carpenter shop have been provided. Such rough lumber affords good experience in manipulation, and its use may help to establish habits of adapting materials as we find them to the purposes we have in hand. This is the natural attack of childhood, and it should be fostered, for children can lose it and come to feel that specially prepared materials are essential, and a consequent limitation to ingenuity and initiative can thus be established.

On the other hand, some projects and certain stages of experience are best served by a supply of good regulation stock. Boards of soft pine, white wood, bass wood, or cypress in thicknesses of $\frac{1}{4}''$, $\frac{3}{8}''$, $\frac{1}{2}''$ and $\frac{7}{8}''$ are especially well adapted for children's work, and "stock strips" $\frac{1}{4}''$ and $\frac{1}{2}''$ thick and $2''$ and $3''$ wide lend themselves to many purposes.

TOYS

THE proper basis of selection for toys is their efficiency as toys,
that is:

They must be suggestive of play and made for play.

They should be selected in relation to each other.

They should be consistent with the environment of the
child who is to use them.

They should be constructed simply so that they may serve as
models for other toys to be constructed by the children.

They should suggest something besides domestic play so
that the child's interest may be led to activities outside
the home life.

They should be durable because they are the realities of a
child's world and deserve the dignity of good workmanship.

FLOOR TOYS

"There comes back to me the memory of an enormous room with its ceiling going up to heaven. . . . It is the floor I think of chiefly, over the oilcloth of which, assumed to be land, spread towns and villages and forts of wooden bricks . . . the cracks and spaces of the floor and the bare brown "surround" were the water channels and open sea of that continent of mine. . . .

"Justice has never been done to bricks and soldiers by those who write about toys—my bricks and my soldiers were my perpetual drama. I recall an incessant variety of interests. There was the mystery and charm of the complicated buildings one could make, with long passages and steps and windows through which one could peep into their intricacies, and by means of slips of card one could make slanting ways in them, and send marbles rolling from top to base and thence out into the hold of a waiting ship. . . . And there was commerce; the shops and markets and storerooms full of nasturtium seed, thrift seed, lupin beans and such-like provender from the garden; such stuff one stored in match boxes and pill boxes or packed in sacks of old glove fingers tied up with thread and sent off by wagons along the great military road to the beleaguered fortress on the Indian frontier beyond the worn places that were dismal swamps. . . .

"I find this empire of the floor much more vivid in my memory now than many of the owners of the skirts and legs and boots that went gingerly across its territories."—H. G. WELLS, "The New Machiavelli," Chapter 2.

Nowhere else, perhaps, not even in "Floor Games" or in "Little Wars" will we find so convincing a picture of the possibilities of constructive play as is to be found in those pages, all too brief, in "The New Machiavelli" where the play laboratory at Bromstead is described. One can imagine the eager boy who played there looking back across the years strong in the conviction that it could not have been improved, and yet the picture of a child at solitary play is not, after all, the ideal picture. Our laboratory, while it must accommodate the unsocial novice and make provision for individual enterprise at all ages and stages, must be above all the place where the give and take of group play will develop along with block villages and other community life in miniature.

Mr. Wells lays emphasis on the great good fortune of possessing a special set of "bricks," made to order, and therefore sufficient in number for the type of floor games he describes. Comparatively few adults

Floor Blocks at the City and Country School

can look back to the possession of similar play material, and so a majority can not realize how it outweighs in value every other kind of toy that can be provided.

Toy manufacturers have seldom attempted to supply adequate sets of blocks. In general, the commercial product is too small in size or too limited in numbers to afford ambitious play schemes. There is at least one set on the market, however, calculated to meet the needs of our laboratory. These are the *Hill Floor Blocks,* designed by Professor Patty Smith Hill of Teachers College, Columbia University, and manufactured by A. Schoenhut & Company of Philadelphia. They are of hard maple, and come in seven sizes, from 3″ squares to oblongs 24″ in length. There are also triangular pieces in two sizes. A set contains 680 pieces. Half and quarter sets are also obtainable. They are used in the Teachers College Kindergarten, in the Horace Mann School, and in many other schools.

Where the budget for equipment is limited, floor blocks can be cut by the local carpenter, or in a school, by the manual training department. When this is done the blocks used in the City and Country School will be found especially well adapted for models. They are of white wood, the unit block being $1\frac{3}{8}″ \times 2\frac{3}{4}″ \times 5\frac{1}{2}″$. They range in size from half units to blocks four times the unit in length.*

Sets of the following sizes are suggested for the minimum building needs of children four years of age. These should be supplemented by as many more as can be supplied. Older children will require a larger number as more elaborate play schemes are developed.

For a Class of Ten Children—

100 half units, $1\frac{3}{8}″ \times 2\frac{3}{4}″ \times 2\frac{3}{4}″$.
200 units, $1\frac{3}{8}″ \times 2\frac{3}{4}″ \times 5\frac{1}{2}″$.
100 double units, $1\frac{3}{8}″ \times 2\frac{3}{4}″ \times 11″$.
24 quadruple units, $1\frac{3}{8}″ \times 2\frac{3}{4}″ \times 22″$.
15 diagonals (half units cut diagonally in half).
15 diagonals (units cut diagonally in half).
20 pillars (units cut lengthwise in half), $1\frac{3}{8}″ \times 1\frac{3}{8}″ \times 5\frac{1}{2}″$.
20 cylinders, diameter $2\frac{3}{4}″$, length $5\frac{1}{2}″$.
20 cylinders, diameter $1\frac{3}{8}″$, length $5\frac{1}{2}″$.
20 curves (10″).
20 switches (13″).

A Single Set for Individual Play at Home—

20 half units.	20 double units.
50 units.	20 quadruple units.

The "curves," cut from $1\frac{3}{8}″$ material, are quarter sections of a circular ring having an outside diameter of 14″ and an inside diameter of $8\frac{1}{2}″$. This gives a width of ring corresponding to the unit block ($2\frac{3}{4}″$).

The "switches," cut from $1\frac{3}{8}″$ material, are quarter sections of an elliptical ring having outside diameters of 22″ and $15\frac{1}{2}″$ with inside diameters of $16\frac{1}{2}″$ and 10″. Their width also corresponds to the unit block ($2\frac{3}{4}″$).

---

*Floor blocks cut from these measurements can now be obtained on order from **Pendleton and Townsend, Patterson, New York.**

Builders and Cabinet Makers at the Gregory Avenue School

The list of blocks published by the School of Childhood at the University of Pittsburgh includes several varieties, some of commercial manufacture, others cut to order. They are as follows*:

A. Nest of blocks.

B. Large blocks made to order of hard maple in five sizes:
   Cubes, 5" x 5".
   Oblongs, 2½" x 5" x 10".
   Triangular prisms made by cutting cube diagonally into two and four parts.
   Pillars made by cutting oblongs into two parts.
   Plinths made by cutting oblongs into two parts.
   Light weight 12" boards, 3'-0" to 7'-0" long.

C. Froebel's enlarged fifth and sixth gifts.

D. Stone Anchor blocks.

E. Architectural blocks for flat forms.

F. Peg-Lock blocks. †

Block Boxes are an inportant part of the equipment. Their dimensions should be planned in relation to the unit block of the set used. Those shown on page 34 are 13¾" x 16½" x 44" (inside measurements) for use with the set described above where the unit is 1⅜" x 2¾" x 5½". They are on castors, and can be rolled to any part of the room. In the City and Country School shelves are now used for storing blocks rather than boxes (see cut page 24). Such shelves are relatively shallow and proportioned in relation to the unit block.

---

*See University of Pittsburgh Bulletin, "Report of the Experimental work in the School of Childhood."
†No longer on the market.

Mr. Wells tells us that for his floor games he used tin soldiers and such animals as he could get—we know the kind, the lion smaller than the lamb, and barnyard fowl, doubtless, overtopping the commanding officer. Such combinations have been known to children of all generations and play of the kind he describes goes on in spite of the inconsistency of the materials supplied.

But when we consider fostering such play, and developing its possibilities for educational ends, the question arises whether this is the best provision that can be made, or if the traditional material could be improved just as the traditions concerning blocks are being improved. For some years past pioneers have experimented in this field in the belief that just as constructive play can be definitely stimulated by an adequate supply of blocks, it may be further stimulated by an initial supply of toys such as dolls, animals, trains, and carts, designed in related series, and consistent in size with each other and with the building possibilities of the blocks used.

The generally accepted hypothesis provides a doll family of suitable size scale, transportation toys, a series of domestic animals and sometimes a series of wild animals, all of construction simple enough to be duplicated by home manufacture, and suggesting, each series after its kind, a host of supplementary toys that can be devised from the plastic materials at hand in our laboratory.

Meeting the Train

Children Re-Create the World as They See It with the Equipment They Have at Hand

On the other hand, enthusiasts raise the question, why supply any toys? Is it not better for children to make all their toys? And as Miss Pratt has well said, "Getting ready to play is mistaken for play itself." Too much getting ready kills real play, and if our purpose is to foster and enrich the actual activity, we must understand the subtle value of initial play materials, of having at hand ready for the promptings of the play impulse, the necessary foundation stones on which a superstructure of improvisation can be reared.

In the City and Country School where children freely devise their "floor games," and where materials for floor play have been at all times bountifully supplied, careful observations have been made of the constructive schemes resulting when different varieties and combinations of floor toys are provided. Evidence so gained supports the conclusion that for the very early age period (3-4 years) blocks are largely sufficient in themselves, at least when supplemented by such plastic materials as paper, clay, bits of wood and nails, pieces of cloth, string, buttons, etc., for at this age imagination satisfactorily endows a block or stick with whatever attributes are desired. At about the age of six, however, floor schemes become more elaborate and appear to be definitely assisted by a supply of toys, especially where the play content is rich and varied. Dolls and transportation toys are the chief need, and domestic animals in suitable sizes are an aid in many schemes.

The whole question of adequate equipment for floor play ties up inevitably with the question of play content and it is, perhaps, not amiss to remind the reader here that the content of constructive play is at all times a reflection of the child's experience. If the educational possibilities of such play are to be fully realized, the adults responsible for the play laboratory must clearly understand the futility of expecting interesting constructive schemes of the type Mr. Wells describes from the child whose experience has been limited to his immediate home surroundings. Except in the very earliest years, play content confined to the dramatization of the details of home life, to the daily round of dressing, eating, sleeping and housekeeping offers comparatively little in educational values contrasted with play content that reflects a broader experience. When definite provision is made to enlarge life's horizon and stimulate interest at first through first-hand experiences and investigations of the community outside the home, and thence, by successive steps to other communities and other lands, play content will be correspondingly stimulated and educational values will be immensely increased.*

The whole working hypothesis of floor toys is as yet but little understood either by those who buy or those who sell play materials. The commercial dealer declares with truth that there is too little

---

*For example see *"Record of Group Six,"* by Leila V. Stott, Bulletin of the City and Country School, and *"Education Through Experience,"* by Mabel R. Goodlander, Bulletin X, Bureau of Educational Experiments.

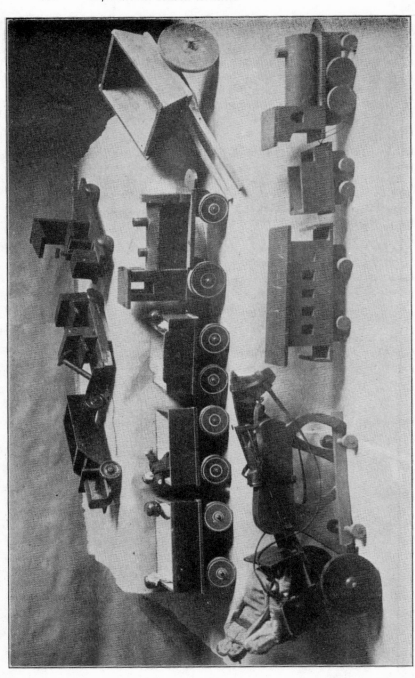

Transportation Toys

A Trunk Line

demand to justify placing good initial material on the market. The wooden animals he does provide are merely wooden ornaments without relation to any series and devoid of playability, immobile, reasonless. Even dolls of suitable size and type are often difficult to secure. Simple transportation toys can generally, though not always, be obtained in the shops. A few well-chosen pieces for initial material will soon be supplemented by bench-made contrivances.

For railroad tracks the block supply offers possibilities better adapted to the ages we are considering than any of the elaborate rail systems that are sold with the high-priced mechanical toys so fascinating to adult minds. Curved blocks corresponding to the unit block in width and thickness are a great boon to engineers, for what is a railroad without curves!

Transportation toys can be perfectly satisfactory when not made strictly to scale. Indeed, the exigencies of the situation generally demand that realists be satisfied with rather wide departures from scale in railroads. Train service, however, should accommodate at least one passenger to a car.

Supplementary

LARGE AND SMALL SCALE TOYS

The floor scheme pictured here is a good illustration of our principles of selection applied to toys of larger scale. The dolls, the tea set, the chairs are from the toy shop. The little table in the foreground, and the bed are bench-made. The bedding is of home manufacture, the jardiniere, too, is of modelling clay, gaily painted with water colors. The tea table and stove are improvised from blocks as is the bath room, through the door of which a block "tub" may be seen. The screen used as a partition at the back has large sheets of paper as panels.

There are some important differences, however, between the content of a play scheme like this and one of the kind we have been considering (see cut page 38). In part they are due to the size and character of the initial play material, for dolls like these invite an entirely different type of treatment. One cannot build villages, or provide extensive railroad facilities for them, nor does one regard them in the impersonal way that Mr. Wells' soldiers are regarded, as incidentals in a general scheme of things.

These beings hold the centre of their little stage. They call for affection and solicitude, and the kind of play into which they fit is more limited in scope, less stirring to the imagination, but more usual in the experience of children, because play material of this type is more plentifully provided than is any other and, centering attention as it does on the furnishings and utensils of the home, requires less contact with or information about, the outside world and its activities to provide the mental content for interesting play.

In the epochs of play development interest in these larger scale toys precedes that in more complicated schemes with smaller ones. Mr. Wells' stress on the desirability of a toy soldier population really reflects an adult view. For play on the toy soldier and paper doll scale develops latest of all, and because of the opportunities it affords for schemes of correspondingly greater mental content makes special appeal to the adult imagination.

Play material better adapted to this latest period than are either soldiers or paper dolls remains one of the unexplored possibilities for the toy trade of the future.

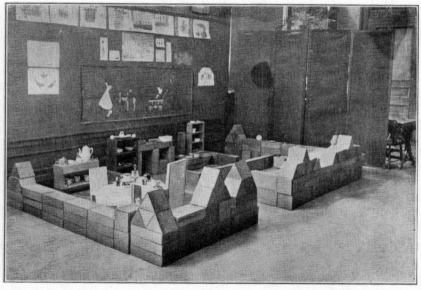

A "Furnished Apartment" at the Ethical Culture School

HOUSEKEEPING PLAY

Materials for housekeeping play are of two general kinds, according to size—those intended for the convenience of dolls, and those of larger scale for children's use. The larger kind should be strong enough and well enough made to permit of actual processes.

Plentiful as such materials are in the shops, it is difficult to assemble anything approaching a complete outfit on the same size scale. One may spend days in the attempt to get together one as satisfactory as that pictured here. The reason seems to be that for considerations of trade such toys are made and sold in sets of a few pieces each. If dealers would go a step further and plan their sets in series, made to scale and supplementing each other, they would better serve the requirements of play, and, it would seem, their own interests as well.

STOREKEEPING PLAY

From housekeeping play to storekeeping play is a logical step and one abounding in possibilities for leading interest beyond the horizon line of home environment.

Better than any toy equipment and within reach of every household budget is a "store" like the one pictured here where real cartons, boxes, tins and jars are used.

A "Grocery Store" at the Ethical Culture School

Schools can often obtain new unfilled cartons from manufacturers. The Fels-Naphtha and National Biscuit companies are especially cordial to requests of this kind, and cartons from the latter firm are good for beginners, as prices are plainly marked and involve only dime and nickel computations.

Sample packages add to interest, and a small supply of actual staples in bulk, or of sand, sawdust, chaff, etc., for weighing and measuring should be provided as well as paper, string, and paper bags of assorted sizes.

Small scales, and inexpensive sets of standard measures, dry and liquid, can be obtained of Milton Bradley and other school supply houses. A toy telephone and toy money will add to play possibilities, and for older children a "price and sign marker" (Milton Bradley) is a valuable addition.

The School of Childhood (Pittsburgh) list includes the following miscellaneous articles for house and store play:

Spoons	Bells
Various sized boxes	Enlarged sticks of the kindergarten
Stones	Ribbon bolts filled with sand
Pebbles	Rice
Buttons	Shot
Shells	Bottles
Spools	

CRAFT AND COLOR MATERIALS

Materials of this kind are a valuable part of any play equipment. Of the large assortment carried by kindergarten and school supply houses the following are best adapted to the needs of the play laboratory:

Modelling Materials—Modelling clay and plasticine, far from being the same, are supplementary materials, each adapted to uses for which the other is unsuited.

Weaving Materials—Raffia, basketry reed, colored worsteds, cotton roving, jute and macramé cord can be used for many purposes.

Material for Paper Work—Heavy oak tag, manila, and bogus papers for cutting and construction come in sheets of different sizes. Colored papers, both coated (colored on one side) and engine colored (colored on both sides) are better adapted to "laboratory purposes" when obtainable in large sheets instead of the regulation kindergarten squares. Colored tissue papers, scissors and library paste are always in demand.

Color Material—Crayons, water color paints, chalks (for blackboard use) are best adapted to the needs of play when supplied in a variety of colors and shades. For drawing and painting coarse paper should be furnished in quantity and in sheets of different sizes. For the older children newsprint paper and "show card" colors, with big brushes, make possible pictures of a size and type calculated to satisfy their enlarging ambitions in this field of expression.

If children are let alone with paper and crayons they will quickly learn to use these toys quite as effectively as they do blocks and dolls.

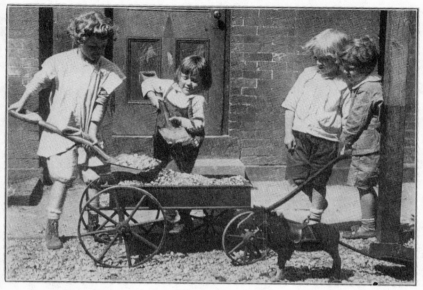

TOYS FOR ACTIVE PLAY AND OUTDOOR TOOLS

Among the many desirable *toys for active play* the following deserve "honorable mention":

Express wagon

Sled

Horse reins

"Coaster" or "Scooter"

Velocipede (and other adaptations of the bicycle for beginners)

Football (small size Association ball)

Indoor baseball

Rubber balls (various sizes)

Bean bags

Steamer quoits

As in the case of the carpenter's bench it is poor economy to supply any but good *tools* for the yard and garden. Even the best garden sets for children are so far inferior to those made for adults as to render them unsatisfactory and expensive by comparison. It is therefore better to get lightweight pieces in the smaller standard sizes and cut down long wooden handles for greater convenience. The one exception to be noted is the boy's shovel supplied by the Peter Henderson Company. This is in every respect as strong and well made as the regulation sizes. A complete series to the same scale and of the same standard would meet a decided need in children's equipment, where light weight is imperative and hard wear unavoidable.

In addition to the garden set of shovel, rake, hoe, trowel and wheelbarrow, a small crowbar is useful about the yard and, in winter, a light snow shovel is an advantage.

JEAN LEE HUNT.

The Historic Playground Described by G. Stanley Hall in His Essay
"The Story of a Sand Pile"

SUGGESTED READING

BOBBITT, FRANKLIN
"*The Curriculum*," Houghton Mifflin, 1918.
  Chap.   I, "Two Levels of Educational Experience."
  Chap.   II, "Educational Experience Upon the Play Level."
  Chap. XVII, "The Function of Play in Human Life."

CHAMBERLAIN, A. E.
"*The Child:* A Study in the Evolution of Man," Scribner, 1917.
  Chap.   I, "The Meaning of the Helplessness of Infancy."
  Chap. II, "The Meaning of Youth and Play."
  Chap. IV, "The Periods of Childhood."

COOK, H. CALDWELL
"*The Play Way*," Stokes Co., 1917.

DEWEY, JOHN
"*Democracy and Education*," Macmillan, 1916.
  Chap. XV, "Play and Work in the Curriculum."
"*How We Think*," D. C. Heath & Co.
  Chap. XII, Section II, "Play, Work, and Allied Forms of
    Activity."
  Chap. XVI, Section II, "Process and Product."
"*Interest and Effort in Education*," Houghton Mifflin Co., 1913.
  Chap. IV, "Types of Educative Interest."
"*The School and Society*," University of Chicago Press, 1916.
  Chap. VI, "The Psychology of Occupations."
  Chap. VII, "The Development of Attention."
"*Cyclopedia of Education*," Edited by Paul Monroe, Macmillan Co.
  Articles on "Infancy," "Play."

DEWEY, JOHN AND EVELYN
"*Schools of To-morrow*," Dutton, 1915.
  Chap. V, "Play."

DOPP, KATHERINE E.
"*The Place of Industries in Elementary Education*," University of
    Chicago Press, 1915.

GROOS, KARL
"*The Play of Man*," Appleton, 1916.

HALL, G. STANLEY
  "Educational Problems," Appleton, 1911.
    Chap. I, "The Pedagogy of the Kindergarten."
  "Youth: Its Regimen and Hygiene," Appleton, 1916.
    Chap. VI, "Play, Sports and Games."
  "Aspects of Child Life and Education," Ginn, 1914.
    "The Story of a Sand Pile." *

HARTMAN, GERTRUDE
  "The Child and His School," E. P. Dutton, 1922.
    "The Place of Activity in Education—Activity as Play."

KILPATRICK, WILLIAM HEARD
  "The Montessori System Examined," Houghton Mifflin, 1914.
  "Froebel's Kindergarten Principles Critically Examined," Macmillan, 1916.

KIRKPATRICK, EDWIN A.
  "Fundamentals of Child Study," Macmillan, 1903.
    Chap. IX, "Development of Adaptive Instincts—Play."

LEE, JOSEPH
  "Play in Education," Macmillan, 1915.

PRATT, CAROLINE
  "Toys: A Usurped Educational Field," The Survey, Sept. 23, 1911.
  "The Real Joy in Toys," in "Parents and Their Problems," National Congress of Mothers, Washington, D. C.

PRATT, CAROLINE AND WRIGHT, LULA
  "Experimental Practice in the City and Country School," E. P. Dutton, 1924.

WELLS, H. G.
  "The New Machiavelli," Duffield Co., 1910.
    Chap. II, "Bromfield and My Father."
  "Floor Games," Small, Maynard & Co., 1912.
  "Little Wars," Small, Maynard & Co., 1913.

WOOD, WALTER
  "Children's Play and Its Place in Education," Duffield Co., 1913.

BUREAU OF EDUCATIONAL EXPERIMENTS
  Bul. I, *"Playthings,"* Report of Committee on Toys and School Equipment, 1917.

---

*The interesting cut appearing on page 48 is shown here through the courtesy of Dr. Frank A. Manny and with permission of Dr. Hall.

Bul. III, *"The Play School,"* Descriptive Report by Lucile Deming, with a discussion of ideals and methods by Caroline Pratt.

Bul. IV, *"The Children's School, the Gregory School, Teachers' College Playground,"* Descriptive Reports by Lucile Deming, with a discussion of ideals and methods by Margaret Naumburg.

Bul. X, *"Education Through Experience—A Four-Year Experiment at the Ethical Culture School,"* by Mabel R. Goodlander.

CITY AND COUNTRY SCHOOL
"Record of Group Six," by Leila V. Stott, with an Introduction by Caroline Pratt and Records of Special Teachers. Bulletin 1, 1922.

PLAYGROUND AND RECREATION ASSOCIATION OF AMERICA
Bul. No. 27, *"Some Inexpensive Playground Apparatus,"* by E. H. Arnold, M. D. (Joint publication with Russell Sage Foundation.)

Bul. No. 102, *"Play for Home,"* by Joseph Lee.

Bul. No. 118, *"How to Equip a Playroom: The Pittsburgh Plan,"* by Alice M. Corbin.

TEACHERS' COLLEGE PUBLICATIONS, COLUMBIA UNIVERSITY
"Experimental Studies in Kindergarten Education," papers by Patty Smith Hill, John Dewey, Meredith Smith, Grace L. Brown, Julia W. Abbott, Luella W. Palmer. Reprinted from *Teachers' College Record,* Vol. V, No. 1, Jan., 1914.

UNIVERSITY OF CALIFORNIA PUBLICATIONS, Vol. V, No. 19, 1914.
"The Demonstration Play School of 1913," by Clark W. Hetherington.

UNIVERSITY OF PITTSBURGH BULLETIN, Vol. 12, No. 19, 1916.
"Report of Experimental Work in the School of Childhood." Papers by Will Grant Chambers, Meredith Smith, Luella A. Palmer, Alice Corbin Sies.